Where the Madness Lies

Where the Madness Lies

Citizen Accounts of Identity and Nationalism

Kishalay Bhattacharjee

Orient BlackSwan

WHERE THE MADNESS LIES: CITIZEN ACCOUNTS OF IDENTITY AND NATIONALISM

ORIENT BLACKSWAN PRIVATE LIMITED

Registered Office
3-6-752 Himayatnagar, Hyderabad 500 029, Telangana, India
e-mail: centraloffice@orientblackswan.com

Other Offices
Bengaluru, Chennai, Guwahati, Hyderabad, Kolkata,
Mumbai, New Delhi, Noida, Patna

First published by Orient Blackswan Private Limited 2023

ISBN 978-93-5442-611-7

Typeset in
Minion Pro 10.5/12.5
by Le Studio Graphique, Gurgaon 122 007

Printed in India at
Thomson Press, New Delhi 110 020

Published by
Orient Blackswan Private Limited
3-6-752 Himayatnagar, Hyderabad 500 029, Telangana, India
e-mail: info@orientblackswan.com

This book is dedicated to the millions of people around the world displaced, killed, maimed, incarcerated, intimidated for being who they are.

Contents

Tables

Abbreviations

AASU	All Assam Students' Union
ABVP	Akhil Bharatiya Vidyarthi Parishad
ADB	Asian Development Bank
AGP	Asom Gana Parishad
ASI	Archaeological Survey of India
BDR	Bangladesh Rifles
BJP	Bharatiya Janata Party
BLT	Bodo Liberation Tigers
BSF	Border Security Force
BTAD	Bodoland Territorial Autonomous District
BTC	Bodoland Territorial Council
BTR	Bodoland Territorial Region
CAA	Citizenship (Amendment) Act 2019
CJI	Chief Justice of India
CRPF	Central Reserve Police Force
CVC	Central Vigilance Commission
FIR	First Information Report
FY	Fiscal Year
GDP	Gross Domestic Product
IMF	International Monetary Fund
INA	Indian National Army
IPC	Indian Penal Code
IRFA	International Review of Financial Analysis
J&K	Jammu and Kashmir
JNU	Jawaharlal Nehru University
LAC	Line of Actual Control
LGBTQI	Lesbian, Gay, Bisexual, Transsexual, Queer, Intersex
LoC	Line of Control
LWE	Left Wing Extremism
MeitY	Ministry of Electronics & Information Technology

MHA	Ministry of Home Affairs
NCPCR	National Commission for Protection of Child Rights
NCRB	National Crime Records Bureau
NDFB	National Democratic Front of Bodoland
NEDA	North-East Democratic Alliance
NEFA	North-East Frontier Agency
NIA	National Investigative Agency
NRC	National Register of Citizens
NSO	National Statistical Office
OCI	Overseas Citizen of India
PLSI	People's Linguistic Survey of India
PSA	Public Safety Act
RBI	Reserve Bank of India
RSS	Rashtriya Swayamsevak Sangh
RTE	Right to Education Act
SKM	Samyukt Kisan Morcha
TMC	Trinamool Congress
UAPA	Unlawful Activities (Prevention) Amendment Act, 2008
ULFA	United Liberation Front of Assam
UNESCAP	United Nations Economic and Social Commission for Asia and the Pacific
UNHCR	United Nations High Commissioner for Refugees
UNLF	United National Liberation Front
USCIRF	US Commission on International Religious Freedom
VHP	Vishwa Hindu Parishad

Acknowledgements

Books like this have mysterious ways of evolving, particularly if one must run into a global pandemic during the final stages of the manuscript. Over years of reporting, teaching, and reading, many colleagues and friends, perhaps unbeknownst to them, helped shape my thinking on identity, citizenship and nationality. But I must mention the names that have directly influenced, helped and contributed to the book's being. I am indebted to my student, Ashima Sharma, who has been an extraordinary support in almost all aspects, from fieldwork to the book's title. I owe greatly to my other students, Akshita Chembolu, Vanshika Ramakrishnan and Anjali Notandas, for richly contributing towards the book's content. Sumedha Maheshwari, who joined us later, has been excellent in maintaining the timeline of incidents, which extended well beyond the expected. My gratitude to Jamila Firdaus for field interviews.

I also wish to thank those who offered useful comments. For sharpening my focus, I owe special thanks to my colleague Shiv Visvanathan, in whose office we conspired to make this book happen. I am deeply grateful to the several voices who agreed to share their family genealogy, speak about themselves and their relationship with the nation. But I could not have reached them without the help of Utpal Pathak, Shahid Ali, Saba Naqvi, Teteii, Sabra Nagi and M. Deepak.

I must acknowledge my dearest friend Sumana Roy, for her inputs.

For her patient and precise editing, I thank Sanna Jain. I always believed that editors are co-authors and I owe that debt to all my editors. Thanks to Roopa Sharma for commissioning the book when it was merely an idea.

A large part of the book was written at the Nehru Memorial Museum and Library and I thank my librarians for all the help. And to the warm hospitality of several people who have hosted me during my travels and guided me with invaluable gossip.

I must not forget the love and support of my sister Sarmistha, my parents, whose family stories are recounted here, my uncle Kulada and my daughter, Bambi, who makes me write and doesn't let me give up hoping for a better world!

Prologue

Outsider[1]
/aʊtˈsʌɪdə/

noun
1. a person who does not belong to a particular organization or profession.
2. a competitor, applicant, etc. thought to have little chance of success.

Migration[2]
/mʌɪˈɡreɪʃ(ə)n/

noun
1. movement of people to a new area or country in order to find work or better living conditions.
2. movement from one part of something to another.

I know who I am...and I know, too, that I am capable of being not only the characters I have named, but all the Twelve peers of France and the Nine Worthies as well.

Cervantes, *Don Quixote*[3]

Becoming, rather than being, is what makes Don Quixote literature's first modern fictional protagonist. While Cervantes created this identity, through his creation, he questioned identity: Do we know who we are any better than others who question or verify who we are? Quixote leaves everything behind: his name, home, cherished books. He flees from his identity in search of another, caught up in his world of fiction, where windmills are giants and peasant women are princesses, where he is an old man in homemade armour, destined to be defeated again and again. Yet, he says—I know who I am, and who I am in my heart of hearts has nothing to do with your ideas and your expectations of me. 'Being' is easy, but 'becoming' is risky because you may tilt at the sight of windmills.[4]

There has been so much scholarly pursuit of the concept of 'identity' that the word has assumed an identity of its own by now. And that is often the problem: we all seem to understand what this word means, but by no means can we fully explain the idea. It is perhaps a little Quixotic!

Locating Identity in History

Historian Nayanjot Lahiri finds evidence of the 'notion of identity in ancient India' in two portrayals of Amrapali—'one as seen in the writings about Buddha, and the other as described in her own telling'[5]—in the *Therigatha*, probably the first anthology of women's literature, authored by Buddhist nuns. Amrapali was believed to have been the most famous woman of Vaishali and was said to have hosted the Buddha, who accepted an invitation to dine with her. Her accounts suggest that individuals of this period had an understanding of plural identities and did express them beyond the voices or edicts of kings and preachers. In India, it is only from the fifth century BCE that we find evidence of people's self-expression.[6] However, these expressions do not yield much information. The need to record personal names can be traced to the second century BCE. But it was not until the 'Buddhist era' in the same century that hundreds of self-descriptions could be seen at places like Bharhut and Sanchi. What one does not see in the epigraphs, however, is how others viewed these people. Varna (caste) is absent from these self-descriptions: caste enters the picture only after the *Manusmriti* and *Arthashastra*. Record-keeping in its modern sense really started only with Emperor Ashoka, but even then it was mostly the king's words and ideas that were inscribed—much like the plaques set up by politicians today when inaugurating infrastructure. There is no real knowledge of commoners or even 'celebrities', as Lahiri observes:

> What were their names, where did they live, which regions were they recruited from? We have no idea. Even of the greatest ancient Indian poet and dramatist, Kalidasa, we know nothing either about his historical persona or the court where he may have served. Nowhere in his works does he say anything about himself, and no one else thought it fit to fill up on his life and relationships.[7]

The English word 'identity' gained currency only in the 1960s, but its roots go back to Plato's *thymos*, as Francis Fukuyama argues in his book *Identity*. In many cultures, the concept may have emerged even earlier.[8] The 'foundations of identity', as Fukuyama claims, 'were laid with the perception of a disjunction between one's inside and one's outside'.[9] This book will hinge on how identity plays out both within and outside of an individual, as well as on the insider-outsider conundrum; 'who am I?' against 'how am I being viewed?'.

The outsider in ancient India was what historians refer to as the 'Other'. Historian Romila Thapar, while delivering the Nemichandra Jain Memorial Lecture, situates identity and the Other through language, rather than ethnicity, caste or religion. Her exposition is timely and appropriate. History, she explains, 'is a dialogue between the past and the present'. Given our present, riddled with interactions involving the Other, she describes the multifaceted relationship between the Self and the Other:

> Those whom we see as essentially different, often help us to define ourselves, both individually and socially. Identifying people by otherness...can be used to marginalise a section of society...even to exile it. Multiple groups all over the world become refugees by denying them citizenship.... Alternatively, the other can be incorporated into one's own society, as was also done repeatedly in the past, and created [*sic*] what we often call civilisations.... The relationship of the Self with the Other can change over time, and move from being distanced to being proximate or the reverse. The identity of each can also change, but the presence of each is an important component of social relations. Every society marks the Self from the Other in diverse ways.[10]

But who is it that determines Otherness? Whether in the past or in the present, it is those in authority who make this decision, along with others who can claim the dominant identity of their society. The identity of 'Other' was not necessarily reserved for people who came from other geographies; it could just as well be a group within the same society.

In the past, as Thapar says, society had 'to accommodate the Other, if need be through argument and discussion, and if no resolution is forthcoming, then agree to a co-existence.'[11] But our current impatience and intolerance (a word that is in greater currency today, but makes me uncomfortable) with the Other determines to a large extent how we live in modern society. This unease has become a recurrent articulation of our times, connecting religion and society.

Although identity, as Lahiri sees it, entered the discourse much later, as Thapar explains, notions of the Other existed as early as the Vedic period. The *Rig Veda* tells us about the Arya varna and Dasa varna. Those who spoke Sanskrit correctly and followed Vedic practices were the Aryas. So the Aryan was not a racial category, as believed in the nineteenth century, but was identified clearly through language. The Dasa, then, was the Other for Aryan society. They were also referred to as '*mlecch*' or '*adevas*', meaning those who did not have gods. However, some of the Dasas were wealthy and may have been inducted into Aryan society. Dasi women, however, were treated as a commodity that could be 'gifted' to others by the chieftain and worked as servants for Aryas. Curiously, some of their sons were accepted into the Arya fold as 'Dasi putra Brahmins'. Several rishis, for example Kakshivat and Kavash Ailush (who was, in fact, given the title of 'the best among Brahmins'), were Dasi putras. Their spiritual qualifications appear to have granted them a higher position in the hierarchy.[12]

In the following age emerged the *Shramanas*. They were the Jains, the Buddhists, and the Ajivikas, and were opposed in varying degrees to Vedic Brahmanism. For the orthodox, the Shramanas were clearly the Other. The Shramanas became popular and the relationship between these groups and the Brahmins was antagonistic. Over time, these Others also largely succumbed to the dominant orthodoxy.

However, there is another Otherness that is entirely imposed from the outside, rather than being a self-proclaimed identity like that of a renouncer. The category of *avarna* or the so-called 'untouchable' was created to ensure a steady supply of bonded labour. Many bonded labour districts actually existed well into our post-independence India. Though the practice has been formally abolished, the bonded labourer continues to exist.

In the ages that followed, a glorious interface of cultures and faiths came together to shape a civilisation of which we are presently a part. The Bhakti movement, and simultaneously the Sufis from Central Asia, attempted to liberate people from orthodoxies. However, they were considered the 'Other' or outsiders to the dominant religious tradition. The 'yavanas', 'shakas' and 'turushkas' came from the West and Central Asia and many of them followed Islam. They were outsiders too. It was purely an ethnic identity and not one determined by religion. Kabir and Ravidas were outsiders even within their own cities. Chaitanya, Durdas, Mira and Laldev were 'Others' as well. And, of course, the most popular of the Bhakti traditions, Krishna bhakti, was adopted by many Muslims (a word not in use then).

Some social relationships, however, remained static. Muslims and other sects treated the avarna in the same way as before, even if s/he converted to the given faith. In some cases, the Other evolved and took different form, and in some cases it developed into the voice of the dissenter. Throughout the book, we will view identity and other such notions from the perspective of the Other.

In this context, it is useful to remind ourselves that the imagined geographical space we refer to as India was actually what 'Sheldon Pollock calls, "Sanskrit cosmopolis", referring to the diffusion of Indian culture across a vast swathe of Southern Asia between the fourth century and the fourteenth'.[13] Richard Eaton, in his recent book *India in the Persianate Age: 1000–1765*,[14] goes on to explain how Sanskrit place names culturally connected South Asia and South East Asia as a Sanskrit world, rather than as an area defined by a common religion. Sanskrit was not 'identified with a particular linguistic or ethnic group or with a particular region'. South Asia was a cultural zone without hard political borders, primarily concerned with maintaining moral and social order and the circulation of Sanskrit texts that dealt with everything from grammar to architecture, and had acquired a trans-regional character.

The Gandhara region, for example, remains to this date a crucible of history. Present-day Uzbekistan, Krygysztan, Tajikistan, Afghanistan, Pakistan and northwest India, taken together, loosely comprised this incredibly diverse region within the 'Sanskrit cosmopolis'. What remains today are mere whispers from that time, but these fragments are adequate to illustrate a very sophisticated exchange of knowledge, language and art. The relationship between Central Asia and the Indus region is marked not only by the spread of the Indo-Iranian languages, but also a certain sense of continuity. This region goes back millennia to the Neolithic period, when human interaction continued across the Himalayas. While new data, archaeological findings, and DNA analysis will refine our knowledge and decipher the stories of those amazing civilisations, the one deduction that will remain untouched is that the world we inhabit today is a result of continuous migration.

From the eleventh century onwards, a similar 'placeless' world was coming into being: what Richard Eaton calls the 'Persianate world', embracing much of West, Central and South Asia. Both these worlds were grounded in language and literature. Today's India is therefore an assimilation of these two worlds, which interacted and mingled with each other for centuries.

Indrani Chatterjee, speaking at 'Beyond Borders', a series of lectures, refers to the monastic civilisation in what is referred to today as 'Northeast India'. From a collection of metal Buddhas kept in a khong in Tripura, she starts reimagining the past of these connected monastic sites, which transcends post-colonial maps and borders:

> ...just by looking at the metal—the brass and the bronze statues, we could begin to imagine a circuit of metal moving, ideas and icons moving, and people moving. So, what we are being asked to imagine... [is] a connection between the routes which had in my mind after '47 been very discrete entities. The western Himalayas, the eastern Himalayas and the coast to me were no longer separate and discrete...but possibly connected geographies.... [T]his is a very well-connected riverine set of movements and trade links. This particular river network was aided by great evidence of technological skill, bridge-building associated with various Buddhist monks from the 14th century....[15]

Interestingly, it is people who decide these matters. And it was people who may have wanted borders as a way of protecting property rights. Chatterjee argues that:

> All borders were effective by local arrangements. For example, the connections between Himalayan and plains Nepal and Indian UP. Nepal's borders with the EIC state in 1816 did not prevent the EIC recruiting many platoons of Nepali men into the Company's militaries. So that by the end of the 20th c [*sic*], and with the work of many citizenship-focused groups, many Gurkhas too had become British citizens.[16]

The Invisible Tribal

Not many studies and discussions take into account the significant population of tribal communities, right from the heart of the 'nation' to the Himalayan foothills. The majority of the waterheads (sources of rivers) and forests 'belong' to them. This is where the energy and natural resources of future India will have to be drawn from. Is there an acknowledged tribal identity in our country? Yes, the Constitution guarantees their rights in its Fifth and Sixth Schedule. But in reality, it is an identity that is invisible, an identity that is perceived as militant, and which must therefore be contained through force.

Tribals have either been studied through ethnography[17] or viewed as exotica, and in both instances, they have been homogenised into one identity. In the upper-caste/class Hindu or Muslim or Christian mind, 'tribal' is a derogatory term, used for groups of people whom they perceived as 'primitive'. Tribals are the avarnas.

As Virginius Xaxa observes in his essay on indigenous people, tribals are not necessarily the 'first people' to inhabit the region, but they retain a prior claim to its natural resources—or at least, that is how the tribal question was envisioned.[18] People who may have come from elsewhere imposed this identity as a mark of differentiation between themselves and these 461 communities; however, it eventually became a vehicle of assertion for indigenous people. Early ethnographers were not very clear about caste and tribe, and it was not until 1901 that they were categorised as communities practising animism. To overcome some of the theoretical problems of understanding 'tribal' as a distinct group, Xaxa says that in 1957, Roy-Burman introduced the word 'indigenous' from his discipline, anthropology. The word slowly gained currency after the year 1993 was declared as the international year of indigenous people. It was acknowledged that these groups were being marginalised and dispossessed of their traditional forms of livelihood. The word 'Adivasi', when translated into English, would mean indigenous, and has been in circulation for a long time, indicating people who were settled in the subcontinent before the Aryans came in. But these conclusions are problematic—tribal communities cannot claim to be original inhabitants either, since the tribals often refer to how their ancestors had migrated into the subcontinent. The Nagas are said to have arrived in Tibet in the first millennium BCE and then moved to their current homeland. That would have been much later than the arrival of the Aryans. The Mizos arrived only in the sixteenth century, and the Kukis came even later. The Bengalis or the Odiyas, for example, have a longer history of settlement in the region. Though most of the indigenous groups are from Dravidian, Austro-Asian or Tibeto-Burman language families, there are some who belong to the Indo-Aryan group as well. The relationship between tribals and non-tribals before the arrival of the British has been left to speculation because of a lack of documented evidence. While many of these groups were being fast absorbed into Hinduism and, with the coming of the British, increasingly into Christianity as well, many of them continued to follow their traditional beliefs. They combined in their lifestyle and faith a pluralism that is unique.

However, the word 'they' would contradict my argument; there cannot be one 'tribal' identity, just as you cannot say that the Brahmaputra is one river or that the Brahmaputra and the Ganga are one. All rivers carry water, but each has a different name and geography. The Ganga may merge with the Brahmaputra in Padma, but there is also a juncture where the Jamuna, Hoogly and Padma merge together, and each has its story, its sources and its histories. The so-called 'tribal' population is spread across different regions and is not tied by any common language, tradition, livelihood or even race. The terms 'tribal', 'indigenous people' and 'ethnic groups' are all umbrella terms and contradict the notion of a single identity.

The dedication of Mahasweta Devi's *Imaginary Maps*, translated by Gayatri Chakravorty Spivak, reads, 'For All The Indigenous Peoples of the World'.[19] Mahasweta Devi spent her life working with tribals and writing about them. In 1965, she began her work in Palamu, fighting against the bonded labour system originally introduced by the British. In 1986, she formed the Adim Jati Akiya Parishad to forge tribal unity. Tribal communities were a part of her life and work. She saw them as oppressed and fought for their rights in whichever way she could. But her stories and work focused primarily on eastern and central India. In Odisha alone there are sixty-three 'Adivasi' 'tribes'. Does each of them have a name? Yes, they do. It is alarming to see how many 'tribal' languages have been removed in the last census. This, to my mind, is a worse form of dispossession than the act of taking over tribal lands in order to get at the mineral wealth, in the form of bauxite or iron-ore, that lie beneath, claiming that these resources belong to the nation-state as a whole.[20]

The Indian 'Self' and the Indian 'Other': The Case of Bodoland

In 2012, I was in Bodoland, lower Assam, reporting a violent turn of events. For the first forty-eight hours I described it as a conflict between two ethnic groups, till I was told that by masking the 'identity' of the groups, I was only creating greater confusion. I went on to report that the violence was between Bodos and Bengali-speaking Muslims. This is a familiar nomenclature in Assam, but it fails to explain why one community is referred to by its ethnicity and the other through religion. As both the Bengali Hindu and Bengali Muslim are clear about their distinct identities in Assam, just Bengali would have been inadequate. Can Bodo be referred to as 'Assamese'? No, the community is clear about its distinct Bodo identity as well. Should Bodos then be differentiated as Bodo Christians and Bodo Hindus? Yes, if we are explaining armed insurgency, but not in the given context. So, who are the Bodos?

For those who have not followed the story of Assam, Bodo assertion started in the 1980s and was followed by an accord, an autonomous council, and then a territorial council in 2003. What does that imply? Under the Sixth Schedule of the Indian Constitution, the educational, economic and linguistic aspirations, land rights, and the socio-cultural and ethnic identity of people inhabiting 'tribal areas' in various states, including Assam, were secured. The Bodos became the primary beneficiaries of these provisions and other communities inhabiting the area were not taken into consideration. The debate on the Sixth Schedule in the Constituent Assembly was originally oriented towards hill tribes. Whichever way you take it, it did not grant reservation to any one community. The Bodos, however, extracted this from the government and reserved 75 per cent of the seats in the Territorial Council, thus denying the area's other residents their legitimate rights. Thus was born the Bodoland Territorial Autonomous District (BTAD),[21] which claimed 35 per cent of Assam's land. The Bodos need another 15 per cent to raise the pitch for their long-standing demand of dividing Assam 50-50.[22]

The BTAD's birth pangs are still being felt. What began as a students' movement turned into a heavily armed group demanding sovereignty (The National Democratic Front of Bodoland or NDFB). That was soon followed by the emergence of a counter force (Bodo Liberation Tigers or BLT) demanding statehood—and now governing the area. The area has been heavily militarised and violence has been the roadmap for this movement, with high stakes and multiple voices.[23] They control the strategic 'chicken's neck' connecting the entire region to the rest of the country. The area under their control borders Bhutan, which was the launching pad for several armed Indian militias.[24] During their surrender, at the time of the 2003 accord, 2,600 cadres gave up less than 500 weapons, many of which were country-made arms.[25] Of the hundreds of 'surrender ceremonies' in the state, this was one of the largest I remember reporting. I was told that the exhibit was only a part of their inventory. The rest of the weapons continue to be in circulation, making this stretch of land bordering Bhutan one of the most weaponised civilian areas in the country.

The NDFB was formed in 1986. One faction is on a ceasefire agreement. A large number of cadres surrendered in January 2020. Twenty-six days before the terrorist attacks of 26/11 in Mumbai, this group had triggered Assam's biggest terror attack, launching serial blasts from the ceasefire camps which were being monitored by the government. Some 100 people were killed and over 500 injured.[26]

Since 1986, hundreds have been killed in violence related to the Bodo assertion. Presciently, the then Union Home Minister Sushilkumar Shinde, in his very first reply in Parliament, referred to BTAD as the 'Bodoland Terrorist Autonomous District'.[27]

The story will, however, remain incomplete without mention of the so-called 'ethnic riots' that have erupted in Assam at regular intervals since the 1990s. When such violence is repeated on the very same issues, with ethnic groups routinely displaced, it assumes proportions of ethnic cleansing. There is no data on how many Assamese Hindu families have fled over the years from these districts. The Bengali Hindus are also not accounted for. But both groups had a significant presence in the stretch. Other communities also question the legality of only Bodos getting autonomy and the government acceding to their demands.[28]

The late 1990s witnessed the worst ruptures, pushing Bodos, Adivasis and Bengali-speaking Muslims into hundreds of relief camps. Several lakhs of people were displaced. Ten years later, the Bodos made their way back, leaving behind the other two groups. Subsequently, the other two communities returned to the region to find that a lot of their land had been usurped. Some of those old relief camps have grown into colonies and slums, with inhabitants still waiting to be rehabilitated.

The violence in 2012 was only part of an ongoing process of ethnic cleansing.[29] This is not unique to Bodoland. In the North Cachar Hills Autonomous Council, India's oldest autonomous council set up in 1952, the Dimasa armed groups have triggered similar outbreaks of violence, targeting Biharis and Nepalis, amongst other groups. Similarly, in the Karbi Anglong district where another autonomous council operates, there has been violence against 'outsiders' and neighbouring communities.[30] In neighbouring Meghalaya, thousands of non-tribals were thrown out of the state between 1979 and 1989.

But Assam's case is different because it is the most heterogeneous state in the country, with seventy-two communities (each with over 5,000 members speaking their own language) living together. Here, it is the dangerous politics of ethnic identities and ethno-exclusivism that has resulted in such divisiveness. Former Chief Minister, the Late Hiteswar Saikia, enabled this by creating seven autonomous councils. His successor Tarun Gogoi went even further, doubling the number (one of these had a population of just 10,000).[31] These councils, twenty-one in all, with their ethnic militias,[32] created a climate of disgruntlement amongst those who felt that the state had discriminated against them. The government followed a policy of ceasefire, talks and appeasement, but the situation remained explosive.

Over time, however, the tone and tenor of the violence has been changing. Amid the chaos, and with the government displaying ambivalence, certain groups have started ascribing their own reasons for picking up arms.[33] The popular Sri Sri Ravi Shankar[34] had issued a statement saying, 'This heinous crime against ethnic people in Assam by fundamentalist immigrants is causing a huge humanitarian crisis. Wake up and join in to condemn this act.'[35] Such statements only serve to deepen the rift between communities.

Leaders from various political parties increasingly descended on the plains and issued statements which divided the population into communal camps.[36] The victims were called 'migrants' by some, 'illegal migrants' by others. Having extensively covered the violence as a reporter, I found that Bodo leaders had allegedly refused an offer by NGOs to come and work in the area, claiming that this would benefit the 'illegal migrants'. They said that rehabilitation could take place only after proper identification of the citizenship of the relief camp inmates. This was said at a time when thousands of children were at risk of disease and malnutrition and 4,000 pregnant women required urgent help.[37] This was long before the exercise of creating a National Register of Citizens (NRC) even got underway.

This strain of analysis—that the violence was triggered by the unabated march of 'illegal migrants'—has many takers across the nation. Simultaneously, a sense of victimhood and 'Muslim brotherhood' has also played out. People were killed in Mumbai in 2012 when members of the minority community took out protests against the killing of Muslims in Assam. Thousands of students from the Northeast had to flee from multiple big cities after rumours of threats and intimidation.[38]

This was also the first such instance of violence where civil society had been mobilised by social media and false news.[39] The jury was out even before the dead had been counted, driving a wedge between communities and bringing back the xenophobic mood of the 1970s to raise the pitch against illegal migration from Bangladesh.[40]

Illegal migration is indeed a reality, but it is the result of a flawed mechanism of detection and gross border mismanagement. Land may be at the heart of the dispute, but the underlying intent behind raising this issue is of ethnic cleansing.

Citizen No. 4018322021290761004 50

Situated between an individual identity and a national identity is the now contentious issue of citizenship, which will, in all likelihood, dominate the future political discourse and impact millions of people. Who is a 'citizen' of India? On the surface, going by the acts and laws of the nation, it seems rather simple. But on the ground, citizenship is not easy to prove, and given how poor documentation is in developing countries, legitimate citizens can be delegitimised very easily. The case in point, of course, is Assam and the massive exercise of updating the National Registry of Citizens to weed out 'termites', as the Union Home Minister had proclaimed in 2019.[41]

Meanwhile, the government introduced the Citizenship (Amendment) Act in 2019 (the fifth such amendment) that grants citizenship (reducing the time for naturalisation) to minorities like Hindus, Christians, Parsis, Buddhists, Jains and Sikhs (but not Muslims) from Pakistan, Bangladesh and Afghanistan. The country broke out into a million mutinies against this Act. The government countered the protests with unprecedented state repression.[42]

Despite being ruled by the Bharatiya Janata Party (BJP), Assam, along with the rest of the Northeastern states (all of whom are ruled by alliances with the BJP or are members of NEDA, the North-East Democratic Alliance), violently opposed the idea of this legislation. Assam revived its agenda of opposing illegal migration and rightfully claimed that the amendment contradicts the Assam Accord, which clearly states that anyone entering the country after midnight of 24 March 1971 will be identified as a foreigner. The Centre remained unmoved and came down heavily against anyone who even spoke against it.

The Bill had fallen through when it was first introduced in 2016, but was passed without much debate at the second instance. However, here is the situation on the ground: if you have entered Assam after 1971, you are not an Indian. You can be considered an Indian if you were born in India, on condition that one of your parents is an Indian (but the other parent cannot be an illegal migrant). You can also become an Indian by living in India for twelve years (terms and conditions apply). If you fail to prove your citizenship and are declared a 'foreigner', you will be deported. But how will you deport people without their country of origin accepting them? Why would the country of origin accept people without scrutiny? So the process can take an enormous amount of time, during which the government will have to feed the 'foreigner' and maintain detention camps—which are presently running in some parts of Assam, even though the Indian prime minister has denied the existence of any such camps.[43] The new Act now creates a crisis; the minority immigrant (only till 2014) of certain eligible religions, barring Muslims, will be granted citizenship, in contravention of the Assam Accord.

The befuddlement does not end here. The NRC updation, implemented at the Supreme Court's insistence and under its supervision, was just short of ludicrous—one had to prove at whatever cost (not money) that either the individual or their father or grandfather had voted in an Indian election before 1971. The government uploaded the electoral list, and if you did not find your name on it, you could be considered a castaway.

I was Stateless

When the exercise of updating the NRC in Assam picked up steam in 2018, I applied for 'citizenship' only to understand the process, which was under a cloud of suspicion and apprehension. At the time of my application, I was not living in Assam, but I had adequate proof of my ancestry there. Or so I imagined. I was told I must upload a 'legacy document' that would prove that my father had voted in India before 1971. I asked my father, a historian by training and a teacher by profession, whether he had voted. He said that he had, but he obviously had no proof of having done so. The government uploaded this data for people to locate their proof. My father's name was missing from the relevant electoral roll, and there was no way of proving that he had voted that year.

By sheer chance, my father dug out a certificate from the 1950s signed by a gazetted officer, verifying his status as a bonafide Indian citizen. The paper was old and the ink was fading. Under the NRC clauses, this appeared to be the only valid proof of my claim to be an Indian citizen. While it worked for my sister, who was working as a doctor in Assam, in the first round of verification they rejected my father, my daughter (born in Delhi) and me. The NRC office at Zoo Road, Guwahati, wanted me to go and present myself, along with my daughter. I was basically summoned. I explained my inability to travel from Delhi. Regarding my father, they argued that he worked in Shillong and therefore had no right to claim citizenship in Assam. I would have thought that this qualified as citizenship of the country. My mother, on the other hand, was already on the rolls. Her legacy came from her father, who was an advocate practising in the Gauhati High Court, and had come to present-day Assam in the early twentieth century. A couple of months later, when the draft was actually published, my name, as well as my daughter's, were there. My father did not make it to that list. He was summoned several times, but given that he was ninety-one years of age, we preferred not to inform him of his new, possibly delegitimised status.

As per the Assam Accord, all residents of Assam who had entered the state till 1 January 1966 would be 'regularised'. Those who entered between 1966 and 25 March 1971 could not vote for the next ten years, and those who came after the midnight of 24 March 1971 would be 'detected, deleted and expelled in accordance with law'. My father was born in undivided Assam, studied in Assam (under Calcutta University), shifted to present-day Assam in 1947 to complete his education, worked in Shillong (previously the capital of Assam and then of Meghalaya) till his retirement in 1992, and is in possession of a certificate identifying him as a citizen (which is not mandatory to acquire, and no such certificate is normally issued). However, his citizenship was in question. How can the same piece of paper that grants citizenship to his children deny him the same? This is not mere oversight. This appears to be a willful process of 'elimination', a word that I would like to repeat in the course of this book, because this is what the exercise really intends to do.

The issue of citizenship is intractable. Apart from the Constitution, there exists a whole set of laws, such as the Foreigners' Act 1946, the Passport Act 1952 and the Citizenship Act of 1956. The rules are a maze of complexities.

The draft list of 400,000 was a vindication of sorts for Assamese nationalist groups like the All Assam Students' Union (AASU), which have fought a long battle against illegal immigration, a battle that often morphed into anti-Bengali and anti-outsider xenophobic campaigns. The erroneous claim of 'indigenous' and 'original' inhabitants of Assam is the pivot on which this movement turns, and this book interrogates the history behind the emergence of this assertion. Without looking back at the several partitions of Bengal and the Chief Commissionership of Assam, this disenfranchisement cannot be explained.

Ironically, in 1978, my father, who now found himself out of the contentious list, had authored one of the seminal works[44] dealing with the separation of Assam from Bengal and the formation of the Chief Commissionership in 1874. I must caution the reader that simply having one's name in the list does not guarantee permanent residence. Someone might just wish to contest this inclusion. Several names have been arbitrarily deleted after such contestations.

What makes us genuine citizens? If the laws are clear, there should have been no cause for anxiety among genuine citizens to claim their rights. There are reportedly many Assamese names that have been left out of the list, but given their 'original' and 'indigenous' status, they were perhaps not as anxious as the other communities, particularly the Bengalis. The racial profiling of Bengalis as illegal refugees and thus 'the other' has been going on for decades, since before the creation of Bangladesh.

29 August 2019

While I was writing this section, the situation in Jammu and Kashmir and Assam was developing. In the past twenty-four days, Jammu and Kashmir was brought under an unprecedented, undeclared emergency. In the eastern theatre, another situation was developing in Assam with the final 'elimination' list under NRC to be announced in less than twenty-four hours.

I recall noting this down: 'Tomorrow I may be rendered stateless'.

Saturday, 31 August 2019

No one objected to my inclusion, so they retained my name and my daughter's name as well. My father, who was initially excluded, now enjoyed a new 'status': 'accept'. His plea (conveyed by my sister, who insisted that they link his Aadhaar card, which they had forgotten) was accepted, and he is now officially an Indian citizen. My small family has finally been granted citizenship, but that will not stop people from suspecting otherwise. Some unknown social media denizens have already asked, in response to my speaking on behalf of the excluded: 'Why don't you take them home?' The shrill hyper-nationalism is only getting worse. In the draft list of 2018, 400,000 people were left out of the list, and the majority were Bengalis. In the final list of the National Register of Citizens declared on 31 August 2019, 190,000 people have been left out. This could be the largest number of stateless people in the biggest-ever disenfranchisement exercise conducted anywhere in the world. Citizenship then becomes a potent instrument of 'elimination'. Political parties are rallying around the figure in the final list, some saying they reject it because it is too small a number, while others say they reject it because 'genuine' Hindus have been included in the list.

But what really is NRC in the context of the subject matter of this book? It is a tool to scrutinise and profile anyone who speaks Bangla, irrespective of religious faith, as a suspect illegal migrant. Even if found legitimate, one is forever seen as a migrant and a refugee.

What has NRC achieved after the publication of the final register?

1. AASU received a fresh lease of life with their statement that 190,000 was too few. Assamese sub-nationalism felt somewhat vindicated, but there was little clarity on whether to celebrate or restart another campaign. It drove a wedge into the Assamese-Bengali relationship.
2. The BJP rejected it, arguing that while they had kept their promise, the list is erroneous because genuine citizens had been excluded.
3. In other parts of the country, BJP state units kept the focus on the Assam situation (and thereby also distracted people from other critical issues). However, massive resistance, followed by a global pandemic, suspended the national project.
4. The NRC is a government policy to control people by rendering them stateless, while not exactly throwing them out.
5. The government pushed through a controversial amendment to the Citizenship Act, ensuring that Muslims are left out.[45]
6. Fear and harassment of children of families excluded from the NRC and the families with an uncertain future.[46]
7. Detention centres (later changed to transit centres), which are disturbingly similar to concentration camps, will create further fear, anxiety and divisiveness.
8. Illegal infiltration and cross-border smuggling continues unabated.[47]

Jammu and Kashmir, Leh and Ladakh For One Last Time

While this book was being written, the BJP government, re-elected to power in May 2019, announced its most dramatic decision yet: the abrogation of Article 370 in Jammu and Kashmir, Leh and Ladakh, consequently derecognising the state as well as bifurcating it. This was welcomed by an overwhelming 'majority' and seen and read as a victory over an unjust historical accommodation in the only Muslim-majority state of India. But the Muslim population of the state, numbed by this unprecedented and unexpected decision, remained under emergency lockdown for six months in what *Time* described as 'the world's longest lockdown'. This was almost immediately followed by another lockdown due to the pandemic.[48]

In today's digital age, we understand that an internet shutdown is a very lethal form of violence. In 2018, there were sixty-five shutdowns; by August 2019, Kashmir was under its fifty-first lockdown; in the preceding eight years, there have been 176 internet shutdowns.[49]

Whatever facts and details I add here today will remain relevant even to readers in the future, because, as a Kashmiri journalist writing for *Time* magazine during this shutdown said, 'Though I write all this in past tense, all of it is still happening'.[50]

In Assam, the emergency is of a different nature. It is exclusion and an unleashing of tyranny to isolate specific individuals, who are no longer allowed to think or demand or argue or fight. The targeted individual may merely survive. This tyranny is not arbitrary. There is a method to it, and it is within the totalitarian concept of lawfulness.

From Kashmir as a place of 'dead eyes',[51] to Assam as the place of absent citizens, the citizen's compliance with the state is compliance against one's own will. In a totalitarian state like India, the citizen is unable to formulate political agency, as was the case in Russia during the Bolsheviks or Mussolini's Italy, where the idea of dissent was exiled. In India, exile is alien—the citizen is coerced into compliance or made to disappear. The body politic claims the body of the citizen. I have earlier written extensively on how citizens without proof of identity in India can run the risk of being abducted and killed.[52] The culture of impunity that we have witnessed over the past seventy years post-independence is numbing. But to detain people for absolutely no reason and to banish people for no fault of theirs is the crisis of our times.

Anecdotal Evidence

Assam-NRC

A 44-year-old farmer from Baksa, Ajgar Ali faced no problems in getting included in the list. But a certain Mridul Das filed a complaint against his inclusion. In the final list, his family was safe, but he found himself excluded, despite the elusive Mridul Das failing to turn up at the hearing meant to explain his objection.[53]

'Basudev Biswas: 55 years, [son/of] Sudarshan Biswas, Village – Faridpur, [Police Station] – Sirajganj, District – Dacca.' The fact is that Basudev Biswas has lived in Assam's Nagaon district and had a citizenship certificate signed in 1964. On 11 May, Basudev died in detention.[54]

In the 1970s in Simlitola Tea Estate, Puna Munda met Kachela. Both Adivasis from Jharkhand, they fell in love and got married. In 2013, the Foreigners Tribunal declared Puna a foreigner. On 10 June, five years into his detention, Puna died fighting cancer.[55]

Two weeks after giving birth to twins, Sahida Bibi from Dhubri's Rowa village was thrown into a detention centre, along with the newborns. A month-and-a-half later, one of the children died in her arms.[56]

Eighty-four-year-old Sashi Mohan Sarkar of Basugaon was picked up in 2017 and taken to a detention centre. He was partially immobile. On a winter morning in 2018, Sarkar died in detention.[57]

Nur Hassan is a marginal jute farmer in Iswarijhar *char* in Assam's Bongaigaon district. While the rest of his family was deemed citizens, his 9-year-old daughter, Sofia Khatun, was a 'declared foreigner' and was summoned for a hearing.[58]

Ten-year-old Riya Das in Bongaigaon district's Kachudola village could not establish any linkage with her parents, so they notified her as a foreigner.[59]

Ten-year-old Siddhartha Saha from Barpeta Road town is also not in the list for failing to prove 'adequate documentary evidence' of parentage.[60]

Nirod Baran Das hanged himself from a ceiling fan in October 2018 in his house in Kharupetia. Not far away in Udalguri, Deepak Debnath committed suicide. Both had their names dropped from the list after having had them verified.[61]

Pradip Kumar Bordoloi, aged sixty-two, was imprisoned for a week during the Assam Agitation, an anti-foreigner movement that gave impetus to this massive ongoing exercise. First he found himself out of the list, then his wife was accused of 'stealing' her legacy proofs; just as they were regularised, their children were excluded.[62]

The stories above are not 'just a few stories'. They are real lives, real people, real bodies piling up over half-a-century of strife, violence and mistrust. Too many bodies have been split open, and others thrown in internment camps to decay. Even memories betray their existence.

(Former) Jammu and Kashmir, Leh and Ladakh—Article 370

In Jammu and Kashmir, where no one trusts anyone any more, where the streets are barricaded, houses locked up, and voices hushed, grieving bodies, warm bodies, sick bodies, burning bodies, frail bodies, palpitating bodies are all chained by a conspiracy of silence.

There are other bodies, too. Uniformed, armed, hated, weary. They carry the burden of the dead, of the sick, of the angry bodies. The issues affecting this region are discussed in the Appendix at the end of this book.

The Body of the Citizen

What is the body of a citizen worth? In its darkest years, the body of a citizen in Assam was worth being chopped up and used to feed the fish in the river, so as to cleanse all traces of murder. Those were the 'secret killing' years.[63] The citizens protested and voted the Asom Gana Parishad (AGP) government out of power. The AGP had indulged in a culture of terror, using surrendered terrorists to target the families of their former cadres who were still underground. Today, in the same place, the bodies of 190,000 citizens will become numbers in detention centres or in notices and summons issued by the state demanding that they prove why their bodies must be preserved. The citizenry is now no longer one; it has been divided into 'them' and 'us'. The 'them' shall disappear if the 'us' so wishes. How does a citizen's mind function in people's democracies? Just because something is familiar, it need not be perfectly natural or acceptable. The citizen's body today is in a battlefield of combatting doctrines, beliefs, arguments and reasoning. It is incredible how many of 'them' and 'us' are eventually led into orthodoxy, conforming to one camp or the other, a process which, thanks to the internet age, is now out in the open for all to see. Troll armies are set up like guerilla units, tracking every dissenter, every 'anti-Indian' and every 'anti-national' and swooping down on them, identifying their bodies for the detention centres. There is an eerie similarity in the way totalitarian regimes across ages control the body of the citizen. When children go hungry, people are homeless, when there are lynchings and rapes, when there is no access to livelihood, when one is othered on the grounds of gender, race, ethnicity and religion, then the citizen loses control over the body. The body of a citizen carries within it the experiences of the oppressed.

When I started reporting in Assam, I wanted to mask my identity. Don't get ghettoised, I was warned. If you are known as a Bengali reporting on Assam, you will be seen as partisan. I ignored this; is it possible for me to bury my identity of class, caste, gender, religion, etc., while approaching a story? I may consciously ignore my identity so as to not colour my story, but at some subconscious level it is quite possible that it may influence me. This constant shifting of consciousness can be disturbing and impact our sense of justice. Does the personal become the political?

Our culture and identity are not of our making. We only participate in it. I was born into a family of teachers, writers, filmmakers, artists; there is a sense, somewhere, of a cultural hierarchy within a space that was 'liberated', and yet confined by caste and class. My father had migrated, but not quite. He only moved a couple of cities, and his migration was simultaneous to the largest migration in human history—the Partition. My mother did not even experience that tectonic movement. Our identities are closely bound to our histories.

'Nationalism': The Ghost Who Walks

Never in recorded history has 'the Indian' suffered as much insecurity and indignity as today. What is causing such anxiety? Clearly, the biggest source of this insecurity and indignity is social inequality, lack of gainful employment, and political mobilisations based on ethnicity, religion and caste. But there is a deeper fear that seems all too pervasive; an impulse to prove our Indianness on every level, something that has been elevated to a crisis of national identity.

In a 75-year-old nation of a billion-plus people speaking 700 live languages and with more than 2,000 ethnicities, identity can be a tricky marker, and the majority community will always be the guardian of the dominant identity, which in India is the caste Hindu.

The debate over identities is not unique, but to dismiss the other's identity altogether is brute violence. We all have multiple identities, but they rearrange themselves according to convenience to forge a national identity, particularly in times of crisis. In India, however, this national identity is in possession of only one linguistic, religious and caste identity, much like what early European nationalism looked like. If the nineteenth and twentieth centuries witnessed simultaneous processes of religious revival and secular democratic reform, the twenty-first century has clearly emerged as a revivalist world, defining identity through religion.

The question of 'What am I', as against 'Who am I' can be well-defined by India's deep-rooted caste and religious bias. If the general elections of 2014 catapulted Narendra Modi and the BJP to the centrestage by spurring on a national imagination of 'development', the general elections in 2019 were about who is a 'good Indian'. It divided the country into the Indian and the 'outsider', the patriot and the 'dissenter', the nationalist and the 'urban Naxal', the Hindu and the 'liberal'.

It is easy to read this narrative in terms of the shrill political rhetoric that marked the run-up to the 2019 elections. However, it is the systematic takeover of institutions and ideas, and the superimposition of the notion of a Hindu India on them, that underpins this book. But beyond that notion, the more insidious dangers are the ideas of a pristine, 'decolonised' past, shattered by events that collided against each other during the process of state formation. For example, the Partition, which is a process that set off a chain of events that 'haunts' us to this day. Although the majority in the country claims to not have been impacted by the Partition, history tells us that much of the nation's 'identity' has been shaped by the idea of it, and will continue to be shaped by this experience.

In the context of the 2019 elections, Bengal's ideological shift from three decades of Marxist propaganda to the Trinamool Congress's flirtation with the right-wing, before the latter emerged as one of the biggest challengers to the BJP in the 2021 elections, may not be lost on observers. Bengal's history of a subtle shift from nationalism to communalism, from anti-British to anti-Muslim politics[64] may help understand the current situation. Nationalist ideology in religious terms has defined Indian nationalism. For example, the Young Bengal Group in the 1840s in Calcutta was probably the first Hindu group to imagine Hindus as a national community. The idea of a Hindu nation was already finding space in the literary texts of Bhudev Mukhopadhyay (1827–94), a social and political thinker, and novelist Bankimchandra Chattopadhyay (1838–94), who gave the nationalist anthem Vande Mataram, preferred by the Rashtriya Swayamsevak Sangh (RSS) and BJP over Tagore's 'Jana Gana Mana', the official national anthem.[65]

> Vinayak Damodar Savarkar in 1923 reinvented a term previously used by the likes of Brahmabandhab Upadhyay to describe this ideology: Hindutva. Hindutva, Savarkar made clear, was not the same as Hinduism, despite what an unthinking Indian Supreme Court was to declare eighty years later. Hindutva was a form of political Hinduism that sought to organize and militarize the Hindus as a nationality.[66]

The dramatic resurgence of the BJP in electoral politics is based on the idea that Indian culture is coterminous with Hindu culture. The nationalist project that was required to create this 'imagined community' rode on anthems and simple images. A study of such iconography is discussed in detail in Chapter 4.

What some of Bengal's nationalist leaders propagated was that being an Indian was being a Hindu, and it is well-known that people like Bankimchandra, Swami Vivekananda and Aurobindo Ghosh were at the forefront of this crusade.[67] Decades before and after Independence, the Bengal Congress also had significant influence over Indian nationalism and this propaganda was critical in shaping Indian identity.[68]

It is a misleading belief that the Partition was entirely a result of the Muslim separatist movement. This is tied to the dangerous suggestion that the roots of communalism lie within Muslim society. Historian Joya Chatterji, in her book *Bengal Divided*, invokes the scientific Hindusim propagated by Pandit Sasadhar Tarkachudamani, the 'Brahmoism' of Raja Rammohun Roy and the more assertive Hindusim of Bankimchandra and Vivekananda. Hinduism, Chatterji argues, was being reconstructed as a 'single and monolithic religion' and nationalism was but pride in the heroic past or *anushilan*, the code word for liberation from subjugation. It is the commitment to Hindu 'culture' that empowers many of the protagonists of the early nineteenth-century literary texts.[69] What makes it important to revisit that era, even if cursorily, is the fact that there has been a strong revival of these notions, as articulated clearly in the general elections of 2019.

The Book: As I See It

It is futile to seek and locate a single Indian identity, but what this book posits is that in the polyadic society we inhabit, it is important to recognise that the idea of an 'Indian' today is one that emerges from various identities: The Migrant Indian, The Stateless Indian, The Anti-Indian, The Tribal Indian, and The Dalit Indian.

The concepts of identity, citizenship and nationality are central to the theme of this book. However, it is important to distinguish between them because of their overlapping features. I propose to delineate each of these ideas before situating the idea of an Indian, which is at the heart of this book.

I shall try, as far as possible, not to dwell on the academic underpinnings of these concepts, but study them as they evolved in the post-independence context, focusing on how they play out in the everyday world. This subject is almost impossible to cover in scope and extent: it is like a self-replicating cell that regenerates as one identity gives way to reveal another.

The book is divided into a Prologue, four chapters, an Appendix providing a timeline of crucial developments from 2020 to mid-2022, and an Annexure with the findings of a questionnaire-based survey as well as interviews on these critical issues. This Prologue has identified the problem of identity, citizenship and nationality, drawing from literature to history and reportage, and set up the content and form of the following sections.

Chapter 1 develops the theme of identity through family histories, genealogy, memories, acts of forgetting, and experiences of migration and forced displacement. The people whose experiences shape this chapter come from various places and converge in one city, only to experience the same displacement, or a sense of it, a second time in less than a quarter of a century. Forgetting is an important aspect of memory, because forgetting and forgiveness, separately and together, imply guilt and reconciliation. Forgetting could be a loss of memory as well.

The sense of one's identity is most acutely felt through language. The incredible work of documenting living languages done by the People's Linguistic Survey of India (PLSI), a rights-based movement, provides an overview of the complexity of imagining a 'national identity', given the cultural and biological diversity of present-day India which is home to thousands of linguistic communities and where the history of language use is shaped by regional dynamics and overarching social structures such as caste. It is not only the staggering number of languages that demonstrates this diversity, but also that there are six distinct language families in India—therefore, it is almost impossible to guess what a speaker from another language family is saying. If language is the most important distinguishing element between human beings and other living beings, recognising languages to recognise identity is imperative. But languages die, and in the twentieth and twenty-first centuries there has been a rapid depletion of words and entire languages.

> When a language dies, its speakers decide to migrate. First, they migrate to another language and then they physically start migrating to another region. The second thing that happens is that their traditional livelihood patterns go down. They may have some special skills and that disappears. Thirdly, a unique way of looking at the world disappears. Every language is a unique worldview.[70]

To understand the scope of linguistic diversity of this land, let us examine the state of Arunachal Pradesh. With a population of only 140,000[71] in an area roughly 84,000 square kilometres, Arunachal Pradesh, or the erstwhile North-East Frontier Agency (NEFA), has thirty-five living languages. If one takes into account the linguistic varieties within these languages, then this figure goes up to almost 100. Consider the Adi language. Adis or Abors, who may have migrated from Tibet along the Siang valley at different periods since the seventh century, constitute ethno-linguistic groups like Minyong, Padam, Pasi, Karko, Shimong, Bori, Bokar, Ashing, Tangam, Milang, Komkar, Ramos, Pailibos and Pangge. It is a Tibeto-Burman language family and as per the 2001 census, the population of Adis was estimated at 1,62,000.

Chapter 2 'identifies' five cities through the eyes of its 'citizens', which inform us of what it means to be a citizen. It begins with Harappa, where the residents of the city have left behind adequate evidence of their lives.

The notion of citizenship comes from the word 'city', a space that claims to provide individual security and dignity, both rare commodities in today's cities. The informal identity of an Indian is now at odds with the formal identity of the citizen. The book travels across cities in India, speaking to its 'citizens' to understand how they perceive their rights and duties in today's India. But to go beyond binary notions of belonging, the citizens interviewed in each city are themselves either from marginal communities within the city, or are considered 'outsiders' in some sense. The narrative travels across Jalandhar, Guwahati, Hyderabad, Hampi and Banaras as a random sampling of cities. It involved extensive fieldwork across the country, connecting with people who form unlikely mouthpieces of their cities. It ties up with the author's earlier fieldwork and reportage across several other regions, particularly some of India's conflict zones,[72] to bring together what constitutes a microcosm of the idea of India.

India does not live only in its villages; the rate at which urbanisation has taken place in India reflects what is probably one of the biggest migration stories in the history of civilisation. By 2030, 590 million Indians are projected to be living in cities. We often forget that while a nation is abstract, its spatial elements are formed by the cities, villages, forests, rivers and mountains. The India of our collective imagination always had populous cities. Even in the sixteenth century, Agra had half a million people.[73] Although Benares is usually considered the oldest continuously inhabited city, several cities here have existed since the Indus Valley civilisation.[74] Madurai has two millennia of recorded past.[75] Some cities continue to prosper, while others have waned with time. Modern Indian researchers often ignore ancient cities like Kamrupa, which has existed since the time of the Puranas, or Kangelipak (present-day Imphal), which joined the Indian state after Independence.[76] Kavaratti in the Lakswhadweep Islands has been an island city since at least the seventh century CE and later came under the Kingdom of Travancore.[77] I know of no volume on the modern Indian city except an anthology edited by Vinay Lal,[78] where yet again the exclusion of these cities is glaring.

A city is not made of history or monuments of bricks and mortar—it is human. In order to understand the mind of a 'citizen', I travelled across different cities.

In all these stories and experiences, the one refrain that echoes is that the politics of exclusion is not a phenomenon of today, but has existed in this society for thousands of years. How does exclusion work? Martha Nussbaum, in *The Monarchy of Fear*,[79] discusses what emotions drive and shape exclusion. 'Fear', she says, drives this emotion, combined with 'anger blame dynamic'. Certain emotions are inextricably linked to law and fear is one of them. Shame and disgust also make up what we are. Both share an intimate relationship with various forms of prejudice, exclusion and misogyny. But what causes disgust? That is said to arise from a sense of contamination. How does political mobilisation use this sense of disgust to drive a wedge between communities? The people inhabiting this book have gone through extensive periods of exclusion and their identities are borne from having been subjected to reactions of disgust and exclusion. Interestingly, this is not just a collective exclusion; while they have been discriminated against on the basis of race, gender, ethnicity and religion, it is pertinent to remind ourselves that they have also been excluded by history and literature, by media and popular culture.

Chapter 3, which is based neither on fieldwork nor on genealogy, is a series of case studies of specific communities that exemplify the problems of a single identity, legal citizenship and nationality. The narrative is like a bridge between the two larger sections, moving from the individual to a more collective sense of identity. Much of the chapter is based on the author's own work on these communities and comes together to raise some pertinent questions.

Chapter 4, the final chapter, questions the notion of the nation through heterogeneous experiences that forge a different identity, where voices meet and collide, and where nationality and citizenship confront each other.

We grew up with the idea that there was a Bharatvarsa with a definite territory, which changed after the experience of colonisation, and then the Partition. This correlation was further reinforced by the Constitution of India, which declares: 'India that is Bharat shall be a union of States'. This is clearly a product of nineteenth-century nationalist imagination and what C. A. Bayly calls the 'Hindu conceptualization of geography'.[80] It is well-known that the first idea of a 'country' was articulated as *Jambudvipa* in the early Buddhist texts, where *janapadas* were placed in different directions. But much of this is an exercise in conjecture and interpretation, because another text, *Anguttara-nikaya*, refers to many Jambudvipas, and so assigning a specific territory is a pointless exercise. The picture becomes slightly clearer from the time of Ashoka, where a country is visible, with some of the janapadas mentioned earlier. Kalinga, for example, was a different country/kingdom and not part of Bharatvarsa. So while there are texts alluding to a karmabhumi that was Bharatvarsa, the idea of an India(n) does not and cannot emerge from the Puranas. Yes, the legend of Naraka Asura has been an abiding motif of the history of Assam since the Puranas. The Kalika Purana is said to have been written in the Brahmaputra Valley. This is the land where Kamrupa was *nayika* (protagonist) and Shiva had hidden the past. But these are in the realm of myths, and while legends and myths go a long way in identity formation, it requires strong revivalist politics to be able to invoke ancient texts and formulate a homogenous, monolithic identity that assumes the anthropomorphic form of, let us say, Bharat Mata.

This book studies the notion through iconisations, popular culture, and personal stories that defy the manner in which nationalism is packaged in today's world. It revisits Nagaland, Manipur, and Jammu and Kashmir as case studies that challenge the limits of Indian democracy.

Shaheen Bagh in New Delhi, which emerged as a voice of new India and the new Indian, will be studied as a symbol later in the book.

The story of millions of Indians today is one of negotiating identity, citizenship and nationality. None of the myth-laden notions of identity and nationality comes to one's rescue when confronted by the state to prove one's Indianness. This book attempts to question the status quo of what now appears to be the standard Indian identity.

Is 'nation' a concept that sustains a citizen, providing her/him with a secure base from which to view the world, or does it restrict their freedom? Is the Kashmir Valley part of a nation? Is Assam leading the way to exclude its own?

Endnotes

1. *Shorter Oxford English Dictionary*, 6th ed., Vol. 2: s.v. 'outsider'.

2. *Shorter Oxford English Dictionary*, 6th ed., Vol. 1: s.v. 'migration'.

3. Miguel, Cervantes de. 2006. *The Adventures of Don Quixote*, trans. J. M. Cohen. London: Collector's Library, 45.

4. The idiom 'tilting at windmills' has come to mean fighting imaginary enemies. Its origin can be traced to the classic Spanish novel, *Don Quixote*, by where the main character becomes obsessed with the idea of chivalry and spends his time fighting with windmills that he imagines to be giants.

5. Lahiri, Nayanjot. 2018. *Time Pieces: A Whistle-Stop Tour of Ancient India*. New Delhi: Hachette India, 145.

6. Ibid., 146.

7. Ibid., 154.

8. Fukuyama, Francis. 2018. *Identity: The Demand for Dignity and the Politics of Resentment*. London: Profile Books.

9. Ibid., 25.

10. Thapar, Romila. 2019. 'The Presence of the Other: Religion and Society in Early India'. Nemichandra Jain Memorial Lecture, India International Centre, New Delhi, 16 August.

11. Ibid.

12. Ibid.

13. Eaton, Richard M. 2019. *India in the Persianate Age: 1000-1765*. London: Allen Lane, 22.

14. Ibid.

15. Chatterjee, Indrani. 2017. The 'Beyond Borders: NFI-IIC Lecture Series', India International Centre, New Delhi, 20 December.

16. Ibid.

17. For instance, see Sir Herbert Risley's *The People of India*, edited by W. Crooke and published in 1915 by Thacker, Spink and Co., an eight-volume study which contained annotated photographs of Indian castes and tribes, currently with Cornell University. Another example is *The Oxford India Elwin*, with an introduction by G. N. Devy, published by Oxford University Press in 2008. See also A. M. Shah, *The Legacy of M. N. Srinivas*. New Delhi: Routledge India, 2021.

18. Xaxa, Virginius. 1999. 'Tribes as Indigenous People of India'. *Economic and Political Weekly* 34 (51): 3589–95.

19. Devi, Mahasweta. 2001. *Imaginary Maps*, trans. Gayatri Charkavorty Spivak. Calcutta: Thema.

20. The long struggle of the Dongria Kondh, a small Adivasi community of about 8,000 people in the Eastern Ghats of Odisha, is the story of grassroots resistance against dispossession from their land and their way of life, pitted against a model of development through mineral extraction that is considered exploitative.

21. As per the accord signed on 27 January 2020, the Bodoland Territorial Autonomous District (BTAD) is now referred to as the Bodoland Territorial Region (BTR). See Talukdar, S. 2020. 'The Third Bodo Accord: A New Deal'. *The Hindu*, 28 February. Available at https://frontline.thehindu.com/the-nation/article30800941.ece (accessed August 2022).

22. On 12 June 1987, in the Judges Field in Guwahati, Bodo leader Upendra Nath coined the phrase 'Divide Assam 50-50', which was a demand not only for a separate state for the Bodos, but also for the land area to be divided equally. This war cry transformed the agitation into full-fledged terrorist activity, making it one of the most violent phases in India's post-independence history. Though the Bodo demand harks back to the glorious Bodo kingdom of the ancient world, their population was only 11.5 per cent when the demand was made. As per the 2011 census, the Bodo population in the BTAD stands at 1.4 million, and after decades of extreme violence and the creation of a BTC, the demand still finds salience. See Baruah, Garima. 2022. 'Socio-Economic Status of Bodo People of Udalguri District of Assam—An Income Level Analysis'. *JETIR* 9 (3): d383–89. Population figures for 2021 are yet to be declared but it is expected to be 1 million, if reports of a decline in population are taken into account. See *NeNow.in*. 2018. 'Assam Records Decline in percentage of Assamese, Bodo, Rabha, Mishing Speakers', 28 June. Available at https://nenow.in/north-east-news/assam-records-decline-percentage-assamese-bodo-speakers.html (accessed August 2022).

23. For more details, see Kashyap, Samudra Gupta. 1997. 'Bodo Stir Takes a Bloody Turn'. *The Indian Express*, 18 August. Available at https://indianexpress.com/article/news-archive/bodo-stir-takes-a-bloody-turn/ (accessed August 2022). See also Kalita, Prabin. 2006. 'Once a Dreaded Force, Now They Want a Role in Govt'. *The Times of India*, 13 May. Available at https://timesofindia.indiatimes.com/india/once-a-dreaded-force-now-they-want-a-role-in-govt/articleshow/1528149.cms (accessed August 2022).

24. Sharma, Sushil Kumar. 2016. 'Operation All Out against Bodo Militants: What Next?' Manohar Parrikar Institute for Defence Studies and Analyses. Available at https://www.idsa.in/issuebrief/operation-all-out-against-bodo-militants_sushilksharma_020210 (accessed August 2022).

25. Kashyap, Samudra Gupta. 2003. 'Bodo Liberation Tigers Disbanded'. *The Indian Express*, 7 December. Available at https://indianexpress.com/article/news-archive/bodo-liberation-tigers-disbanded/ (accessed August 2022).

26. *The Hindu*. 2009. 'Assam Pays Homage to October 2008 Blast Victims', 31 October. Available at https://www.thehindu.com/news/national/other-states/Assam-pays-homage-to-October-2008-blast-victims/article16889587.ece (accessed August 2022).

27. *Hindustan Times*. 2012. 'Gaffe After Gaffe Mark Shinde's Week as HM', 10 August. Available at https://www.hindustantimes.com/delhi/gaffe-after-gaffe-mark-shinde-s-week-as-hm/story-kHocVH4YThEeNra82PjgmO.html (accessed August 2022).

28. *The Hindu*. 2020. 'Bodos Jubilant, Other Communities Miffed', 29 January. Available at https://www.thehindu.com/news/national/other-states/bodos-jubilant-other-communities-miffed/article30678385.ece (accessed August 2022).

29. See Mander, Harsh. 2012. 'Assam's Tragedy'. *The Hindu*, 25 August. Available at https://www.thehindu.com/opinion/columns/Harsh_Mander/assams-tragedy/article3820732.ece (accessed August 2022). See also Johari, Areefa. 2014. 'The Killings of Muslims in Assam Amounts to Ethnic Cleansing, Claims Report'. *Scroll.in*, 14 November. Available at https://scroll.in/article/689548/the-killings-of-muslims-in-assam-amounts-to-ethnic-cleansing-claims-report (accessed August 2022). See also Bora, Bijay Shankar. 2014. 'The Killing Fields of Assam'. *The Tribune*, 28 December. Available at https://www.tribuneindia.com/news/archive/features/the-killing-fields-of-assam-23325 (accessed August 2022).

30. Kashyap, Samudra Gupta. 2009. 'No End in Sight to NC Hills Violence; Toll Rises to 50'. *The Indian Express*, 18 June. Available at https://indianexpress.com/article/news-archive/web/no-end-in-sight-to-nc-hills-violence-toll-rises-to-50/ (accessed August 2022). A ground report about the violence was broadcast by NDTV in 2009; a video clip of the same is available at https://www.youtube.com/watch?v=wzFnJdK31vQ (accessed November 2022).

31. See https://assam.gov.in/government/410. See also *The Hindu*. 2013. 'I Am Not Going to Divide Assam: Gogoi', 9 August, Available at https://www.thehindu.com/news/national/other-states//article60038799.ece (accessed August 2022).

32. Sanjib Baruah observes that '[m]ost militant groups are best described as ethnic militias. Even people living in the region may not have heard of all the ethnic groups in whose names these struggles are being fought.' 'Durable Disorder'. *The Telegraph*, 22 September 2003. Available at https://www.telegraphindia.com/opinion/durable-disorder/cid/1018590 (accessed August 2022). For a more detailed account, see Baruah, S. 2020. *In the Name of the Nation: India and its Northeast*. Stanford: Stanford University Press. See also Srikanth, H. 2015. 'Ethnic Militancy in Assam: Whom to Blame?' *Economic and Political Weekly* 50 (5): 17–19.

33. For example, see Borpujari, Priyanka. 2015. '"Nobody Asks Us Why We Took Up Arms": Confessions of a Former Adivasi Militant in Assam'. *Scroll.in*, 23 February. Available at https://scroll.in/article/703553/nobody-asks-us-why-we-took-up-arms-confessions-of-a-former-adivasi-militant-in-assam (accessed August 2022).

34. Shankar founded the organisation 'Art of Living' in 1982 and quickly amassed a following as a spiritual leader and yoga guru, with followers generally referring to him as 'Sri Sri Ravi Shankar' or 'Gurudev'. See The Art of Living. 'Gurudev Sri Sri Ravi Shankar'. Available at https://www.artofliving.org/in-en/srisri (accessed August 2022).

35. Shenoy, Jaideep. 2012. 'Sri Sri Ravi Shankar, Founder Art of Living (AOL) Reacting to Assam Crisis States, "This Heinous Crime Against Ethnic People in Assam by Fundamentalist Immigrants is Causing a Huge Humanitarian Crisis. Wake Up and Join In to Condemn this Act"'. *The Times of India*, 25 July. Available at https://timesofindia.indiatimes.com/sri-sri-ravi-shankar-founder-art-of-living-aol-reacting-to-the-assam-criris-states-this-heinous-crime-against-ethnic-people-in-assam-by-fundamentalist-immigrants-is-causing-a-huge-humanitarian-crisis-wake-up-and-join-in-to-condemn-this-act-/articleshow/15139946.cms (accessed August 2022).

36. See Bhatnagar, Gaurav Vivek. 2012. 'As Calm Descends, Kokrajhar Groups See Hidden Hand Behind Violence'. *The Hindu*, 5 August. Available at https://www.thehindu.com/news/national/other-states//article60458117.ece (accessed August 2022). See also Hussain, Bonojit. 2012. 'The Bodoland (Assam) Violence and the Politics of Explanation'. *Kafila*, 8 December. Available at https://kafila.online/2012/12/08/the-bodoland-assam-violence-and-the-politics-of-explanation-by-bonojit-hussain/ (accessed August 2022).

37. See Sinha, Samrat. 2016 'Our Forgotten Wars: Victimisation and Survival in Bodoland'. *Indian Defence Review* 31 (2), April–June. Available at http://www.indiandefencereview.com/spotlights/our-forgotten-wars-victimisation-and-survival-in-bodoland/ (accessed August 2022).

38. For news coverage of this, see Srivatsa, Sharath S., and Deepa Kurup. 2012. 'After Rumours, Northeast People Flee Bangalore'. *The Hindu*, 16 August. Available at https://www.thehindu.com/news/national/karnataka//article60457480.ece (accessed August 2022). See also Makkar, Sahil, Shamsheer Yousaf and Liz Mathew. 2012. 'Despite Govt Assurances, Exodus to North-East Continues'. *LiveMint.com*, 17 August. Available at https://www.livemint.com/Politics/LQiW35WX6NEeRQzFYNseJL/Exodus-to-NorthEast-continues-even-as-officials-try-to-alla.html (accessed August 2022). For a detailed discussion, see Overdorf, Jason. 2012. 'India: Are Riot Politics Back?—Update'. *Theworld.org*, 16 August. Available at https://theworld.org/stories/2012-08-16/india-are-riot-politics-back-update (accessed August 2022).

39. For more details, see Radin, C. J. 2012. 'A New Social Media App: Cyberterrorism'. *Longwarjournal.org*, 4 September. Available at https://www.longwarjournal.org/archives/2012/09/pakistan_is_not_normally_noted.php (accessed August 2022). See also Meschenmoser, Patrick. 2019. 'Virtual Bombs: The Weaponization of Social Media'. *Meshandmoser.com*, 2 March. Available at https://www.meshandmoser.com/2019/03/02/virtual-bombs-the-weaponization-of-social-media/ (accessed August 2022).

40. This description of the Bodos has been previously published by *The Outlook*, dated 3 September 2012, in an article written by the author of this book. Available at https://www.outlookindia.com/magazine/story/there-we-see-only-the-stumps/282079 (accessed August 2022).

41. *India Today*. 2019. 'Illegal Immigrants are like Termites, Will Throw Them Out if BJP Comes Back to Power: Amit Shah', 11 April. Available at https://www.indiatoday.in/elections/lok-sabha-2019/story/bjp-amit-shah-hindu-refugees-mamata-bannerjee-1499691-2019-04-11 (accessed August 2022).

42. For more details, see reportage from this period. For instance, Tiwary, Deeptiman. 2019. 'Protest Damage Notices: Uttar Pradesh Goes Where No State Has Gone Before'. *The Indian Express*, 31 December. Available at https://indianexpress.com/article/india/protest-damage-notices-uttar-pradesh-goes-where-no-state-has-gone-before-6192271/ (accessed August 2022). See also M. S., Nileena. 2020. 'How the Police Prevented Medical Volunteers from Working at the CAA Protests'. *The Caravan*, 1 January. Available at https://caravanmagazine.in/politics/how-the-police-prevented-medical-volunteers-from-working-at-the-caa-protests (accessed August 2022); Khan, Aiman. 2021. 'Two Years since Killing of Anti-CAA Protesters in UP, NHRC Conducts Spot Inquiry'. *The Wire*, 29 December. Available at https://thewire.in/government/caa-protests-uttar-pradesh-killing-nhrc (accessed August 2022). For international coverage of the issue, see *Human Rights Watch*. 2019. 'India: Deadly Force Used Against Protesters: Police Target Anti-Citizenship Law Demonstrators', 23 December. Available at https://www.hrw.org/news/2019/12/23/india-deadly-force-used-against-protesters (accessed August 2022).

43. Bagri, Neha Thirani. 2021. 'India's Anti-Immigrant Crackdown Has Torn Apart Families and Locked Up Hundreds. 1.9 Million People Fear They Could Be Next'. *Time*, 5 September. Available at https://time.com/6092299/india-anti-immigrant-crackdown-assam/ (accessed August 2022).

44. Bhattacharjee, K. K. 1983. *Northeast India: A Study*. New Delhi: Cosmo Publications.

45. *BBC*. 2019. 'Citizenship Amendment Bill: India's New "Anti-Muslim" Law Explained', 11 December. Available at https://www.bbc.com/news/world-asia-india-50670393 (accessed August 2022).

46. See Agarwala, Tora. 2021. 'Will They Take Me Away?' *The Indian Express*, 28 December. Available at https://indianexpress.com/article/north-east-india/assam/assam-nrc-list-supreme-court-parents-children-6270105/ (accessed August 2022), and 2022. 'After Foreigners' Tribunal's "Stop Interfering" Letter, NRC Coordinator Says: "List Not Final"'. *The Indian Express*, 17 May. Available at https://indianexpress.com/article/assam/foreigners-tribunal-letter-nrc-coordinator-7919726/ (accessed August 2022).

47. For more details, see *Hindustan Times*. 2020. 'Post Lockdown, Infiltration Dips but Smuggling Continues Across Porous Indo-Bangla Border'. 12 June. Available at https://www.hindustantimes.com/india-news/post-lockdown-infiltration-dips-but-smuggling-continues-across-porus-indo-bangla-border/story-IQpsYZqCTjT6gU0VMh2gvN.html (accessed August 2022). Another report about smuggling appeared in *The Hindu*. 'Smuggling Only Motive for Infiltrators from Bangladesh: Border Security Force', 2 December. Available at https://www.thehindu.com/news/national/smuggling-only-motive-for-infiltrators-from-bangladesh-border-security-force/article33229615.ece (accessed August 2022). See also *NeNow.in*. 2021. 'Cattle Smuggling Continues Unabated Along Indo-Bangla Border, Reveals Govt Data', 11 March. Available at https://nenow.in/north-east-news/assam/cattle-smuggling-continues-unabated-along-indo-bangla-border-reveals-govt-data.html (accessed August 2022).

48. Khan, Ahmer and Billy Perrigo. 2020. 'What Life Is Like Inside the World's Longest Lockdown'. *Time*, 5 May. Available at https://time.com/5832256/kashmir-lockdown-coronavirus/ (accessed August 2022). See also Fareed, Rifat. 2021. 'Two Years of Kashmir Unrest, Political Void and a Sinking Economy'. *Al Jazeera*, 5 August. Available at https://www.aljazeera.com/news/2021/8/5/kashmir-special-status-india-two-years-human-rights-economy (accessed August 2022).

49. According to internetshutdowns.in (accessed August 2022).

50. Bashi, Shahnaz. 2019. 'The Indian Government Insists All is Well in Kashmir. But as the Communications Shutdown Continues, Its Citizens Are Struggling to Reach the Outside World.' *TIME*, August 23. Available at https://time.com/5659671/kashmir-indian-government/ (accessed August 2022).

51. See Barry, Ellen. 2016. 'An Epidemic of "Dead Eyes" in Kashmir as India Uses Pellet Guns on Protesters'. *The New York Times*, 28 August. Available at https://www.nytimes.com/2016/08/29/world/asia/pellet-guns-used-in-kashmir-protests-cause-dead-eyes-epidemic.html (accessed August 2022).

52. Bhattacharjee, Kishalay. 2015. *Blood on My Hands: Confessions of Staged Encounters*. New Delhi: Harper Collins India.

53. Saikia, Arunabh. 2019. 'Humans of Assam: This Farmer's Name was Struck Off the NRC—After an Unknown Man Filed an Objection'. *Scroll.in*,

1 September. Available at https://scroll.in/article/935834/humans-of-assam-this-farmers-name-was-struck-off-the-nrc-after-an-unknown-man-filed-an-objection (accessed August 2022).

54. Saikia, Arunabh. 2019. 'In Assam, Two Men Tagged as Bangladeshis Died in Detention—One was an Adivasi from Jharkhand'. *Scroll.in*, 30 August. Available at https://scroll.in/article/935456/in-assam-two-men-tagged-as-bangladeshis-died-in-detention-one-was-an-adivasi-from-jharkhand (accessed August 2022).

55. Ibid.

56. Saikia, Arunabh. 2019. 'A Newborn Died in a Detention Centre in Assam. His Mother was Later Found not to be a Foreigner'. *Scroll.in*, 28 August. Available at https://scroll.in/article/935337/detention-in-assam-a-baby-and-old-man-died-despite-their-families-having-proof-of-citizenship (accessed August 2022).

57. *Hindustan Times*. 2019. 'A Case for Posthumous Citizenship for NRC Victims', 27 November. Available at https://www.hindustantimes.com/analysis/a-case-for-posthumous-citizenship-for-nrc-victims/story-V8vkdnT6HmkWd3T7n8qTxL.html (accessed August 2022).

58. Saha, Abhishek. 2021. "'They Called Us Illegal. How is it Possible?' Family Declared Indians after Year in Detention'. *Indian Express*, 1 January. Available at https://indianexpress.com/article/north-east-india/assam/assam-nrc-detention-centre-7128303/ (accessed August 2022).

59. Saikia, Arunabh. 2019. 'Assam's NRC: These Children could be Stateless Soon'. *Scroll.in*, 27 August. Available at https://scroll.in/article/935195/assams-nrc-these-children-could-be-stateless-soon (accessed August 2022).

60. Ibid.

61. Saikia, Arunabh. 2019. 'Death by Citizenship: They made it to NRC, but were Dropped Later—Tagged as Suspected Foreigners'. *Scroll.in*, 17 July. Available at https://scroll.in/article/930730/death-by-citizenship-they-made-it-to-nrc-but-were-dropped-later-tagged-as-suspected-foreigners (accessed August 2022).

62. Saikia, Arunabh. 'Humans of Assam: A Crusader against "Illegal Migrants" Now Finds Himself Left Out of the NRC'. *Scroll.in*, 1 August. Available at https://scroll.in/article/932414/humans-of-assam-a-crusader-against-illegal-migrants-now-finds-himself-left-out-of-the-nrc (accessed August 2022).

63. The Assam killings, referred to as 'Secret Killings', were recorded between 1998 and 2000. They led to three inquiry commissions under India's Commission of Inquiry Act of 1952. On 3 November 2005, the K. N. Saikia Commission was constituted, and it submitted its report to the government on 15 November 2007 (to be presented to the Assembly). The Saikia report

investigated thirty-five cases of secret killings. According to the report, most of the killings occurred in the dead of night and the assailants spoke in the local language. 'The assailants were invariably armed with sophisticated firearms of prohibited bores, and masked with black wrappers or caps to avoid being identified,' notes the report. 'The vehicles used were mostly Maruti Gypsies and vans always without registration numbers. There was police patrolling in the crime areas prior to and after but not during the killings.' See Bhattacharjee, Kishalay. 2013. 'Close Encounters of the False Kind'. *Open Magazine*, 17 October. Available at https://openthemagazine.com/features/india/close-encounters-of-the-false-kind/ (accessed August 2022).

64. Haimanti Roy writes:

> *Amrita Bazar Patrika* (henceforth, *ABP*), 23 April 1947, 1, 5. The newspaper published its intentions of conducting a Gallup Poll to ascertain 'as far as possible, public opinion on the question of proposed partition of Bengal for the creation of a separate homeland for Bengal Hindus' on March 23 1947. The polls closed on 15 April 1947, and the results were published on 23 April. To maintain the credibility of the poll, the paper also published comments in support from Surendra Mohan Ghosh, the president of the Bengal Provincial Congress Committee, and the reputed Calcutta based charted accountant company of Messrs. Gupta and Mitra.... Scholars have argued that that this particular poll was indicative of the communalization of the Bengali bhadralok public opinion and was part of wider organized campaign towards the partitioning of the province.

See 2009. 'Partition of Contingency? Public Discourse in Bengal, 1946–1947'. *Modern Asian Studies* 43: 1355–84. Available at https://dspace.mit.edu/bitstream/handle/1721.1/51358/Multiple%20Nations-Draft02.pdf;sequence=1 (accessed August 202). See also Joya Chatterji. 1996. *Bengal Divided: Hindu Communalism and Partition, 1932-1947.* Cambridge: Cambridge University Press, 240–41.

65. Nandy, Ashis. 2009. 'The Demonic and the Seductive in Religious Nationalism: Vinayak Damodar Savarkar and the Rites of Exorcism in Secularizing South Asia'. Working Paper No. 44, Heidelberg Papers in South Asian and Comparative Politics. Heidelberg: Heidelberg University.

66. Ibid., 3.

67. For further details, see Sarkar, Tanika. 1994. 'Imagining a Hindu Nation: Hindu and Muslim in Bankimchandra's Later Writings'. *Economic and Political Weekly* 29 (39): 2553–61. Available at https://www.jstor.org/stable/4401824 (accessed August 2022). See also Nanda, Meera. 2009. 'Hindu Triumphalism and the Clash of Civiliations'. *Economic and Political Weekly* 44 (28). Available at https://www.epw.in/journal/2009/28/special-articles/hindu-triumphalism-and-clash-civilisations.html (accessed August 2022). A detailed discussion can also be found in Chatterji, *Bengal Divided.*

68. Propaganda, or upper-caste Hindu mobilisation against Muslims and lower castes. By the 1930s, the bhadralok-dominated Bengal Congress had already distanced itself from the Muslim leadership and the lower-caste Hindus. When Savarkar launched the Hindu Mahasabha on 27 December 1939, it quickly changed its colour and became a caste-Hindu organisation defending bhadralok interests.

> Election results in late 1945 and early 1946 demonstrated that the Bengal Congress was still the party of choice for Hindus. Those who had joined the Mahasabha during the war had come back to its fold. They were convinced that the Congress, with its all-India influence, would prove to be a far more effective champion of Hindu causes. The Congress did not disappoint them in Bengal. Joining hands with the Hindu Mahasabha, it began a vigorous campaign for partitioning Bengal. It is hardly remembered today that it was not the Muslims of Bengal who wanted the Muslim-majority districts of eastern Bengal to be taken out of the province and merged with Pakistan. The initiative came almost entirely from Hindus led by the Congress and the Hindu Mahasabha, and supported, very significantly, by the Communist Party of India.

Mukherjee, Ishan. 2019. 'Battle for the Bhadralok: The Historical Roots of Hindu Majoritarianism in Bengal'. *The Caravan*, 29 November. Available at https://caravanmagazine.in/politics/historical-roots-of-hindu-majoritarianism-in-west-bengal (accessed August 2022).

69. Chatterji, *Bengal Divided*, 156, 159, 165.

70. G. N. Devy, speaking in an interview. Roychowdhury, Adrija. 2020. 'There are 600 Potentially Endangered Languages in India… Each Dead Language Takes Away a Culture System'. *The Indian Express*, 3 May. Available at https://indianexpress.com/article/research/international-mother-language-day-2018-ganesh-devy-indian-languages-5072487/ (accessed August 2022).

71. See Census 2011.

72. Including Jammu and Kashmir, Assam, Manipur, Nagaland, Tripura and the states of what is generally called the 'Northeast' and the 'Maoist corridor'.

73. Frank, Andre Gunder. 1996. 'India in the World Economy, 1400–1750'. *Economic and Political Weekly* 31 (30): PE50–64. Available at https://www.jstor.org/stable/4404438?seq=1 (accessed August 2022).

74. 'For over 2500 years this city, also called Varanasi, has attracted pilgrims and seekers from all over India…. Banaras is one of the oldest living cities in the world, as old as Jerusalem, Athens, Peking…its present life reaches back to the sixth century B.C. in a continuous tradition.' Eck, Diana L. 1983. *Banaras: City of Light*. New Delhi: Penguin Random House India. See also https://www.britannica.com/place/Varanasi (accessed August 2022).

75. Kundu, D., B. Lahiri, A. Pandey and P. Sharma. 2019. 'City Profile: Madurai, India.' *Environment and Urbanization Asia* 10 (2): 308–30.

76. Bhuyan, R. R. 2021. 'Religious Interaction in Early Medieval Kamarupa: An Insight into the *Kalikapurana*'. *Indian Historical Review* 48 (2): 218–32. See also Mazumdar, Prasanta. 2020. 'Manipur's Titular King in Rajya Sabha, Feels He Can Serve People'. *The New Indian Express*, 21 June. Available at https://www.newindianexpress.com/thesundaystandard/2020/jun/21/manipurs-titular-king-in-rajya-sabha-feels-he-can-serve-people-2159252.html (accessed August 2022).

77. See https://lakshadweep.gov.in/about-lakshadweep/history/ (accessed August 2022).

78. Lal, Vinay (ed.). 2013. *The Oxford Anthology of the Modern Indian City: Making and Unmaking the City, Politics, Culture and Life Forms*. New Delhi: Oxford University Press.

79. Nussbaum, Martha C. 2018. *The Monarchy of Fear: A Philosopher Looks at our Political Crisis*. London: Oxford University Press.

80. Bayly, C. A. 2000. *Empire and Information: Intelligence Gathering and Social Communication in India, 1780–1870*. Cambridge: Cambridge University Press.

1 The I of Identity

Genealogies from Sialkot, Sylhet, Mithila, Cannanore and Shillong

Identity[1]
/ʌɪˈdɛntɪti/
1. the fact of being who or what a person or thing is.

Tribal[2]
/ˈtrʌɪb(ə)l/

adjective
1. of or characteristic of a tribe or tribes.
• DEROGATORY
characterized by or reflecting strong group loyalty.

noun
1. members of tribal communities, especially in South Asia.

Indigenous[3]
/ɪnˈdɪdʒɪnəs/

adjective
1. originating or occurring naturally in a particular place; native.

Ardhoporinoto Bortoman

i
Going through old papers I have calculated and identified
Relations between ancestors and descendants
For example, with my great grandfather's paternal aunt's grandchild

They were experts at clerical work
How much ration each soldier will require
How much to be paid to labourers for laying the rail to the tea estates
They would do that entire math for their masters

My grandfather was then teaching at Sonaram school
Great Grandfather's paternal aunt's grandchildren arrived

With history in suitcases, ilish from Padma and
Kalibabu's Chandimandap

I can still calculate and tell you
The son-in-law of the granddaughter of a nephew

ii
In our house the sun was imprisoned on a plate smeared with sandalwood
Since time was displaced, this god has been there in our house
In our language it was called Bhavani Shankar—the dual image of Shiv and Parvati
A strange tale of our genealogy
Every evening we would pray to Bhavani Shankar

Slowly one by one everyone left for different towns and cities
The dew of lonely youth had accumulated in the sky
I stayed home restless unable to play football
Emotionally read letters by my aunts and uncles
Time betrays some of us, stays indifferent
I smear sandalwood on my heart every morning

iii
For the sake of conversation
Consider my father is a German and my mother Assamese
I wasn't sure whether I should learn German or Assamese
Mother wanted me to learn Assamese and dad thought I would learn German
Read Schopenhauer and Goethe
Mom would make me tilor pitha and laru
And bought me kuhipaat.

I was confused in this dilemma
I wanted both my father's perspective and my mother's emotion
The road I stood on
Had an unbridgeable distance with my past
And a terrible distance with my present

iv
What is my difference with you?
Just like you, in the blinding rain
I can navigate the alleys of Guwahati
To decipher the voices amidst high rise apartments
Like you, I too shuddered to see bus full of people speeding by
Fear in our faces were reflecting on the rear view mirrors

The day we were introduced in Cotton College
You took me home and sang me Parbatiprasad's sangeet

I brought home Bina Baruah's Jibonor Batot
And a lot of dreams from ardhoporinoto time

Kishore Bhattacharjee[4]

Two kinds of memory jostle against each other: one, memories of the place where communities reside, and two, family memories, genealogies interrupted by the events of one's life. Together they mourn a time that is otherwise separated from the history of the city as we know it. Identity locates itself in these memories and in acts of forgetting.

Since the 1950s, scholars with anthropological training have studied community life, committed to extensive fieldwork to understand identity. In the following pages, I attempt to weave together the acts of remembering and forgetting of several families who have travelled from distant places, as well as the 'neighbourhood', to 'settle' in a promised land, Shillong, which they imagined would be their own. One day, they were told that this land belongs only to some people. They stayed on till they were hounded out; some stayed on despite the odds. They belong to different communities, and while some came here in search of livelihood, others arrived in search of shelter. This chapter explores peoples' perception of time and memory, of the past and the living present, with unsentimental nostalgia. Their memories are different, yet bound by a common ground—a new home, Shillong.

For millions in South Asia, the decades after the Partition transformed their lives in a way they had never imagined. Shillong's story and history, however, moved beyond the pale of reason and imagination. Why are some major historical events neglected despite their magnitude? Is historical narrative not a product of perception of the experience?

The context for these events is firmly rooted in the Partition and post-Partition holocaust, how eastern Bengal became East Pakistan and, later in 1971, India's role in the creation of Bangladesh, which remains the biggest stumbling block in India-Pakistan relations. However, India's relations with Bangladesh soured soon after the Liberation War. This affected India both internally and externally, a body blow that left the state fighting insurrections or mutinies in Nagaland, Manipur, Mizoram, Assam, Tripura, Meghalaya, Arunachal Pradesh, Bengal, the tribal heartland in eastern and central India, and later in Jammu and Kashmir. The challenges to democracy that emerged from the imposition of internal emergency only intensified, with political violence, caste-based and communal conflict, and the sustained rise of authoritarianism.[5] It also helped to create a political landscape and soundscape that has echoed in various parts of the country, most recently in the general elections of 2019.

Interrogating the facts and oral memory of the last century may help us understand better the identity of the Indian, which remains mostly ambivalent and absent even while its workings become increasingly visible in our everyday life.

What are you?

I am an Indian.

I mean, what are you truly?

I am a Bengali.

I didn't ask you that.

What do you want me to say? I am an English-educated Bengali Brahmin, but not from Calcutta.

Then where are you from?

Shillong.

How did you get to Shillong?

I was always there.

I mean, how did your parents arrive there?

Oh! Now I get you. So, my father moved from East Bengal/East Pakistan just after the Partition.

Ah! So you are a Bangladeshi.

Nowai, Dhaka Dakshin, Sylhet

My father, a historian who lived in Shillong for most of his life, was born in a part of Assam that is now Bangladesh. Technically, he merely moved across towns within the same administrative unit. However, its impact was profound, given that his place of birth and childhood was suddenly partitioned, and he and his family chose to 'cross over' to India from Pakistan, both new nations formed in 1947.

April 1972. Twenty-three years since he left his home.

That morning, he packed some clothes in a beige leather suitcase and left for the Dawki border. The journey (in a red, yellow and blue Bedford local bus) took him more than two hours. After so many years in exile, he could now visit home.

The house was situated on a mound (*tila*) in a big estate with a *tongi ghar* and a Shiv temple.

The house was built in the 'Bangla Batton' style of architecture typical to the city; 'a timber frame with plastered bamboo surface'.[6] The idea was to have lightweight structures and a pitched roof to protect against the frequent seismic activity and high rainfall of the region. They are very close to what is popularly seen as the 'Assam-type House'. The house had one storey, with indoor and semi-outdoor spaces held under one pitch. The rooms had high ceilings. The walls were 'painted in white lime and the modular wooden panels coated with black bitumen' to create an aesthetically pleasing contrast. The walls were made of 'ekra', a bamboo fence baked with a mixture of mud and lime.

The main house had an annexe with many rooms to receive guests. The 'forsho' was the main room in the outhouse, and other rooms were allotted according to hierarchy. Hookah was offered to visitors, and a separate hookah was kept for Muslim visitors. Moin Chacha was a regular visitor, but restricted himself to the outhouse. It was understood that Muslims would not cross this boundary; Hindus followed the same practice when they visited a Muslim house.

The house had a vegetable garden, where they grew cauliflowers, cabbages, and other vegetables. The common kitchen was managed by his mother and other women of the family, and more than thirty people sat to eat on the long verandah on any given day.

Although they were not zamindars, they were affluent and had landed property, and thereby dependent families as well. Some of the property was disposed of to maintain the large household, but the majority was lost in litigation.

Although his father was a qualified teacher and an academic administrator of repute, much of his time was taken up in fighting cases to retain the land. As was common practice then, the existing land would be sold at throwaway prices to finance these litigations and maintain family status. Lavish festivals like Durga puja and Kali puja drained their resources and landed them in heavy debt. He could not reconcile with his father's style of living, and this impacted his studies. Education was primarily about admitting the sons to schools (daughters came second), but the family hardly ever cared about how their children were faring in their studies. They were strict disciplinarians of a strange kind. Returning home late was punished, and he once had to escape to a neighbour's house with the help of his mother after his father found him playing cards with seniors.

Later, he moved to the reputed Duttarail Middle English School, which, although located in a Muslim-majority area, was under the supervision of a revered headmaster, S. C. Hom Chaudhuri. In 1942, he had joined the Quit India Movement and organised strikes in school that usually failed to mobilise support. He would have been expelled had not the president of the school governing body intervened and given him a last chance. Many years later, he had a chance encounter with the topper of his class, Gopendra Das, who had gone on to Murari Chand College. He learnt that Gopendra had become a ticket collector, having given up studies during the riots of 1950. From Middle English school, he went to Bhadeshwar High School, another well-known institution, but consumed by the prevailing mood of pre-independent India, immersed himself in student politics instead.

The village was free of communal unrest, and he could not recall even a single incident of violence. Though Muslims were not permitted to join the Durga puja rituals, they would volunteer to clean the compound. Only dry prasad was distributed amongst them. Despite the limited social intercourse between the two religious groups—or even amongst different castes—the few interactions there were, were warm and without malice. Aslam Chacha, a peasant in the village, was the one who caught him smoking and counselled him. He never smoked again in his life. He did not know the word secular, but remembers the village as a space that was truly secular in spirit. Clashes happened only over land, and did not assume a religious colour.

Sylhet gets its name from 'Sree Hotto' or 'a beautiful market', and it was an ancient commercial hub.[7] After the Mughal invasion in 1612, it got its first culvert, road network and a clock tower. In 1765, the East India Company acquired the Diwani of Bangla Suba and Sylhet, along with Karimganj, came under its rule. Cachar was annexed in 1832. On 12 September 1874, it was partitioned from Bengal and integrated as a revenue district to the Chief Commissioner's Province in Assam. In 1836, Bengali became the language officially in use in the schools and courts of Assam. In 1905, when Lord Curzon forcibly pushed through the partition of Bengal, another restructuring took place, and on 16 October 1905, a new 'province of "Eastern Bengal and Assam" was created…with an area of 1,06,540 square miles and a population of 31 million'.[8] The people of the Brahmaputra Valley protested this and Bengal violently opposed the decision as well. By 1912, the decision had been annulled and Assam went back to its Chief Commissionership status with Cachar, Goalpara and Sylhet.[9]

Although everyday life in the 1940s was unaffected by the political fallout of post-war Europe and events at home, the impact was bound to be felt sooner or later. As William Van Schendel writes in *A History of Bangladesh*: 'In the 1940s the Bengal delta went through breathtaking change. World War II shook the established order as the Japanese advanced and the terrible famine of 1943/44 struck. Soon afterwards the social and political system started to crack up.'[10]

The Bengal Famine and the Great Calcutta Killings (also known as Direct Action Day) of 1946 are critical to understanding how Bengal evolved over the next decade.[11] There were peasant revolts across Bengal and the Tebhaga movement peaked in 1946–47. The majority of landowners were Hindus. In Sylhet, this was called the Nankar movement. Hindu-Muslim differences were being reinforced. Bengal's privileged Hindu landowning groups, who also formed the intelligentsia and controlled big businesses, saw this as a challenge to their control.[12] From erstwhile Bengali nationalism, the focus shifted to communal politics. The partition of Bengal became inevitable.

> …the second and definitive partition of Bengal was preceded by an organised agitation which demanded the vivisection of the province on the basis of religion. This movement was led by the very same section of Bengali society that had dominated its nationalist politics since the time of Bengal's first partition: the so called bhadralok or 'respectable people'. In less than forty years, bhadralok politics had come full circle, moving away from nationalist agendas to more parochial concerns.[13]

The first indication that their home may not be in India came when Lord Mountbatten proposed on 3 June 1947 that the people of this Muslim-majority district should decide which country they wished to belong to. The rest of Assam would remain with India. While Mountbatten believed that the people here should decide, the same courtesy was not extended to the Hindu-majority Sindh province.

The Assamese leadership seized this opportunity to shake Sylhet off their back. Sylhet, however, was completely taken aback. The people here had no prior history of communal violence, and had to come to terms with their newly awakened religious 'identity'.

6 July 1947. The Sylhet Referendum

It was raining very hard that morning. He recalls that most members of the family went out to vote to decide whether their district (Sylhet had been part of Assam for seventy years by then, since its separation from Bengal) would join India or Pakistan. The election symbol for staying with India was a *ku(n)re ghar* or hut, and for joining Pakistan, a *kudall kuthar* or axe.

At the Dhaka Dakshin polling booth in north Sylhet, Shailendra Shekhar Dutta, a lecturer in Murarichand College, was the senior presiding officer. Dhaka Dakshin was a Zamiyat stronghold, and he remembers that they were in favour of joining India.

On 14 July 1947, Sylhet decided to be part of Pakistan. Government employees were given the option of choosing which government they wished to serve, but it would not be an easy transfer of population. The subcontinent was in chaos.

It is believed that the Congress had already decided to give Sylhet away. Bengali-speaking Sylhet had been severed from Bengal, and therefore the Bengal Provincial Congress Committee did not take it into consideration. Assam did not want the region, so the Assam Provincial Congress Committee remained disinterested.

TABLE 1.1: Results of the Sylhet Referendum, 6–7 July 1947

Name of the subdivisions	Total Muslim electorate	Total general electorate	Vote for East Bengal	Vote for remaining in Assam
Sadar	92,268	48,863	68,381	38,871
Karimganj	54,002	46,221	41,262	40,536
Habiganj	75,274	60,252	54,543	36,952
South Sylhet	38,397	41,427	31,718	33,471
Sunamganj	51,846	39,045	43,715	34,211

Source: Bhattacharjee, 1990.[14]

The referendum left out more than 200,000 valid votes of tea garden labourers from 190 out of 221 tea estates. Widespread rigging was also alleged.[15] Except for 3.5 *thanas*, the district joined Pakistan. At the stroke of midnight, Assam lost only an eighteenth of its area but a significant third of its population, as well as its tea gardens and lime and cement industries.[16] Of course, the worst blow was losing access to sea ports. Suddenly, the region was landlocked. The new borders became hard mental boundaries that only created new antagonisms. All natural movements of tribes across the hills in this new landlocked region were suddenly restricted. Several tribes raised demands for political autonomy.

The differences between the Brahmaputra and Surma Valleys over this district can easily be viewed as the genesis of the identity and citizenship debate in Assam, and what came to be 'identified' as the Northeast region. The Barak Valley was known as Surma Valley, together with Sylhet, before the Partition. Situated in the southern part of Assam, it is made up of Cachar, Karimganj and Hailakandi. The political rearrangements involving this region fuelled antagonism and ethnic contestations between the Assamese in the Assam Valley, which is now referred to as the Brahmaputra Valley, and the Bengalis of Barak/Surma Valley.

Although the Sylhet referendum is an invisible footnote in Indian history, its impact has been manifold, the most significant being that the Bengali Hindu population from Sylhet relocated to Assam. The plan to keep Sylhet out was aborted. The Assamese-Bengali faultlines would only grow worse from this point onwards. In a couple of decades, multiple violent assertions based on identity emerged, jostling against each other for hegemony. On the other hand, an apolitical Hindu Sylheti identity was already a threat to many communities and tribes as Bengali settlers started spreading across the region.

The Bengali-Assamese relationship was strained because historically, once Sylhet came to Assam, the Assamese saw Bengalis, who began dominating the region, as usurpers of land and jobs. Even though Assamese leaders were relieved that Sylhet went to Pakistan, the Partition did not help; the Bengalis had already created their own pockets of influence and swiftly moved in and settled inside Assam, deepening the antagonism between the two communities. Language became the trigger and the Assamese started the *bhasha andolan* demanding their right to their language. This was one of the first instances of identity mobilisation based on language and it took place on both sides of the border—in Assam, the Assamese language over Bengali, and in East Pakistan, it was the clash of Bengali over Urdu that eventually formed a new nation, Bangladesh.

While historians usually see the Partition as a line that cut through Bengal and Punjab, they often forget that it went right through Assam and Tripura as well. Bengal was partitioned 201 times that included 197 enclaves.[17] Unlike West Pakistan, in the East the Long Partition started in 1947 and continued till 1971.

While a new homeland was created for the Bengali Muslims which eventually became a country with no territorial loss, the Bengali Hindu was destined to be a refugee. Unlike Punjab, the Partition in Bengal was a long-drawn and unending process. People had to change their citizenship multiple times. In many cases, they were not (and are still not) sure of their citizenship. Nor are they certain of their identity—refugee or migrant or outsider.

While a new national identity based on religion was taking shape in Pakistan, East Pakistan was still stuck in limbo. The majority of the population of this new country lived in East Pakistan, but was being governed from a distance of 1,500 kilometres. Pakistan's state-formation challenges were far greater compared to those of India. The biggest challenge at the time of the country's birth was its obduracy in imposing Urdu as a national language. The Bengali language became a rallying point, although this linguistic identity was not strong enough to avert the genocide of 1950. The irony, however, is lost to history: a Hindu Bengali, Dhirendranath Datta of the Pakistan Congress, was among the first to raise the demand for Bengali as national language in the Pakistan Constituent Assembly. Datta and his son were allegedly tortured and killed by Pakistani authorities in 1971 on charges of seeking to disintegrate the country.[18] Their bodies were never found. Interestingly, in independent Bangladesh Datta's family property was confiscated, and he was never duly acknowledged.

Bangladesh's relationship with the 'Bengali' has been paradoxical, moving between a kind of longing and hatred, a tension that has forged an absent Bengali identity which moves between victimhood and anxiety. The East Bengali or the Bangal's (almost a pejorative in West Bengal, referring to the Bengalis of East Bengal/Pakistan/

Bangladesh and to refugees in Assam, the Hindu Bengalis are called Bongals and the slur for a Muslim Bengali is Miyah) relationship with Bangladesh has been paradoxical, moving between a kind of longing and hatred, a tension that has forged an absent Hindu Bangal identity that moves between victimhood and anxiety. The Bangal in absentia has detached her/himself from the process of history to cling to some moments in the past.

In the four days of 16–19 August 1946, unprecedented communal killings in Calcutta were reported. Some 5,000-10,000 people died, around 15,000 were injured and there is no authentic casualty figure to this day.[19] Witness testimonies in this massacre were considered partisan and therefore lack clarity. Private, public and official memory all remain buried in the Great Calcutta Killings.

The killings and hostility seemed to have vanished with Independence, but tensions between the Hindus and Muslims continued to simmer after the Partition. From 1947 through 1950, sporadic incidents were reported, but large-scale rioting was avoided.

News of Muslims killed in Howrah in West Bengal incited passions in East Bengal. On 10 February 1950, Dhaka observed a 'protest' day.[20] Self-styled leaders made speeches at Paltan Maidan, calling upon Muslims to avenge the Calcutta killings. Hindus across East Bengal were attacked with blood-for-blood slogans. Ownership of shops changed hands swiftly. It was now that the Muslim middle class also engaged in violence. Barisal was the worst affected. All Hindus under Muladi thana were killed. Hindus in Bhairab Bazar in Mymensing district were also wiped out. The Hindu families who survived were forced to leave now. The exodus began. Bengal and Assam witnessed a surge in refugees. During the period 10 February–16 April 1950, some 14,00,000 refugees fled East Pakistan. At the same time, around 400,000 Muslims left India.[21] The movement of refugees continued for months. Home Minister Sardar Patel suggested that Pakistan provide land to resettle the refugees. On 8 April 1950, the two prime ministers of India and Pakistan, Nehru and Liaquat Ali, signed the Nehru-Liaquat Pact defining the position of minorities in both countries. Under this agreement, minorities of both countries would enjoy every right granted to a citizen. It also ensured that migrants could move freely from East and West Bengal, Assam and Tripura with as many household goods as they wished to carry with them. Migrants could also return to their homes if they chose. If they returned by 31 December 1950, ownership rights would not change and they would be able to dispose of their property, exchange land, or otherwise claim their land. The provision included every single person who had left since August 1947. The Pact had other provisions for inquiry committees, the search for abducted women, etc., none of which was implemented on the ground. Almost all prominent Hindu families and professionals were forced to leave East Pakistan.

My father took his matriculation exams in 1947 from Calcutta University. The Partition was still not a reality. Then the line was drawn; he has no recollection of specific details regarding the date or time of the family's relocation because they decided to move gradually, and never faced any riots or oppression. Some members of his extended family required financial help, but he and his family were safe. They did not witness the horrors of refugee camps. They were educated and had jobs. When they met neighbours and relatives, they hardly ever reminisced about the village. Those days seemed like a past life that appeared only in dreams.

He settled in Shillong, working in the office of the Accountant General and then as a teacher of history in the town's most respected college run by Irish Christian Brothers.

1971. India was at war with Pakistan, helping the Mukti Bahini of Bangladesh. Aircrafts would fly low and Shillong would be under perpetual 'blackouts'. Even children played war games. But the longing for a home left behind was not as intense. The sense of Indianness was more dominant.

On 25 March 1971, Bangladesh was born. The Indira-Mujib (Treaty of Peace and Friendship) pact was signed on 19 March 1972. His family nominated him to go across to the new country of Bangladesh and claim 'enemy property'.

Twenty-three years since he left 'home', the memories are a blur. Flashes of his childhood dissolved into his youth, which coincided with the birth pangs of a newborn nation. It felt like a long sabbatical from home. The house, its people, the neighbours all must be more or less the same. When was the last time he had visited home?

At the last moment, however, he stepped back from the customs check-post. He was told that the 'Muslims' had plundered the town, but did not touch the Shiv mandir inside their home. After all, they had been 'friends'!

He did not look beyond the check-post guards but turned towards 'India' and started walking. By tea-time he was 'home', because this was home. What used to be home was now 'alien'. 'Deshbari' had lost its spatial existence and remained only in memory and nostalgia. At ninety-one, he remembers only the name of the village, Nowai. He says everything else is a dream interrupted.

So while the Sylhet referendum remains a footnote in Partition studies, it is a critical introduction to understanding identity.

Shillong, 1969

I was born in the spring of 1969 and grew up among plum and cherry blossoms. We would go for Sunday picnics in the park nearby with sandwich baskets. I often walked up the side of the Crinoline Waterfalls behind our house to read. At first, we lived in a smaller accommodation that was part of a rather large house owned by a Bengali engineer. They were like grandparents to me, even though the owner-tenant relationship was firmly acknowledged. I spent hours hanging out with Amma, our landlady, who taught me how to blow into the chulha to get the fire burning. Our landlord, whom I called Jethu, would take me along to discover nuts and bolts that eventually became my tool kit, stored in a broken suitcase that I owned with an absolute sense of pride. My mother, proud of my knack for engineering, believed for a long time that I was destined to build bridges, until my high school grades assured her otherwise.

The branches of the plum tree covered the entire kitchen roof, which was made of asbestos. The house had two rooms: at a slight elevation from the kitchen was the only bedroom. The other room was the living room, which had a bed where my father slept. The bedroom was for my mother and her two children. It was a less than modest living, but it did not seem out of the ordinary. The town was made up of similar homes. My father taught in a college and my mother was at home, mostly trying very hard to further her love for the performing arts. She happily organised plays and events for the *para/mohalla* (locality). She was known as Kakima, and dad was Kakababu. Many years later, I was told that while we were not exactly poor, we did not have adequate money because dad had to send money-orders to seven different families every month: relatives who couldn't manage their lives after the Partition. Similar stories were to be heard in every home. No one made a fuss.

In 1975, Amma and Jethu moved to Calcutta and we became the proxy owners (in reality, tenant and caretaker) of a large campus, a front garden full of flowers such as forget-me-nots, sweetpeas, chrysanthemums, ginia, and sunflowers, a courtyard, and a bamboo grove in the backyard. It was a house of plums and pomegranates; from the road named Sylheti para, a stone staircase (I forget the count, but remember counting it several times) would lead to the house made on two levels. The house had wooden floors and distempered walls with pretty lace curtains that my mother had stitched. Every bit of the house was well-kept, and books occupied most shelves. Eventually, my mother took up work as a teacher and spent a lot of time collecting folktales. She continued with her work in the performing arts, but her priority was her children. The backyard was later transformed into a vegetable garden. Fermented fish, or *shutki*, is an East Bengal delicacy that was often cooked with some of these vegetables. Journalist Amrita Dutta has a brilliant description of this strong-smelling dry fish that became synonymous with 'Bangladeshis', even though most tribals in the region had their own delicious recipes, the most famous being the Manipuri variety:

> Growing up in the tiny Sylheti community of Shillong, I knew there was something not kosher about shidol and shutki (dried fish). The preserved fish eaten by Bengalis who originally belonged to the Sylhet and Chittagong districts of what is now Bangladesh was—if not a secret—then definitely an embarrassment. For one, it marked us out as ungainly, rustic outsiders—much like our angular Bengali accent—as we ventured out of our tiny outposts in the Northeast and into Kolkata. Its cooking was preceded by nervous shutting of windows and worry at neighbours' noses wrinkling in disgust. Those who know not how they sin have associated the fragrance of shutki with that of mildewed, rotting socks or decaying animals.[22]

We did not have boundary walls between neighbours and wandered at will to whichever house we wished. It was a completely Bengali para, but there were subtle differences; we were 'upper caste' and one amongst only three Brahmin households. This fact did not provide any privileges, but it was acknowledged. At home, this discussion was either avoided or they did not consider it important enough to educate us on caste. I did not know about Dalits and had not read Ambedkar. Shillong was truly isolated, and its own traditions and cultural practices were not discussed either. For example, we all knew of the Khasi matrilineal tradition, but it was not till this millennium that Khasis themselves started writing about how patriarchal the matrilineal Khasi society is. Caste, class, religion, race, and ethnicity were alien concepts to us, even though we were victims and perpetrators at the same time.

However, looking back, the 1970s were really good.

Shillong: The First Rumblings

It was in 1866 that Shillong came into being. Some twenty years before the British moved the Sylhet Light Infantry here, a Welshman named Thomas Jones brought the gospel and introduced the Roman script to the Khasi language. The British created this town out of almost nothing. In its early days, some affluent Bengali entrepreneurs who came from Sohra helped in establishing the town. Golan Haidara, Haki Kasimuddin Molla and Abdul Gaffar, among others, were prominent citizens. However, the town would not get water or power supply for another decade. By 1875, churches of various denominations had been set up, as well as a mosque. Beyond the territorial control of the British, in Laban the first Laban Sanatan Dharma Sabha (Laban Harisabha) was established by Bengali Hindus. Soon, the Shillong Hindu Dharma Sabha came up. There was a Brahmo Samaj as well. Slowly, many schools were set up. The Shillong Zilah High School, set up in 1876, had a Sylhet centre.

The last decade of the nineteenth century and the beginning of the twentieth century transformed Shillong in more ways than one. Natural disasters and the movement of people reconfigured the Khasi hills. On 12 June 1897, late in the afternoon, a 'quarter of a minute' changed everything. The Great Earthquake[23] devastated the town and the destruction stretched as far as Sylhet, where flooding rivers, mostly in Sunamganj, killed many. The Deputy Commissioner made an attempt to connect Shillong via railway to Sylhet, but this was eventually abandoned due to financial reasons. During this period, the Shillong sector was overwhelmingly Bengali. The population in 1881 was only 4,288 persons. It is significant, in the context of today's India, that in 1901 Swami Vivekananda visited Shillong to preach a 'universal religion'. Even as late as 1914, the Assam Secretariat had more Bengali Hindus than Assamese or Khasis. The town was multi-ethnic, but linguistically it maintained English and Hindi as the languages of communication.[24]

Some of Shillong's early history is found scribbled in memoirs and journals, but what has been virtually obliterated is the pathology of prejudice that came to control relationships from the 1970s. At first this was subdued, but later it ran through the hills like wildfire.

But the Shillong I knew in the 1970s was straight out of a story-book: zig-zag roads, church bells, pine cones and the rain on tin roofs. The monsoon was long and incessant. We chased clouds into our rooms. During spring, autumn and winter, the skies were clear and seemed so close that one could touch and smell them, like the Cherra oranges that came home in woven bamboo baskets.

Shillong back then was a vibrant place. A blind singer would sing in front of the Shani temple—he sang Bengali songs in a very strong voice. People dropped coins in an old cigarette can placed on his harmonium. The music of church choirs melded with the rustling of pine trees. The hills emerged as if from subterranean depths, towering over the big lake Umiam or the Barapani. The Khasi folktales my mother read out to me transformed themselves into living beings and helped me escape. These hills were the perfect secret hiding places for a child's imagination.

Can a city exist without memories?

By the late 1970s, there was trouble. In the 1980s, there was more trouble. The Khasi,[25] Jaintia and Garo tribes who claimed indigenous rights over Meghalaya, the state formed out of Assam in 1972, considered others as threats to their land and occupation. These hills were soon in the throes of xenophobic violence targeting non-tribals. But Shillong never mourned. We loved. That was the only way to confront and counter. Every day we walked around the lake to the city centre and discussed poetry. Shillong was not poetic, but it had poetry. The binaries were obvious: the public and the private, family and social space, cultural and institutional space, leisure and work. But what Shillong offered was also space for our dreams, passions and anxieties. It was the space we discovered in the sacred groves of Mawphlong, or when I saw the pebbles at the bottom of a stream, the clear water flowing with a murmur.

Shillong was where Amit Ray met Labanya. Tagore visited Shillong at least thrice and set his epic love poem, *Shesher Kobita* or *The Last Poem*, there, probably the most famous invocation of Shillong in world literature. He is also known to have written his famous poem *Raktokorobi* during one of the visits. In *Shesher Kobita*, on a visit to Shillong, an arrogant barrister from Calcutta, Amit Ray, falls in love with a strong-willed and educated governess, Labanya. Both fulfil each other's intellectual desires, but there is an incommunicable distance between them that both recognise as being difficult to bridge.

Later, in 1960, Ritwik Ghatak would shoot his poignant and popular *Meghe Dhaka Tara* in Shillong and Cherrapunjee. Nita, his protagonist, symbolises the pain of separation and sacrifice. The film tells the story of Partition from a perspective that only Ghatak could have dared to portray. Nita's piercing, echoing scream, '*Dada, ami bachte chai*' or 'I want to live', is a cry for all experiences of displacement, forced migration and partition.

The external space in which we lived and worked, where time and history functioned, and where sets of relations were defined, gave us our perceived identity. Our community governed our relations in every aspect of life. In my case, I was a *dkhar*, non-tribal, Bengali. The domestic help was a *kanchi* from the Nepali basti below our para. Nepali women would work at most homes as domestic help. The Nepali *daju* would deliver firewood to our home. Hard labour, like ferrying firewood, charcoal or heavy household goods, was the exclusive territory of Nepali men. The Khasi *kongs* had an impeccable reputation as being reliable nannies. I had one too. The Punjabi Sikhs were cleaners. The Marwaris were traders monopolising the entire supply chain. The Sindhis had sophisticated shops selling clothes. Bengalis were engaged in a lot of activities, from teaching to government employment and small trade. The city's ethnic and gender identity was very visible, given the role of women in Khasi society and an enviable dignity of labour. Fish, vegetable markets, fruits, even pork and beef would be the Khasi woman's domain. Biharis provided specialised labour.

The town had definite markers. Mistrust ruled the city, and localities were demarcated into safe and unsafe zones, depending on where one resided. We didn't ask many of our friends where they lived, lest we disassociate from them. I lived in Laban, where we imagined tribal and non-tribal communities lived together. But safe distances were maintained. Rilbong was predominantly Bengali, whereas Bishnupur was largely Assamese. Mawlai was perceived to be 'dangerous' for the non-tribals. In the 1970s, Bengalis inhabited Umpling, Jailroad, parts of Pologround, Rilbong, Kenches Trace, New Colony, Motinagar and Laban. My para was entirely Bengali. But Mawkhar, Mawlai, Garikhana (where Bengalis lived as well), Laitumukrah (which had a Bhat Colony of largely Bengali-speaking people), Nongthmai, etc., were predominantly tribal areas. Nepalis resided beyond Bishnupur, but they were in greater strength in Jhalupara. Marwaris lived in the centre of town and many Sindhis lived in Polo Ground. The town's apparent cosmopolitanism was only a facade; some places were just a shade safer by day, but were to be avoided by evening. The code was well-known: enter your safe zone by evening and pray there are no emergencies.

Communal violence changed the city's character. It was now imperative that all land be tribal and within legal and extra-legal jurisdictions, these were established.[26] With availability of land and property in the state capital, Shillong, Khasis from rural Meghalaya were drawn to the city, filling the vacant non-tribal spaces/localities. Soon, the names of these localities were undergoing change to make them sound more indigenous.

Cultural spaces were strictly demarcated along lines of community and gender. For example, the Sunday Study Circle in the Laban Bengali Boys High School had only Bengali men. Bangiya Sahitya Parishad, a Bengali cultural body created in 1937, was also very insular, though in its early days it had been vibrant and had enjoyed the support of other communities. The Assamese community in Laban met at the Nam Ghar and in Laitumukrah, they gathered at Krishti Kendra. The affluent and well-connected visited the Shillong

Club or the Golf Club, where we were not even allowed to venture. So we picnicked instead on the golf course, which was open to all and was used as a thoroughfare. The Khasis and other tribals would meet at the churches. The Wards Lake, Lady Hydari Park, and the various waterfalls were places everyone visited without fear. There was only one zone, the European Ward, where non-tribals could purchase property.

The common areas where different communities exchanged courtesies were places like bookstores and the fish market. Later, many of these community areas turned into battlegrounds.

The only visible Hindu-Muslim-Christian differentiations were of funeral grounds and cemeteries. These were dark resting places that courting couples often visited. These are important spaces in a city where members of each family have been cremated or buried. They were now part of the earth, but their identities suddenly take on a religious tone. They were real flesh and blood people who were part of the city, but Shillong's community wanted to erase their existence.

Shillong inspired a collective imagination of a pleasant refuge. But cities can be a source of authority and repression, just like the state. Authority secures identity, but at the same time, gives rise to tensions between the two. What was the social contract the communities or individuals residing here had with this city? The authority of one community to dominate the others based on their indigenous rights became the new narrative of identity. The spatial form of the city was now divided into localities of 'us' and 'them', and the city assumed its own power. This exercise of power was possible because of an absent state and order was maintained through curfews, provocation and intimidation. Control and identity are familiar partners and identity-formation in Shillong was coercive. The relationship between city spaces and the construction of identity has been widely written about and studied.

Many literary characters achieve self-realisation in ordinary city spaces. Those extraordinary moments in one's life constitute the city. My self-realisation comprised of crushing inadequacies framed almost entirely by the 'othering' I experienced. To heal myself, I loved. The forests and liberated spaces became my refuge. Poetry and love helped to disengage the complex textures of the city. Shillong is not a city of great monuments or creative architectural spaces, nor is it extravagant.

There is no colour except olive green and rust-red tin roofs. Those were the Assam-type houses that gave the city some character.

Shillong can be a stranger to its own residents. Alienation grows in its spaces—as much as belonging. Both the insider and the outsider felt alienated in their own ways. It was a strange, shared process, but this shared experience did not offer comfort or closure. It only divided us further. It failed to offer a 'political imaginary' of 'the being together of strangers'; the self and the city were divided, there was no interweaving of different communities and the city no longer offered itself as a site for imagination and representation. Shillong at best could survive as a stereotype.[27]

The benign imagination of Shillong came under attack in the murderous years that shaped its identity in opposition to the identity of 'the other'. From 1979 right up to the 1990s, the city's intolerance towards 'outsiders', which found expression in brutal violence backed by impunity, has been the lingering image in the minds of people who were displaced. There is no accurate figure of the number of people who may have disappeared or been eliminated during this torturous period, even at police stations. Racial and ethnic prejudice, resulting in violent 'othering', constructed a social imaginary of ethno-nationalism. From a space of refuge and liberation, Shillong slowly transformed into a space of anxiety and fear.

We never visited tribal homes, and therefore never realised the differences. We met them in school, and that was how it stayed. Only much later was there some interaction amongst us, but by then an invisible but deep chasm had already developed.

By 1979, my community and I were labelled 'foreigners' and 'Bangladeshis' in a campaign that turned into a violent 'anti-outsider' crusade. Over time, this turned to an ethnic cleansing.[28] It was only then that I developed a clear 'identity'—that of an 'Outsider/Insider'.

This history is not complicated, and yet not documented well. No police stations in the state have any First Information Reports (FIRs) of murders, abductions, attacks or intimidation. I was raised in a beautiful hill town destroyed slowly by ethnic divides and physical constructions that defy any aesthetic appeal. Shillong, the then capital of Assam and later of Meghalaya, is not far from the international border with Bangladesh, the 'land' of my ancestors. (In terms of geographical contiguity and territorial and administrative jurisdictions, Meghalaya would also very much be the 'land' of my ancestors.) The label of 'Bangladeshi' embarrassed me, and I wanted to deny being a Sylheti-Bengali. If my parents spoke in Sylheti, that embarrassed me even more, and I would make concerted efforts to avoid such a situation. The slur I grew up with referred to us as refugees from a poor country, who have come to take 'our' land. For whatever reason, back then, I did not want to be identified as a refugee. I was not one and nor were my parents.

Curiously, I read and spoke Bengali and fared better in it than in other subjects at school. I cannot say that it was a source of pride for me, but it gained me the respect of my peers, who generally excelled in the main subjects and struggled with the 'second language'. The Irish Christian Brothers ran this school, where students were taught everything except diversity. It was a good school by many standards, but school education in India has often been problematic; schools prefer to avoid basic questions like, 'who am I?'. The histories we learnt failed to inform and contextualise our experiences. The Partition was not even part of the curriculum, even though the town was filled with survivors of several partitions. An 'apolitical' education does not have to be divorced from reality.

By the time I was in middle school, the anti-foreigner agitation in neighbouring Assam had gathered steam and spilled over to Meghalaya, where violence was unleashed on the 'non-tribal'. It will be useful to explain these terms for the uninitiated. The colonial ethnographers' definition of 'tribes' was not very clear and that conceptual problem was later overcome by the use of the term 'indigenous', which demarcated the tribes from the alleged 'settlers'.[29] After independence, this tribal/non-tribal clash led to the word 'indigenous' gaining a lot of currency.

In these volatile growing up years, I developed an acute need to avoid confrontation, because the 'minority' should stay quiet. It has taken me a long time to recognise the differences between minority and majority. I was part of a minority community in Shillong, but part of the majority in other parts of the country.

The 'trouble' in Meghalaya broke out between October and November 1979, just after Kali puja or Diwali. Some 'miscreants' beheaded the image of Kali. The faithful retaliated. In one stroke, the town was paralysed: the Central Reserve Police Force (CRPF; we had never seen this uniform) and columns of the army marched through our streets.[30] This escalation of violence and state control did not come out of nowhere; my guess is that the elders (and the school) had avoided this conversation, and so we were unprepared and taken completely by surprise. There is still no clarity about what went wrong, nor is there any sense of closure. The situation persisted in various phases for over a decade-and-a-half till the exclusion of non-tribals from every aspect of work and life had been institutionalised. Once that was achieved, peace returned to Shillong, which later branded itself as an international rock concert destination.

At school, our relationship with tribal classmates was ambiguous. There was more than one set of relationships: the tribal vis-à-vis the non-tribal, and the non-tribal vis-à-vis other non-tribals. For example, the Khasi-Bengali relationship was straightforward. The Khasis looked upon the Bengalis with suspicion, viewing them as 'usurpers' who should be thrown out. The Bengalis looked upon the Khasis with condescension and saw them as 'aggressive tribals' who should be avoided at any cost. (Interestingly, written Khasi language had initially used the Bengali script, before they moved to the Roman script introduced by Thomas Jones.)

The Bengalis, Khasis, Garos and the Jaintias have always lived together, given that they share contiguous land, and so the sudden escalation in animosity is interesting for many reasons. Local differences and identities were being reinforced and articulated in most uncomfortable ways.

The sets and subsets of ethnicities, living in the shared—though segregated—space, are subsumed at various levels. Assamese-Bengali relations were already strained, a direct fallout of the Sylhet story. The Assamese-Khasi relationship was also double-edged; they both hated the Bengali, but the Khasis had their own issues with the Assamese, and eventually broke away from Assam to form the state of Meghalaya with the people of the Garo and Jaintia hills. It was only a matter of time before the Assamese and Bengali both became targets and the tribal/non-tribal divide was exposed. In retrospect, these turbulent years laid the foundation for understanding upper-caste and upper-class hegemony. In Assam, for example, following the victory marches of a students' agitation that took over state power, what emerged was an even more fractious region, with each ethnicity asserting nationalism through aggressive methods. The caste Hindu 'Assamese' sub-nationalism came to be challenged by tribes who claimed greater ethnic rights over the others.[31] These concepts came in suddenly: identity, sub-nationalism, ethno-nationalism, ethnicity, indigenous rights, separatism, right for self-assertion, etc.

Many I knew fled the town and settled elsewhere. We continued to live amidst intimidation and insecurity, which became very much a part of our lives. That was the new normal. We were exhausted of living with fear.

Violence between neighbours is not new to humankind, but for someone stepping into their teenage years, the experience of being cast as an unwanted 'outsider' who 'eats fish' and is too weak to hit back can be debilitating. We learnt vigilance on the job; be alert when walking alone, even in your neighbourhood. Gangs of young non-tribal boys with bicycle chains and iron rods would move stealthily in dark alleys, and counter-attacks were normal. The administration was lax and partisan. Delhi was too far away to take notice. The alienation that the tribals felt vis-à-vis the capital made them feel like the 'other' in the eyes of Delhi. The non-tribal was the true castaway, because they neither belonged to Delhi nor to the tribal homeland, even though, in several cases, generations of their families had been born and raised there.

I belonged to a Shillong that would not let me live there. I had legitimate claim to call it my home, but the idea of 'homeland' had by then assumed multiple meanings.

The 'I' of 'identity' is not the only facet of this concept. There is a wider anthropology of the word that emerges from a study of nation-building, ethnic conflict and the constructivist critiques of the state. It also marks arguments on gender, sexuality and culture. This cultural paradigm enables researchers to understand how identity is expressed in various socio-historical conditions.

Shillong, 1984

I finished school in 1984. The same year, my sister left for medical school.

I languished. By 1986, most of my friends had left town to pursue technical education, apart from a few who hung around. We had to bond better in order to survive.

By 1988, the house had been sold. We did not have the money or the right to buy land, so a Khasi coal mine owner from Cherrapunjee bought our house. At first, they just sent their youngest daughter (as the one who inherits property amongst the Khasis) to Shillong. Kongna was very pleasant, but her love interest did not meet with the family's approval, so her brother was sent to keep vigil. Her brother played the guitar effortlessly without being trained, and loved to paint the walls of the house more than anything else. The family was not happy with him either, so now they sent across their elder daughter, Rulby. She was shrewd and asserted the landowner–tenant relationship. They had broken up the house and constructed an ugly two-storey accommodation in the backyard. We occupied the first floor. The hedges were gone. All the trees were hacked down. The garden was flattened. I saved some lampshades and doorknobs and refused to let go of the wooden letter-box where we received our long-awaited letters. The Assam-type main house was no more. It came down right in front of my eyes. I think that on that day, I lost my home.

Through the 1980s, several people left. Some sold their homes for a pittance in distress sales. Others retained them, believing they would return some day. The atmosphere was tense. I left in 1991, but I returned and left for good in 1993. My parents continued to live there.

They kept vacillating over the question of where to 'settle'. They bought a house in Guwahati: my mother had been born there, so she thought that would be where she would like to spend her retired life. They later sold it and bought a house in Calcutta. That was seen as the safe place. This was a ten-year project that finally bore fruit. They agreed to spend winters in Calcutta and summers in Shillong. They disliked Calcutta because the city was not theirs, even though they had familiar networks, relatives, and no one there would ever abuse them for being Bengali. They yearned for Shillong. That was their real home.

However, their health started failing and the cost of maintaining two houses was heavy. So they finally decided to let go of Shillong and in the spring of 2015, they left the city. All of the last day in that house, they welcomed guests who stopped by to meet them. Around 4 PM they happily sat inside the car waiting to pick them up. Half the locality was there to bid them a final goodbye; the other half had passed away, or had relocated elsewhere. Kakima and Kakababu would be gone for good. They sat inside and simply drove away. They did not look back even once, nor did they break down. They just left. My mother had come to live here after her marriage. They had celebrated their fiftieth wedding anniversary earlier that year. My father had been living here since his bachelor days. He had spent sixty-five years in the same house, first as a tenant, then as a proxy owner, and finally as a tenant again.

I have not visited the city since. Do I miss it? Yes. But only because of an 'organic solidarity' with the larger Shillong community, now made possible through social media networks.

Shillong forms the locus of my identity when I am located outside of it. In Assam, for example, Shillong boys were stereotyped as being 'immoral', who drank and did drugs. In other places of India, Shillong meant 'cool' and musically inclined. Within Shillong, however, this 'I' was an unwelcome lingering outsider who was despicable and had to be discarded. Inside the city, the identity changes between localities: in my own para, I was a bona fide para boy; in Laban, I moved between an insider and a peripheral figure, depending on which group I was with. Beyond the immediate sphere of influence, identity becomes suspect and only physical strength can overpower that. I knew my escape routes.

The Mithila Family Tree

My paternal genealogy is not well-documented and therefore I could narrate only phases from my father's memoirs that provide a lens on the Partition. However, my maternal genealogy does trace the family tree to a few generations, providing an in-depth narrative of migration and identity formations.[32]

Kings in India had a strange fetish. Some of them would apparently import Brahmins belonging to five gotras from Kannauj.[33] Kannauj was a cauldron, a Buddhist country, and Harshavardhana was a generous king who is said to have graciously accepted the requests of other kings. How much of this is history and how much myth, it is difficult to say. Their ancestors, however, came from Mithila (as the family tree indicates) and are believed to have been brought by the king of Tripura.

Bhottorgaon, their village, had Brahmins from the same gotra—Bharadwaj. The house they lived in was in Mashorbari or Nowabari. The family tree begins with Parameshwar Acharya; next came

Chandrashekhar Acharya. My mother's paternal uncle Chandrashekhar was a renaissance man who had a well-known library, the Chandrashekhar Bani Bhawan, and was an art collector. Her father had three brothers, the eldest of whom died of cholera; his widow was harassed by his younger brother and sent off to Kashi. They never heard about her again, and this part of the history was not discussed within the family. The next uncle married Kusum Manjari Devi, who was illiterate. He carried the title of Annada Kumar Shankhatirtha, a title he earned from Behrampur in Shankha philosophy, which believed in justice and not in god. Her other uncle, Nalinikumar Bhattacharjee, was a doctor.

How did her ancestors migrate in the first place? Jagannath Shiromoni, the next in line, was angry with his older brother, who looked after the property while he travelled across principalities to perform rituals. In his absence, his two brothers gave away his daughter's hand in marriage. The older brother wanted his niece to be happy, and chose a rich man's son as her husband. However, he married his own daughter to a poor Brahmin boy. When Jagannath returned, he was furious: his son-in-law was a useless brat, whereas his brother's son-in-law was a diligent boy who knew the shastras. So accompanied by his younger brother, he left the village and settled in Nowabari.

A few generations later, the family assumed the title of Bhattacharjee, beginning with Ramgati Bhattacharjee. His son, Kalikumar, was their grandfather, who was an astrologer as well as an astronomer who studied the planets and stars. He was very poor. He would walk during the nights and then prepare astrological charts in the morning. He never met any of his clients. Once, he was invited to the court of the king of Rangpur, where people soon learnt of his clairvoyance. A gold image of the Devi was once stolen from the palace and he was requested to help recover it. He promised to locate the image, but refused to reveal who had stolen it. The king was delighted and as a reward, promoted him to the position of Rajpurohit. Two years later, however, he returned home, tired of the opulence of the palace. All he brought back was a copper coin; he had no greed for land. He died of a stroke; while his house no longer stands, the neighbours still refer to it as the doctor's house.

Her father, Kaliprasanna, came to the Brahmaputra Valley at the age of fourteen. He had lost his mother as a toddler, and grew up in his maternal home. When his uncles, busy with the estate, discovered that he had failed Class VII, he was severely reprimanded. This was when his sister started taking care of him.

His sister, Jogomaya Devi, married Dwarakanath Roychoudhury, who wrote poetry and published a book, *Sukhosorbori*. They had five daughters and a son. Dwarakanath was transferred as magistrate to Sibsagar.

After his matriculation in Gauhati, he stayed on in Assam while his sister and brother-in-law moved away. He rented a house near Ugratara temple and, at twenty-three years of age, married Kamala Devi, who was only ten at the time. Kamala Devi had not attended school and had learnt whatever she could at her maternal uncles' home. When she turned twenty-four, Kaliprasanna became a lawyer. From Jorpukhuri, he moved to Kamarpatty and then Panbazar, till he purchased his first house in Rehabari. In Panbazar, they stayed in three different houses, the last of which was the wooden double-storey where the Bhattacharjee family lived for twenty-two years. It was known as *ukilbabur bari*.

Since they had no relatives in Gauhati, Tinkodi Bandapadhay took them under his wing. Along with teaching at Sonaram School, her father was a private tutor in the Bandapadhay household and eventually he became part of the family.

Some members of the extended family tried to remain in Sylhet even after the Partition. Others moved to Dharmanagar in Tripura. After the first riots of 1950, the family confronted her uncle, the head of the family, demanding to know why he had forced others to stay. He discussed the matter with a Muslim elder, who asked him to place his trust in him, and stay on. Her father also tried to persuade him to leave, but he was sure that India was not his home and they would not be acknowledged there. The brothers visited the ancestral house in 1948, 1952 and 1954. The families slowly started migrating after 1954. When it became evident that India is where one would have to reside, they slowly crossed over.

They were three brothers and two sisters. Only two of them are alive: the youngest sister, Shobhona, is eighty-one, and her elder brother, Kulada, is eighty-six.

Like all her siblings, Shobhona was born in Gauhati and moved across three homes: Panbazar in Gauhati to Laban in Shillong (101 km away), where she lived for fifty years after her marriage, and then to Narendrapur in Calcutta, where she currently lives. So while she identifies herself completely as a 'Panbazar girl', she spent the greater part of her life in Shillong.

When Shobhona came to Shillong, married to a teacher, they lived in an annexe. She transitioned from a more affluent family to a modest living. But soon this para became her home and she invested all her time in encouraging young people to stage plays and musical events. She occupied herself with her family and society. She had an all-consuming interest in talking to people and collecting oral literature in languages she could not follow. She started researching Khasi folktales and published them regularly in Bengali literary journals. She could not pick up the Khasi language like most of her kin, but her interest was deep and she would sit with domestic workers, vendors and colleagues and pester them for folktales. Though she started teaching and was fulfilled by sharing her time with young minds, the folktales never left her. She published volumes of Khasi, Mizo, Nepali and other folktales, besides a kind of memoir about her city of birth.

Shobhona, like many others, made Shillong her permanent home. Even during the intense anti-Bengali and anti-outsider agitation, she did not feel partisan. She feared for the tribal as much as for the non-tribal. Amidst all the trouble, she found the time to visit neighbours, pick up vegetables and fish, enquire about new books from Basanti store and return home before tea-time. Occasionally she would buy a saree at Prakash's Mohini Store and collect her daughter's school blazer from Lila Brothers. It was a routine she had perfected to the last detail.

She never uttered a word against any other community and always endeared herself to people she met. None of the violence she witnessed affected her empathy and concern.

Then, just like that, she left one day, never to return.

Sialkot to Shillong

Inam Elahi Nagi's ancestors had come to Assam from the village of Kotli Loharan in Sialkot, which was then in Punjab, over 100 years ago. Kotli Loharan was known for blacksmithing and producing fine quality surgical instruments.

His mother was born in Tezpur, where her parents lived. They were in the business of repairing guns. Their main clientele were the tribals of Assam and Arunachal, who used guns for hunting. Elahi's paternal grandfather had worked in the British Army workshop as a foreman, and was posted in Jabalpur when his father was born. Their first business was a bicycle shop in Nowgaon, after which they had a car workshop in Guwahati. A branch of the workshop, A. A. Nagi and Sons in Shillong, was handled by his father's cousins. Later, they moved to Dhaka (in what was then East Pakistan) after the Partition, and Elahi's parents came to Shillong to manage the workshop, shutting shop in Guwahati. Theirs was the first workshop in Shillong, and they still have bills dating back to 1928, which can be used as evidence and documents for the NRC!

The other Nagis eventually decided to return to Karachi, but Elahi and his brother continued to live here. Non-tribals inhabited the main town of Shillong, which was a really small area in those days. The local tribes lived in the neigbouring bastis on the outskirts. Their garage started the first taxi service, and he even drove a taxi. There used to be a mere ten or twelve cars in the entire town. He recalls that people had to wait for hours to get a passenger.

Elahi was married in Dhaka because his wife was a Pakistani from Lahore. She later became an Indian citizen. They were the only importer of motor parts in Pakistan, and that is how they acquired businesses in Dhaka.

Their ancestral home in Kotli still exists, though it has been renovated and rebuilt now. A cousin and his family still live there.

His brother first went to Pakistan in 1977, a very nostalgic trip. It is very difficult, almost impossible, to get a visa now to visit Pakistan. It is even harder for his sister (who is married there) to come to India. She has visited India only twice in forty years. The last time that members of Elahi's family went to Pakistan was around ten years ago.

They did not migrate under duress, so there is no trauma of leaving home under pressure. However, any migration is sad. You lose your roots.

Elahi's passport is from Shillong. He cannot relate to any other place but Shillong. The anti-outsider movement here did disturb business. Non-tribals are still targeted. But at his age, it is easier to imagine that these disturbances are temporary. Where else will he go?

The anti-Muslim sentiment has not really affected the Nagis, or other Muslims in Shillong. He feels that this is his cocoon, even though he is not sure when the next agitation will happen, and they may have to pack their bags and leave someday soon.

Remember, there is no place which is permanent.

Cannanore to Shillong

The Mathummals lived in the left wing of a wooden cottage on Keating Road, which connected the Civil Hospital area and Police Bazar. The town, like any hill town, had many lanes and by-lanes crisscrossing the landscape. A Bengali family occupied the right wing.

Keating Road had a mix of communities: Bengali, Khasi, Nepali and Marwari. Interestingly, its Durga Puja Committee had a Bengali Muslim as the club's secretary. It was a residential area, but since the road connected Police Bazar and the Civil Hospital general area, it was a thoroughfare of sorts and had high traffic.

Sometime in the late 1930s, M. P. Sukumaran joined the British Indian Army and was posted to Amritsar, all the way from Cannanore, Kerala. He was subsequently posted to Lahore, Quetta, Abbottabad and Peshawar. When Japan attacked the eastern borders of India, Sukumaran's company, the Royal Indian Supply Corp, moved to the Northeast and was stationed in Shillong. As soon as Partition was announced and riots broke out, they were sent to Calcutta. After India's independence, Sukumaran decided to take voluntary retirement from the army and moved to Shillong, just because he liked the place. He started working with the Goenkas because he knew about film distribution, and ended up managing all their film business. The Goenkas of Shillong had several businesses, from film theatre to automobiles.

A couple of years later, his younger brother M. P. Karunakaran, who had got a job with the central government, moved to Shillong. From the 1950s to the year 2000, both brothers lived in Shillong, though M. P. Sukumaran had moved back a little earlier.

Cannanore was part of the erstwhile Madras Presidency. When Sukumaran left Kerala, the family comprised of four sisters, his younger brother and his parents. His father was a businessman who imported goods from England until the Quit India movement, when he gave it up. He was fascinated by Gandhi. He died while Sukumaran was away and the responsibility of the family fell to Karunakaran, who was studying on a scholarship. He finished college and soon took up a government job. He was posted to Shillong and then to Arunachal Pradesh. The wives, too, moved to Shillong, and they lived together as a joint family. Both brothers had two sons each, and they all attended the same Christian Brothers School, St. Edmunds. Wooden floors were the common architectural feature across all houses in the town, along with tin roofs and a corner room. My friend Deepak's mother (Karunakaran's wife) and his aunt would both appear mysteriously from behind the curtains and amiably serve tea and snacks. It is here that the sons brought their friends to discuss books and music. Politics was hardly ever the topic of discussion. Sukumaran would occupy the window chair and Karunakaran would arrive from work with a broad smile; both loved to interact with their sons' friends.

Interestingly, both brothers picked up the local language and developed a very strong relationship with the people who came from all parts of the country. For visitors from south India, this family was the first port of call. Sukumaran initially stayed in Garrison Ground and Happy Valley and later in Nongthymai and Malki, where they were tenants in the house of the Deputy Commissioner, Mr Booth. Shillong presented an opportunity that was not available in Kerala. The cosmopolitan character of the town must have played a role in their decision to make it their home.

When trouble broke out in the late 1970s, they were not really affected, and like other residents, considered it a passing phase. They were non-partisan. The sons barely identified themselves with Kerala. They did not speak the language fluently and could not pick up the nuances of life there, like they could in Shillong. But somewhere, like other non-tribals, they lost their connection with friends from school. Today the circumstances have changed. The older of the younger brother's sons is married to a Khasi girl and they live in Bengaluru.

By and large, the south Indians, predominantly from Kerala, never hesitated to mix with the local people. Unlike other communities, they would eat in tribal households as well. In the south, they had witnessed enough caste segregation and were conscious of differences. The first mosque in India came to Kerala; Christianity and even Judaism came to Kerala early as well. Perhaps they take to the 'Other' easily. That could be why the Mathumals never found it too difficult to assimilate.

Karunakaran retired when his sons were in college and decided to stay on, while Mathumal moved back to Kerala to look after his ageing mother. Within a year, Sukumaran had returned. Eventually, both left. Both have passed away, but till their last day they missed Shillong: the weather, the vegetables, the numerous relationships they developed, and the carefree life that was Shillong. Karunkaran's wife, who now lives with her son in Bengaluru, mourns the loss of her home in Shillong.

The Identity of a Citizen

These families and individuals came from disparate backgrounds, motivated by a common purpose. They did not get lost in the larger crowd; instead, they retained their individual identity. They absorbed the culture of the region, but did not wholly assimilate within it. When acting together, they created group identities. Thus, individual, social, regional and national identities were in play. It is the regional and national identities that have been in tension. So, while individually and socially they may have connected with others, their regional identity was at cross-purposes.

The demand for recognition and the idea of difference lie at the heart of a plural identity, a concept reflected in the opening line of the Indian Constitution: 'We, The People of India'. But this was merely a document and made little sense when contestations about identity challenged the fundamental rights for the protection of identities and diversities based on religion, ethnicity, language, caste and gender. When Ambedkar handed over the draft of the Constitution, he prophesied that inequality in social and economic life, as against political equality, would one day blow up in our faces. We are witnessing this implosion in our everyday lives.

Shillong, or any other city, for that matter, is the sum of the people who inhabit the place. The assertion of one group identity and the exclusion or elimination of others is a challenge that the Indian state did not anticipate. For example, despite its recognition of caste, it failed to include the Scheduled Caste, tribal, minority and marginal communities in the ambit of citizenship and the rights of a citizen. The social inequality that Ambedkar highlighted is a huge ticking time bomb. And while there is an acknowledgment of this in terms of caste and tribe, minority and the marginal, there is an absolute silence and lack of study in cases where those identified as 'non-tribal', in a place like Shillong, become the victims of ethnic cleansing, or where the tribal is held hostage and excluded by other tribals.

In connecting the dots for Shillong, Sylhet is an obvious starting point, as this is where an overwhelming number of families moved to India from during the long Partition. The connection between Shillong and Sylhet was geographically inevitable and carries within itself a history of continuity. The genealogy of two Sylheti families connected by marriage becomes a study in identity as well as of migration and displacement. Within a very short span of time, Shillong had become home to a large number of communities, giving it a cosmopolitan grace. It was only later that this multi-cultural veneer began to erode as contestations between majority and minority communities stood exposed. It is fascinating how a family from Sialkot and another from Cannanore would also make Shillong their real home. All but one of these families have reluctantly departed from the city. They still long for the beautiful hills, fresh air, green vegetables and a rhythm that sits so naturally to a good life. If there is any bitterness at all, it hardly surfaces in their conversations. Their own sense of homeland stands in conflict with the majority community, who consider them outsiders usurping their land. Their doomed longing is an intense exploration of belonging that is at once personal as well as communal.

In the following pages, a cross-section of Indian citizens (who might end up losing their citizenship under the laws currently being framed) responds to a set of questions about their perception and notion of identity, citizenship and nationality. Chapter 2 brings together encounters with citizens from marginal or minority communities across five Indian cities in order to understand how identity and citizenship intersect. Is it enough to be recognised as a citizen by law, while being rejected and excluded by society at large?

Endnotes

1. See Oxford Languages definitions, s.v. 'identity'.

2. Ibid., s.v. 'tribal'.

3. Ibid., s.v. 'indigeneous'.

4. Kishore Bhattacharjee is a poet and folklorist. This poem is from his book, *Mukhamukhi Aspastatat*, 2021, page 1, published by Koel Prakashan, and has been reproduced here with permission. Translated into English by the author of this book.

5. Mitra, Subrata Kumar. 1992. 'Democracy and Political Change in India'. *The Journal of Commonwealth & Comparative Politics* 30 (1): 9–38.

6. Sobhan, Rezwan, Kawshik Saha and Md. Nahyan. 2013. 'The Architecture of "Bangla Batton" Houses in Sylhet City: An Ethnographic Study on Vernacular House Form'. Commonwealth Association of Architects Conference 2013, Dhaka.

7. Batuttah, Ibn. 2013. 'A Visit to Sylhet', (trans.) Samuel Lee. In *The Bangladesh Readers' History*, (eds) Meghna Guhathakurta and William van Schendel. Durham and London: Duke University Press.

8. Choudhury, Mousumi. 2011. 'Partition in the East: Resettlement and Rehabilitation of Refugees in Cachar, A Case Study of Karimganj.' Ph.D. diss., Gauhati University. Available at https://shodhganga.inflibnet.ac.in/bitstream/10603/116402/10/10_chapter%202.pdf, (accessed August 2022).

9. See http://hbvdassam.gov.in/history.html (accessed August 2022). For a more detailed discussion, see Bhattacharjee, K. K. 1983. *North East India: A Study*. New Delhi: Cosmo Publications. See also Sengupta, Jayita (ed.). 2020. *Barbed Wire: Borders and Partitions in South Asia*. New Delhi: Routledge India.

10. Van Schendel, William. 2009. *A History of Bangladesh*. Cambridge: Cambridge University Press, South Asian Edition, 88.

11. Janam Mukherjee writes: 'The Calcutta riots of 1946 are revealed not as an isolated episode of unprecedented "communal" violence, but as a complex epiphenomenal event arising out of the ruin of Bengal's famine.' 2015. *Hungry Bengal: War, Famine, and the End of Empire*. Oxford: Oxford University Press. Available at https://academic.oup.com/book/2861 (accessed November 2022).

12. See Chatterjee, Partha. 1986. 'The Colonial State and Peasant Resistance in Bengal 1920–1947.' *Past & Present* 110: 169–204.

13. Chatterji, Joya. 1996. *Bengal Divided: Hindu Communalism and Partition 1932-1947*. Cambridge South Asian Studies. Cambridge: Cambridge University Press, 1.

14. Bhattacharjee, J. B. 1990. 'The Sylhet Referendum (1947): Myth of a Communal Voting'. *Proceedings of the Indian History Congress* 51: 482–87. Available at https://www.jstor.org/stable/44148264 (accessed August 2022).

15. Ibid.

16. Choudhury, 2011. 'Partition in the East'.

17. The cartographical maze of Bengal's border was the result of several partitions, some due to political rearrangements and others apparently due to games of chess played between nawabs who wagered their land, creating numerous enclaves that festered, till 2015 when 111 enclaves were eventually transferred between India and Bangladesh.

18. For more details, see Mitra, Arnab. 2021. 'International Mother Language Day: Remembering Dhirendranath Dutta and Others Who Died for Bengali Language'. *The Indian Express*, 21 February. Available at https://indianexpress.com/article/lifestyle/art-and-culture/international-mother-language-day-remembering-dhirendranath-dutta-and-others-who-died-for-bengali-language-5072149/ (accessed August 2022). See also Tripathi, Salil. 2020. 'Alternative Facts from the Conflict of 1971'. *Livemint.com*, 22 February. Available at https://www.livemint.com/mint-lounge/features/alternative-facts-from-the-conflict-of-1971-11582261953512.html (accessed August 2022).

19. Claude, Markovits. 2007. 'The Calcutta Riots of 1946'. *Sciencespo.fr*, 5 November. Available at https://www.sciencespo.fr/mass-violence-war-massacre-resistance/fr/document/calcutta-riots-1946.html (accessed August 2022).

20. For more details on the events of 1950, see Trikamdas, Purushottam. 1965. *Recurrent Exodus of Minorities from East Pakistan and Disturbances in India: A Report to the Indian Commission of Jurists by its Committee of Enquiry*. New Delhi: The Indian Commision of Jurists.

21. See the section 'Influx and the Counting of Refugees', from Dasgupta, Abhijit. 2016. 'Residues of Parition: Displaces Bengalis in West Bengal'. *Displacement and Exile: The State–Refugee Relations in India*: 17–91. New Delhi: Oxford University Press.

22. Dutta, Amrita. 2018. 'The Fiery Flavours of East Bengal's Dried and Fermented Fish are all the Notes of Life'. *The Indian Express*, 23 December. Available at https://indianexpress.com/article/express-sunday-eye/smells-like-a-secret-5504173/ (accessed August 2022).

23. Bhattacharjee, J. B. 2004. 'A Missionary Account of the Great Earthquake of 1897 in Northeast India'. *Proceedings of the Indian History Congress* 65: 607–15. Available at http://www.jstor.org/stable/44144775 (accessed August 2022).

24. Sen Gupta, S. 2003. 'Urban Social Structure: A Study of Urbanization in Shillong'. Ph.D diss. North Eastern Hill University. Available at https://shodhganga.inflibnet.ac.in/bitstream/10603/60780/6/06_chapter%202.pdf (accessed August 2022).

25. The tribal or indigenous community from the East Khasi Hills, where Shillong is located.

26. See https://megrevenuedm.gov.in/acts/land-transfer-act-1971.pdf (accessed August 2022). Under the Meghalaya Land Transfer Regulation Act, 1971, land ownership had already been granted to the local tribes, but the communal violence of the late 1970s changed the town's character; most non-tribals started fleeing and allegedly there was adequate pressure on non-tribals to dispose of their immovable property at very low prices.

27. Bridge, Gary and Sophie Watson. 2003. 'City Publics'. In *A Companion to the City*, (eds) Gary Bridge and Sophie Watson, 369–79, especially page 377. UK: Wiley-Blackwell.

28. See Dutta, Amrita. 2018. 'Shillong: Impossible Homeland'. *The Indian Express*, 13 June. Available at https://indianexpress.com/article/opinion/columns/shillong-clashes-tribals-khasi-sikh-xenophobia-violence-impossible-homeland-5214845/ (accessed August 2022). See also Das, Abhinash. 2020. 'Native or Outsider? Mob Attack on 6 Boys in Meghalaya Reignites the Debate'. *Business Standard*, 18 August. Available at https://www.business-standard.com/article/current-affairs/native-or-outsiders-mob-attack-in-meghalaya-raises-questions-of-belonging-120081800244_1.html (accessed August 2022).

29. Xaxa, Virginius. 1999. 'Tribes as Indigenous People of India'. *Economic and Political Weekly* 34 (51): 3589–95.

30. See Gill, Preeti and Samrat Choudhary. 2018. *Insider Outsider: Belonging and Unbelonging in North-East India*. New Delhi: Amaryllis Manjul Publishing. For reportage from this period, see *The Indian Express*. 2019. 'Forty Years Ago, December 23, 1979: Shillong Tense', 23 December. Available at https://indianexpress.com/article/opinion/editorials/forty-years-ago-december-23-1979-shillong-tense-6180036/ (accessed August 2022). For a detailed account, see Choudhury, Soumyadip. 2019. 'A Riot that Changed a City: 40 Years of 79'er Gondogul—the 1979 Shillong Anti-Bengali Riots'. *Cuttingthechai.com*. Available at https://www.cuttingthechai.com/2019/10/8567/a-riot-that-changed-a-city-40-years-of-79er-gondogul-the-1979-shillong-anti-bengali-riots/ (accessed August 2022).

31. Sharma, Nabanita. 2019. 'Ethnic Boundaries During and After the Assam Agitation of 1979–1985'. *International Journal of Scientific and Technology Research* 8 (12): 1850–52. Available at http://www.ijstr.org/final-print/dec2019/Ethnic-Boundaries-During-And-After-The-Assam-Agitation-Of-1979-1985.pdf (accessed August 2022).

32. All family histories reproduced in the book are through long semi-structured interviews recorded by the author.

33. There have been at least three big waves of migrations within India, beginning with the Brahmin migrations between 500–1000 CE. These Brahmins came with skills like performing *yagnas* and establishing new villages that increased the revenue of the rulers. Thus, kings across India would invite Brahmins to come create temples and transform local deities into mainstream Puranic gods and establish villages and towns. See Pattanaik, Devdutt. 2020. 'How the Migratory Patterns of the Brahmins, the Weavers Shaped Indian Culture'. *Economic Times*, 2 May. Available at https://economictimes.indiatimes.com/news/politics-and-nation/how-the-migratory-patterns-of-the-brahmins-the-weavers-shaped-indian-culture/articleshow/75497810.cms?from=mdr (accessed August 2022).

2 The City in Citizenship
Jalandhar, Banaras, Guwahati, Bhagnagar/Hyderabad and Hampi

Citizenship[1]
/ˈsɪtɪzən ʃɪp/

noun
1. the position or status of being a citizen of a particular country.

Stateless[2]
/ˈsteɪtləs/

adjective
1. (of a person) not recognised as a citizen of any country.

On the periphery of France, Strasbourg changed nationality five times in three generations, but was never truly French or truly German.[3]

Harappa

She is a middle-aged married woman, around 165 centimetres in height and wearing a few shell bangles on her left arm. Arranged near her head are funerary objects like pots and pans, to take with her to the next life. She has been kept at New Delhi's National Museum, and hers is one of the most well-preserved Harappan burials excavated at Rakhigarhi, now considered the largest Indus Valley site.[4] Who was she? What was her name? We will never know, even though every day there are new excavations and theories to explain who these people were and where they may have come from. The most recent theory that emerged in the September 2019 issue of the science journal *Cell*[5] suggests she lived sometime between 2800 to 2300 BCE. Interestingly, the buried woman's genome closely matched DNA from eleven other individuals found at sites in Iran and Turkmenistan. Since there is evidence that the Indus Valley traded with those regions, these individuals could well be migrants. These eleven samples were considered outliers from the dominant ancestry pool found in that area. The *Cell* article challenges the hypothesis that the Indus Valley Civilisation had genetic connections with Anatolian farmer ancestry. However, it suggests that there is genetic similarity between the Rakhigarhi woman and the eleven 'outliers' because of a gene flow from South Asia to Central Asia. This supports the conjecture that the 'outliers' found in Turkmenistan and Iran 'are migrants from Indus Valley living in non-Indus Valley towns'.

'The Harappan or Indus (Sindhu) Valley question has been central to many debates about the origin of the "Indian" people. The oldest major Upper Palaeolithic cultures seen in…[this landmass] developed in the Indus Valley.'[6]

The concept of 'city' is ancient and has archaeological roots in this land. We do not know who inhabited the cities of the Indus Valley Civilisation, but surely they were inhabitants of well-defined cities as understood by modern architecture: roads at right angles, a drainage system, the great bath and a granary. Mortimer Wheeler explains in his book, *The Indus Civilisation*: 'The irony of the Indus Valley civilization is that whilst it sustained a metaphysics that has endured it failed utterly to transmit the physical civilization that is its present monument'.[7]

The 'city' of Harappa was first discovered on the banks of River Ravi in the Punjab. However, the Indus Valley civilisation remains till date a faceless society: there is no evidence yet of a state, bureaucracy or religion. The city is situated where the river expands into areas suitable for large-scale agriculture. Archaeologists have claimed that the population density may have been around 200 people per square hectare.[8] It is an extraordinary city: there is a 9,000-square foot 'Great Granary' and elaborate cemeteries, baked brick walls, mud platforms, painted pottery, and inhabitants who wore etched carnelian beads. Most of the Harappan ruins were destroyed by railway construction over 100 years ago, but the sites that could be excavated show a definite street plan and a society engaged in large-scale food production. It is not only architecture and governance, but also the art that points to a highly evolved stage of civilisation. The red jasper male torso found in Harappa, for example, is a striking frontal nude with circular indentations for arms, unlike any other anatomical references from that area, except for a broken torso of a male dancing figure.

Was there a sense of citizenship in Harappa? There is every possibility that there was a sense of Harappan identity and a 'seal' of citizenship as well. What we can say with certainty is that its people were not nomads and had urban housing, they were engaged in regular work and lived under a protocol and as a community, all elements of a bona fide inhabitant of a city.

According to experts, the earliest cities of the world had certain characteristics:

> [A] population that is often hundreds of times larger than any village; full-time specialists such as craftsmen, merchants, officials and transport workers; a ruling class that accumulates the surplus production of the peasants; monumental public buildings; systems of recording and writing without which it would be impossible to manage a city; full-time artists—sculptors, painters, seal engravers—who created things that is unique and specific to the particular civilization; and foreign trade to get materials not available locally.[9]

By these yardsticks, Harappa had all the characteristics of a city by 2800 BCE. Given the scale of the ruins and the robust foundations, it is reasonable to think that these cities were the flourishing first cities of the world. Interconnected reservoirs, wells, a public bath, private toilets in every house, common weights and measures, the standardised size of bricks (in the ratio 1:2:4)—one can conclude from these that the civilisation had well-governed cities.[10] However, the city's hierarchies and system of governance are yet to be understood.

The Indus Valley will continue to excite and engage archaeologists, anthropologists, scientists, linguists, historians and geneticists. However, deciphering the script or arriving at conclusive decisions about the genetic ancestry of the Indus Valley people should have no bearings on our present-day identity. Who the citizens of this civilisation were matters to race science and race politics.[11] With increasing evidence, one thing is clear, as Tony Joseph pithily summarises: 'What we know today…is that we are a multi-source civilisation, not a single-source one, drawing our cultural impulses, traditions and practices from a variety of heredities and migration histories. We are all Indians. We are all migrants. And we are all mixed.'[12]

Mahajanapadas

Between the Harappan civilisation and the late Vedic period, the 'Indian' landmass developed a complex system of citizenship that was not necessarily monarchic. From Buddhist texts like *Anguttara Nikaya*, we know that there were sixteen Mahajanapadas or cities: Kasi, Kosala, Anga, Magadha, Vajji, Malla, Cetiya, Vamsa, Kuru, Pancala, Maccha, Surasena, Assaka, Avanti, Gandhara and Kamboja.[13]

In the proceedings of the Indian History Congress, 1995, Irfan Habib and Faiz Habib presented a map of India, dated 600–320 BCE,[14] where they refer to various texts and archival material indicating territories, tribes, or principalities like Dakhinapatha, the Licchavis of Vesali, Sakyas, and Videha.

> In the *Mahaparinibbana-sutta* Ananda lists six great cities, viz., Campa, Rajagaha, Savatthi, Saketa, Kosambi and Baranasi (SBE, XI, p. 99). Along with these cities, one should probably class Ujjeni, the capital of Avanti (SBE, XVII, pp. 186-7) and Takkasila, the capital of Gandhara (ibid., pp. 174-5; Jatakas, transi, ed. E.B. Cowell, I, London, 1895, pp. 173, 217).[15]

Later, in another paper titled 'The Envisioning of a Nation: In Defence of the Idea of India',[16] Habib invokes the Mahajanapadas as the first firm evidence of the 'idea of India'. He refers to Alberuni's *Kitab-ul-Hind* as the first recorded study of the Indian civilisation. The word 'Hindu' was coined by the Iranians, who pronounced Sindhu as Hindu, and India was a name that came either from the Greeks or the Chinese. As Habib observes, however, it was not until Amir Khusrau, who poetically recounted the various languages of India, and only with the coming of the Mughals that the idea of India as we understand it today emerged fully.

JALANDHAR

> I came to Jalandhar from Delhi in 1954. On 30 July 2019, I turned ninety. I came here when I was thirty-five. I was born in the Punjab. Punjab has three parts, Doaba, Majha and Malwa. Jalandhar is in Doaba. *Do* means two and *aab* means water, so Doaba means 'lying between two rivers', Satluj and Beas. I was

> born in Nawasher in Doaba. Now its name has become Shaheed Bhagat Singh Nagar. Earlier it was under zilla Jalandhar.

Lahori Ram Balley, a Dalit writer, journalist and activist, settled himself in a chair in the corner of his living room, which was decorated with commendations he had received and books he had written. He walked with support and his vision seemed blurred, but none of that had affected his spirit. Jalandhar has the highest proportion of Dalit population in India, and Balley described himself in his own city as an outlier.

> In 1947, I completed my matriculation from Panjab University, Lahore as a first division holder. Then the Partition took place. Though we were from east Punjab, our business was in west Punjab. Our family used to supply raw material to Shri Gopal Paper Mill in Jagadri. Jagadri is now in Haryana. At that time, I was in Kasoor, Pakistan with my uncle. On 15 August 1947, we came to the Nawanshahr railway station and hoisted the Indian flag. Then I left for Delhi.
>
> I was with my wife and we took up residence in Delhi's Bhogal area. I stayed there from December 1948 to 1954. I stayed on rent in the same house, located on Church Road, for all those years. My elder brother also stayed in Delhi. He was in government service. Till 1954, I worked in the printing press for the Government of India. I used to work in the Gazette of India. The address was Government Press, Minto Road, New Delhi.

Balley's memory is vivid; he recalls his journey from Nawanshahr to Jalandhar via Delhi without the usual emotion that many from his generation are now accustomed to. And he relates it down to the last detail, as if he has been tasked to map his life's journey. For Balley, his own journey is like a mirror that he wants to hold up to the nation. The violent partition of British India created an era of strife, poverty and divisiveness, where the ordinary citizen was denied her/his fundamental rights. Balley is in many ways their voice, asserting the rights of the citizen.

> There was a family problem. One of my sisters was not getting married. That's when I left, came to Jalandhar and got her married. When I came here, I stayed in a rented house. It was in the same locality where we are now—Abadpura. For two years, I worked in the postal and telephone departments. I liked this city; it was small, but had all the modern facilities, like the

telegraph office, post office, and the railway. This is where I entered public life.

While I was in Delhi, I had met Dr Ambedkar. I met him last on 30 September 1956. He had taken ill at the time and I gave him my word—I said I would work lifelong to carry out his mission and his vision. So, when he died on 6 December 1956, I left my permanent government job and joined the Ambedkar mission.

Since 1958, I have published a newspaper without a break.[17] Initially it was printed in Urdu, then Punjabi and English. Since 1965 till date, it has been printed in Hindi as well. Basically, I always loved reading and writing. I can speak and write Urdu, Persian, English, Hindi and Punjabi.

Balley is a prolific writer, journalist and publisher. He held on to the written word and never gave up, despite the systematic exclusion of and atrocities against Dalits in India. The media representation of Dalits has been abysmal, and Dalit participation has never been on the media's agenda. Balley waged a lone battle.

I have been printing 1,000 copies [of my newspaper] since the beginning. Now, the circulation in Hindi is around 3,000 copies. This paper goes to England, America, France, Germany and Canada. You will not find a single Ambedkarite paper in India, other than this. We write about atrocities faced by the lower-caste people, about the mission and thoughts of Ambedkar, and other caste issues. I read five newspapers daily. Other than that, Nirmal, my son-in-law, who is in charge of the Ambedkar Bhawan, collects information daily around these topics and issues, and I compile and edit everything myself. Now you find things online as well.

In 1959, I was arrested. I was the National Secretary of the Republican Party of India for six years. We started an agitation. That's when I was arrested. The police picked up my record from my office without any information. So when I came into public life, I stood for parliamentary elections twice, in 1962 and 1967. In 1967, I stood against then Defence Minister Swaran Singh.

By this time, Balley had become a prominent Dalit voice of the city.

Like Dr Ambedkar, I also converted to Buddhism. We have a good majority in this town. When I fought elections, it was a general seat. Now it is a reserved seat. Now, Santokh Singh Chaudhary is

> the Lok Sabha member here. That time we had around ten lakh voters. Today it is two times as much.

Dalit populations across villages and cities are always ghettoised and confined to designated localities.

> The house that I currently live in used to be just gutters. Worms and rats used to crawl here. It was a *basti*. I organised a mission and called for some members of the Municipal Corporation. They started fixing things here. I would do everything for the basti because of a sense of belonging. I think I have had a role to play in the development of this city. That sense of belonging is then bound to be present in me. The poorer bastis did not have electricity, and the alleys you took to reach here were dark and unsafe.

Abadpura is certainly more affluent and organised than most Dalit bastis one encounters in the country. But Balley is acutely aware of caste dynamics, which is also apparent in the way the city was designed. Affluence and numbers have not changed the attitude of the upper-caste residents towards the Dalits.

> From this area, a lot of people have migrated to different countries. So they are better off than other Scheduled Caste (SC) families in the country. This area has 99 per cent Scheduled Caste families. I am also an SC. The upper-caste people from this city have always looked down upon us. They simply have no love lost for our community. The first introduction about us is always through caste.
>
> This entire area was an agricultural field before I bought the land and made this house. At that time, too, these plots of land were segregated. There is a place called Ali Mohalla nearby. That was an area on the outskirts of the city. But as the city continued to expand on all sides, we became the centre. Now the Municipal Corporation is only 2–3 km from here.

The centre, in this case, is literally the periphery.

> There is not a single Hindu family that lives here. However, they do have their shops around the area. So they come here for work, come to earn, but go back to sleep in their own locality. They would never want to live amongst us. But within Hindu localities, they could not stop our people [from] moving in. Now, in the urban estates, for example, many have bought plots [of land] there.

The Dalits may have moved in, but do the upper castes treat them as equal neighbours? In most cases, they are still kept at a distance.

> In our area, there have hardly been any inter-caste marriages. You see, Ambedkar, in his address to the Rajya Sabha, had asked, 'What is untouchability?' Then he explained it as a 'mental twist'. Twist, in that context, meant a knot. The knot that is now there in the head of the Hindus cannot be undone. They are only tying the knot tighter.

Jalandhar's Dalit domination has helped somewhat. Despite the sharp division amongst its residents, there have been no reports of caste-related violence in this city in the last seventy-five years.

> I will explain why we have never had caste violence here. The Scheduled Caste [people] here are well-educated and well-established. They are also financially well-off. So the upper-caste knows that they will be resisted. They can't get away [with violence], unlike most other places. There is a village called Tehlan, from where a case of untouchability was reported. The villagers announced a curfew for eighteen days and did not give up till the victim was accepted back in the village by other castes. This is just an example of how our community can fight back. The intensity of the fight has decreased, but small quarrels among upper- and lower-caste [groups] haven't disappeared altogether. The difference is that slurs like 'chamar' or 'bhangi' are not used to abuse us. If something like this is reported, people will fight back. This empowerment has come about only because of Ambedkar and how we helped spread his vision.

Dalits have historically shared an uncomfortable relationship with Sikhism, and Jalandhar bears testimony to this dynamic. Balley minced no words when he explained why Sikhism could not do away with caste.

> See, Sikhism is represented incorrectly. Sikhism is an outgrowth of Hinduism. It is full of Brahmanism. The Constitution of India states that no person can be a Scheduled Caste unless they profess the Hindu religion. Then came the Kabir panthi, Mazhabi, Sikhs, Ravidasia and Buddhists.[18] Buddhists came into the purview after V. P. Singh came to power. These are the exceptions [to the general rule] that you have to be Hindu if you have to take a reservation for Scheduled Caste. This is in the Constitution. Govind Vallabh Pant wanted it to be included.[19]

> The Sikh Scheduled Caste has two communities, the Ravidasias and the Mazhabi Sikhs. The Doaba region does not have Mazhabi Sikhs, but Malwa and Majha have a greater population [of this community]. They are as poor as they were. They are as segregated as they were. The Mazhabi Sikhs are treated like slaves in the upper-caste Sikh households.

In my formative years in Shillong, I knew that Sikhs only lived in the *methorpatti*, or in other words, in the locality of scavengers and 'jamadars' or sweepers.

> The SC Sikhs were taken as far as Shillong to clean the city. They were called 'bhangis'. They were taken to Shimla as well. There, they were called 'churas'. The Scheduled Caste list has 'bhangi', 'chura', 'valmiki'. In Sikhism, it is 'chamar', 'ravidasi' and 'adharmi'. The British promised these Sikhs land and money and took them to Shimla, Shillong, and other such places.

The Partition also changed the character of Jalandhar; earlier, it was predominantly a Muslim city.

> For as long as I have been here, hundreds of mosques in Punjab [have been] converted to gurudwaras. Old masjids were either taken down or converted into Sikh areas of worship.... For many years after the Partition, Muslims did not come here. Now the population has grown, and the centre for Muslims is now the Imam Nasser Masjid. The bulk of the Muslim population lives there.

Jalandhar barely finds mention in Indian school history books, but it has an incredibly rich multicultural past that can help us imagine the world differently. For example, Balley's relationship with Buddhism may have been shaped by considerations of caste, but Buddhism has ancient roots in this city.

> Let me tell you that Jalandhar was a major Buddhist place. Have you heard of Lama Lopzang? He was a member of the Scheduled Caste mission. He used to say that the bells in the monasteries in Tibet were exported from Jalandhar. It is written in his accounts.

Balley is a proud Jalandhari and claims to have contributed to the city's evolution. At the same time, he is pragmatic about the limits of caste consciousness. Balley's Jalandhar is neatly divided into caste and religious quarters, but there is hope here and empowerment.

So, what is my primary identity?

On 30 September 1956, the Republican Party of India, under the presidentship of B. R. Ambedkar, was raised. I became the national secretary of that party. On behalf of the party, we led many agitations. For seventy days, I was in jail with my family. I have travelled all the way from Kashmir to Kerala, campaigning for the party. So [how I am] known now is as an Ambedkarite author. But I also identify myself as a social and political worker. I have translated all his work. I have briefed[20] seventeen volumes of Ambedkar's work in Hindi and nineteen in Marathi into two volumes in Hindi. These books are so widely read that seven editions have come out till date. My identity in this city has become such that from any place in India, if you send a letter without an address, it will reach me. Just write, 'Lahori Ram Balley, Jalandhar!'

So, am I an Indian citizen?

Yes, of course. By birth, I am a citizen. I have a birth certificate from the Nawanshahr Municipal Corporation.

See, if you go to Canada, you can apply for citizenship after five years. In America, you can do the same .... So you can be made a citizen and your citizenship can also be revoked. In our country, citizenship cannot be revoked because there is no law. So in my opinion, the citizenship agenda is a calculated move against the Muslims.

Do you know of an American author called [Noam] Chomsky? He said, 'Nationalism is to oppress others.' In Japan, Tagore said that nationalism is dangerous. My son and daughter were born in India, but have been in Canada for thirty-five years. They are Canadian citizens now. What connection will they have with Indian nationalism? In a country where people die of hunger or where 50 per cent of the population does not have drinking water,[21] what will they do with nationalism? A hungry man needs food; he doesn't want to know what the governments are doing for nationalism.... What will Indianness do for a hungry man? When women are not free and safe in our society, *to nationality ko kya khana hai* (what is the point of nationality then)?

Balley's description of his city sums up the spatial and historical character of Jalandhar, where even the collective memory of losing one's home does not help overcome the prejudices of caste and religion.

After meeting Balley saab, I tried to meet Mool Raj, whose hide business goes back to pre-Partition days, but he was away. This was the tannery sector and the demarcation of the city in terms of smell and caste occupation was apparent; this was where Dalits resided and traded in animal hides.

I then took a rickshaw to the alleys of Saidan Gate. This city is full of alleys. A shop called 'Sialkot' stood prominently in the market. It is believed that almost the entire population of Sialkot migrated here. At the end of the road stood an old mansion, all its rooms pulled down, with only a door and three windows that opened out into nothing. Vegetable vendors crowded below the mansion, where two large posters advertised 'Heaven Salon and Spa'. The rest of the market had clothes, ranging from cheap *phulkari* to wedding lehangas. Both cycle and electric rickshaws negotiated through congregations of cows and speeding two-wheelers. The noise and the heat made for an unbearable combination. I could not spend a lot of time exploring the alleys.

In the adjoining Charanjitpura market of the old city, rows of book shops make for an interesting observation: most of the shops bore inscriptions of the year they were established—around 1948–50—and many of them sold texts from ancient India, including those published by the Gita Press.

By the evening, I had ended up in the office of Desh Raj Kali, a journalist and author from Jalandhar, who also invoked the Buddhist past of his city.

> I am from Mithapur, the village of Indian hockey star Pargat Singh. I have always visualised my city as an ancient Buddhist centre, as recounted by Fa Hien and Hiuen Tsang. In the philosophy of Jalandhar, there is a huge contribution of Naths and Sufis. Imam Nasser came from Iran in the eleventh century. Buddhists influenced Sufis as well. This city's tradition has always been a philosophical challenge to Brahmanism.
>
> In the village, I am a 'chamar'. But in the city, I would wear a dhoti at home and neighbours would try to assess my caste through my attire. My wife is a Brahmin and I am a Dalit. I live in an urban, cosmopolitan area, but in more than sixteen years, I haven't been able to assimilate. I prefer the village. The city repels me, but it is my city.

> Spatially, the city is neatly divided into three parts. It had a 90 per cent Muslim population before Partition. [The population of] Bara Basti was all Pathans. Doaba had 80 per cent Muslims. After Partition, the city changed. Now there are twenty slums in the city, all inhabited by Dalits. Bhargav camp, Garha village, Gandhi camp, Gopalnagar, etc., have Ravidasias, Kabirpanthis—it is like the entire [population of] Sialkot is here. Valmikis were brought to this city to clean it. They live in areas like Ali Mohalla, Togri Mohalla, and some [other] eight to ten mohallas. They are looked down upon and virtually fenced out by the city. You know something; no one, even today, gives a loan to them. Then there are areas of *pappe* Sikhs or *sheheri* Sikhs, who are traders. Interestingly, the city doesn't have any upper-caste area. Hindus were anyway in smaller numbers here, and [even] after Partition when some of them came, it was never a Hindu city. Today's Jalandhar and its villages have another spatial aspect to it; the affluence of NRIs leaving behind the elderly has converted us into a city of mortuaries and widow homes. The youth left behind are unemployed, and it has become a hellhole of alcohol and narcotics. This is my city.

Interestingly, both Balley and Kali, as Dalit Punjabis, see their city as a symbol of resistance to Brahmanism.

The following day, I set out in the unbearable summer heat to discover Jalandhar. My first destination was the Imam Nasser dargah, the new Muslim centre, as Balley had explained. Navigating through the Telwali galli, you encounter the aesthetic past of the city, with decadent colonial facades of the erstwhile elite. The dargah, hardly visited by even Jalandharis, is a spectacular piece of architecture. Part of the original dargah, built in the twelfth century by a thief who became the Imam's disciple, stands along with the new structure that came up in the 1930s.

Jalandhar is an ancient city, mentioned in texts like *Padam Puran*. Various stories abound around the naming of the city, the most popular being that of the demon. In *Kalika Puran*, the city is mentioned as Jullunder, where Sati's breasts fell; hence, the city landmark—Devi Talab. The city finds mention in the accounts of Greek thinker Ptolemy as well as the Chinese pilgrim Hiuen Tsang, but the earliest historical material referring to the city is from the reign of Kanishka.[22] According to historical sources, the Fourth Buddhist Council, which attempted the reconciliation of different Buddhist sects, was held in this city. The Council also gave itself the task of collecting all Buddhist texts.

The genealogical study of Jalandhar and Kangra's royal family reveals that it is amongst the oldest in the subcontinent.[23] In 1519, after the Turks and the Lodhis, Babur attacked Punjab. But it was during Sher Shah Suri's reign, when the Grand Trunk Road was built and Jalandhar became part of its route, that the famous *sarais* and kos minars were constructed. The sarais were originally the idea of Sher Shah Suri, and were constructed at a distance of 10 *kos* (about 32 kilometres). Trees were planted on both sides of the road and wells dug to provide water and shelter to travellers. But it was Jahangir who actually converted the temporary sarais into structures made of bricks and stone. And he reduced the distance between the shelters from 10 to 8 kos.

I could not miss visiting Nur Mahal, built on the remains of what may have been an ancient city. It is named after Noor Jahan, queen of Emperor Jahangir. It is a quadrangle of 140 rooms on all four sides.

> The Sarai is 551 feet square outside, including the octagonal tower at all the corners. The western gateway is a double-storeyed building faced on the outside with red sand stone from Fatehpur Sikri quarries. The whole front is divided into panels ornamented with sculpture; but the relief is low and the workmanship coarse. There are angels and fairies, elephants and rhinoceroses, camels and horses, monkeys and peacocks, with men on horseback and archers on elephants. The sides of the gateway are in much better taste, the ornament being limited to foliated scroll-work with birds sitting on the branches.[24]

Before Nur Mahal, I drove up to Dakhini Sarai on the right bank of Chitti Bein in Jahangir village. The village still retains the name of the emperor, who had built a fort here. This fort was converted into a sarai during the time of Shah Jahan. This used to be part of the Grand Trunk Road, and en route one can still find the Tut Kalan Kos Minar, built probably during Jahangir's reign.

In the evening, I met a 100-year-old resident of the city, Sardarilal Sharma, whose story of the city started and ended with the Partition.[25] He quickly went back to that day when they had left their home and started walking from Shakargarh to Kathua.

I was born in 1917. We lived in the district of Gurdaspur. Pathankot, Batala, Gurdaspur and Shakargarh were the four tehsils. We lived in Shakargarh. It is a village in Pakistan's Punjab.

In 1947, Pakistan was formed. In 1944, my eldest son Tirath Ram was born. He was three years old when we came to India. We had lived in Hallan village, Punjab, Pakistan. So we crossed over to India from Jammu and Kashmir because that was nearer. We walked all the way to Jammu. Raja Hari Singh's police was patrolling the border so that Hindus crossing over from Pakistan did not face any problems. Once we were in India, we could go anywhere to settle down. We kept walking till we reached Kathua. We had only brought along some jewellery and clothes. I remember spending a night at Kathua, along with my family. We encountered a few relatives there as well. We became a group of fifty familiar people, as more Hindus came to India from Pakistan.

On the way, there is a dry river called Khad. My grandfather was walking with us. He was old and couldn't see at night. All of a sudden, grey clouds gathered in the sky. There was lightning. I was worried thinking of my wife and son, because we had no shelter if it rained. My grandfather held Tirath's hand and took him to my grandmother. They made him lie down on the sheet in which we were carrying clothes. A scorpion started crawling over his body so Baba threw it away, and it crawled on the ground and bit my elder brother. He was in a lot of pain and started crying. I was furious. Our entire family, especially women and children, were in pain after walking for so long. I saw it was about to rain and was wondering what to do with all of us out in the open.

My grandfather called for water. I told him it is a dry place, even the Khad is dry, we cannot find water here. He told me to find a low-lying spot near the river and dig the soil with my hands to find water. He was certain that we would find it. I just kept following what he said. I dug the soil away and found very little water. I poured it into a small steel bowl that dadi [grandmother] carried with her. I came back and told him that it was hardly one sip of water. He asked me to keep quiet. He took that water, sprinkled some drops on his face and washed the tips of his fingers, and held the water droplets on his palm.

After performing this small ritual, he said it wouldn't rain anymore. And he was right. The sky was dark grey, there was heavy lightning, but my grandfather stopped the rain from pouring down till the next morning.

We started walking again. In Kathua, there was a school building. The women could rest there for a while, so we entered the building and as soon as we got shelter, it rained.

We had no idea where we would go. We just kept walking and Gurdaspur happened to be the first place where we could stay. We were dependent on the locals to empathise with us. So we came to Gurdaspur and someone told us, there's a village here called Lamin. We knew this person. He was a lawyer in Pakistan. The lawyer told the sarpanch that we are a Brahmin family. From Lamin, a number of people had migrated to Pakistan, so a lot of houses were empty. These were mud huts, not pakka houses. So, through that lawyer, we settled down in the village.

We had to eat something every day, right? We sold the jewellery and soon ran out of money. There was no source of income. For a few days, all the villagers provided some food for families coming in from Pakistan. But how long could that practice sustain [us]? Then my grandmother sold all her silver coins to provide for another few meals. But this did not last for long [either]. So I left the house in search for some job. I went to Amritsar and looked for any possible job to sustain my family. I did not find anything. Then I looked for a job in Batala, and did not find any there either. Next on my list was Delhi. For the first seven days, I did not eat one roti. I would sit and cry all night. A few days later, I found a friend. I can't recall his first name, but we used to call him Mahajan.

I was sleeping on the footpath one night. In the morning, Mahajan recognised me while I was sleeping. He hugged me immediately and told me about what he had gone through and how he came here. I told him about my situation. He took me along to the place where he worked. It was a printing press. For three years, I stayed at Kashmiri Gate and worked for the Gita Press. Every month I sent some money for my family in Gurdaspur.

Then, once I went home, I met a relative, my 'behnoi'. He used to work in Jalandhar in a press. He got me a job in Jalandhar. I kept working in Jalandhar in the press. The owner of the press promoted me [and made me] the manager. The newspaper was called *Veer Pratap*.

Pakistan main hum ameer aadmi the. Humare ghar main naukar the. Kaafi zameen bhi thi. Hindustan main hum gareeb ho gaye.

> *Kuch bhi nahi raha. Magar aaj fir baadshah hain.* ('I was a rich man in Pakistan. Our house had servants. We had quite a lot of land too. We became poor when we came to Hindustan. Nothing of that wealth remained. Yet, today we are kings once again.')
>
> Back in Pakistan, we had our own land, around 25 acres. We were farmers. Since the land was so big, we farmed some of the area and sub-let the rest of the land to people of a lower caste who wanted to work and earn.
>
> There was no school in that area. It was a mile away and we had to walk. There were no bicycles then. So we were a group of five to six boys who went to school together. We balanced a *fatti* (slate) on our heads and we walked all the way. Near the tree where we all gathered to study, there was a small pond. When the slate was dirty, we used to run and dip it in the pond.
>
> Pakistan is where I was born. That place will always be closest to my heart. That is my motherland. But the land which nurtured me, gave me money, food, where my family settled, is Jalandhar. So naturally, that place is also dear to me. For more than sixty-five years, I have been in Jalandhar.

I asked him what being an 'Indian' meant to him.

> I now have no links with Pakistan. What is left for me is Hindustan. The entire country is mine. I have no distinction for people within my country. I could go and fight for my country. That is my commitment to my country. That is why I call myself a Hindustani. I call myself a Hindustani because I am a Hindu. I am not a 'chamar' or a 'rajput'. I am a Hindu. Just like the Muslims are together in Pakistan despite people from other religions living there, in Hindustan it is the land of Hindus. I also love all my Hindu brothers—I am a Hindustani. Even a Muslim in India is my own, but not the ones from outside who are trying to threaten my country. It is the feeling of being a Hindu that makes me more Indian.

After this spirited display of nationalism, Sharma immediately turned despondent about his nation.

> During our time, there was peace. Now that is gone from our lives. People no longer feel content. They are always sad and unhappy. Money is there, but no happiness. This transition is not good. How will we achieve this peace? This will happen through knowledge. We have to spread this knowledge. For most people, politics dictates their lives. If someone does not get to eat all

through the day, how can we expect her/him to be content? This was a very, very small city. There were hardly any people. This place was all agricultural land and trees. Now it is as big as any modern city. Look at the number of people today!

Banaras

Talilla Banaras chashme baddoor / bahishte khurram-o-firadaus mamoor

(From the evil eye, may God in his greatness / save Banaras as it is a grove in paradise).[26]

Alleys and more alleys. Cobbled alleys with sharp turns. Sacred cows, Banarasi *paanwala*, women with holy water, sweet-makers, loudspeakers relaying chants, rows of parked two-wheelers, overhead wires, ancient doors and windows, children in bright clothes, gatherings of the young and the old, weary travellers, pious pilgrims, the infirm and the agnostic, the policemen and the priest on duty. A city woven with ancient alleys that exhaust you, till you arrive at the Ganga, where millions have attempted to reach for salvation.

Above a flight of stairs on Panchaganga ghat rises the once-resplendent Dharhara mosque, the only mosque amongst hundreds of temples on the ghats of Banaras. It stands tall; they say that from its minars, now long gone, you could once see Dilli's lights.

A few metres away is a Durga puja pandal full of people. It is the night of Navami, and everyone is celebrating. The drums refuse to stop.

Not very far away, loudspeakers crackle with noise and distasteful music in the name of celebration. Standing obscured by the loudspeakers and tents is a statue of the Sufi saint Kabir. This is Kabir chowk, named after the Sufi saint, and this is where he lived, although he died in Maghar, having cast aside his own city of Kashi, choosing hell over salvation. Kabir's dissent against superstition and fanaticism led him to leave his beloved Kashi. He wrote, '*Kaasi Maghar Sam Bichari; Ochchi Bhagat Kaisey Utras Paari*—I regard both Maghar and Kashi as the same. How can you swim across with inadequate devotion (be it in Kashi or in Maghar)?'[27] Kabir's *sufiana* is another *ras* of Banaras that continues to influence generations and lifestyles. But today, in the din of an overcrowded city, Kabir is difficult to locate.

Across the city, near Assi ghat, some residents have come together to discuss an impending crisis—the new political dispensation. One of the first 'outsiders' to make this city his own is the renegade Hindu god Shiv, who appears to light a chillum and sit down with a *kulhad* of chai at Pappu's chai *dukaan*. It is a 100-year-old city centre of dissenting intellectuals.

To know Kashi,[28] one must understand the mythology of Shiv. They say it is his city. That is not entirely true. Long before he descended from the mountains after his marriage to Parvati to find a place on earth, Kashi's religious history was already being written. Historically, Shiv is not just an outsider to the Indo-Aryan pantheon, but beyond that, he contradicts Hindu customs. In mythological representations, he has no concern for purity, is not a believer of the auspicious, has no lineage, wanders naked and makes cremation grounds his home. He is casteless. Even the Vedic hymns on him are ambiguous. He is the anthropomorphic image of the city of Kashi and his *baraat*, with which he arrived in the city, constitutes the multicultural Banaras.

Banaras is perhaps the oldest cosmopolis made up of migrants. Eighty-four ghats garland the city where more than 50,000 Mallas dominate the population. Brahmins, Yadavs and Doms inhabit the ghats.[29] The Yadavs made their entry only in the last 100 years, replacing Bengalis, who had made Banaras their home long before Calcutta became the capital of British India. The Bengali involvement with this city goes deep: from religion to spiritualism, from music to philosophical debates. Bengali zamindars built the city; their havelis are now falling apart in most places. The Marathas also invested in the city, but primarily for strategic interests. Mughals, Gujaratis, and the British—everyone contributed to this city, not only because of its spiritual cosmos, but also as a mercantile base. For centuries, this was one of the most important trading centres in the region.

Choudhary, popularly referred to as Dr Choudhury,[30] a young Dom, enters the chai dukaan and joins Shiv in a corner. They are both residents of Harishchandra ghat, one of the two cremation grounds where the pyres are never doused because of the unending procession of the dead.

> We are not just burning the dead, we also perform the last rites for unclaimed bodies without any payment. Every year, we perform the *pind dan* for them. But since the time you [Shiv]

> came to our shamshan ghat nothing has changed for us. Our children are not studying, because [are we to] pay school fees, or buy our daily bread? Thanks to you that Manikarnika and Harishchandra ghats have remained the heart of the city, unlike other cities, where cremation grounds are outside.

Shiv listens with indifference. He rarely speaks. Dr Choudhury continues to speak.

> Ninety-nine per cent of people in our community are alcoholics because, you will know, it is impossible to carry on disposing corpses all day without being inebriated. You have been around for 3,000 years and the governments have been here 300 years, but did you or the government care to improve our situation? What about our children? Shouldn't they get educated, compete for employment like everyone else? We earn only that much to run a family, but we don't have enough to provide children a good education. One cremation is around 3,000 rupees. People pay lakhs of rupees to doctors, but when they come to Doms, they suddenly become poor. Are Doms the cheapest in society? We earn the least, but we are content.

Others join in the conversation. Someone new to the city observes that Banaras ghats are unique because unlike other cities, here Doms, Mallas, Brahmins and Muslims all live together on the ghats.

> **Dr Choudhury**: Our work is divided. Doms will burn the bodies, pandits will offer the pind-dan, the Mallahs will take the *ashthi* and the people around. Our tradition, our *parampara* goes back centuries when Kalua Dom purchased Harishchandra who worked in the cremation grounds after having given his kingdom to Vishvamitra.[31] This is the adi Manikarnika and the oldest cremation ghat. This is older than mythology, because since the beginning of society, the first human being had to be cremated with rituals and rites. You sit and smoke, but we make sure that the rites of passage are performed.

A journalist sipping chai takes a dig at Dr Choudhury: 'Haven't you or your community benefitted from the new government?' Dr Choudhury replied, 'No, we haven't in any way. The Prime Minister must think of us now. We are in a desperate situation.'

Shiv does not seem perturbed at all. He had declared that Kashi would never be destroyed, that nothing can touch this city that rests on his trident, suspended between heaven and earth. He may have made dying more dignified, but the people who deliver *moksha* seem unhappy.

The journalist quips, 'But you might have to prove your Indianness. Is the Dom an Indian?'

> Indian? Does the government itself have citizenship proof? We have thousands of years of history behind us. You cannot change that. The soul of Banaras resides in the ghats. No one has the right to ask us whether we are from Kashi or from Hindustan. Read my history first. Till you don't get fire, you can neither die nor be born. In both cases, it is the Dom that breathes life and death in your body. And the government will come and ask a Dom whether he is a citizen? That would be a shame.

Veer Bhadra Mishra, an engineer who taught at the Indian Institute of Technology, Varanasi and inherited the position of Mahant of the ancient Sankat Mochan temple on Assi ghat, listened to Dr Choudhury speak.

An amused Shiv appears to pull on his pipe and asks Mishra, 'How long have you lived in this city?' By now, the tea shop was fully occupied and everyone's attention was drawn to this table. The Mahant was addressing his audience. The people respected him and were keen to listen, even though Shiv seemed indifferent.

> In 1653, Goswami Tulsidas surrendered his position. I am from the same *parampara*. Now imagine how he must have envisioned the state of his affairs after him. It was during Mughal rule and *Ramcharitmanas* was his greatest work. In *Ramcharitmanas*, our relations have been defined between father and son, husband and wife, brother and sister and it speaks of our *modus operandum*. Many people at that time were not educated, so he brought in the concept of open theatre and started [the] Ramlila. What I want to say is, our traditions have continued for so long and they have been inclusive. People benefit from it.
>
> The concept of '*Vasudevam Kutumbhakam*' is that [the] whole world is a family and all are brothers and sisters. Now, how does the concept of NRC fit in here? Then you are contradicting that concept of Vasudevam Kutumbhakam. India is from Kashmir to Kanyakumari and from Gujrat to the Northeast.

The journalist then asked, 'How would you describe a citizen of Banaras?'

> There is a word in Hindi, *manwar*, [which] means they have a very open mind. The entire area in Assi and Bhadaini Ghat is

> a prototype model of India. All types of people live here. You have all the people of different states living in close proximity, and that too, freely. These communities together have exposure in Banaras. Does this not give character to the city? All the kingdoms that have been there in India, they have all had a haveli or temple or a house in Banaras. They moved between the commoners. The people of Banaras have walked along such a rich history of important people .... a Banarasi has a mind of her/his own. Banaras rests on the trident of Shivji, it is not a part of this globe. Only this place will survive.

Shiv had a glint in his eye. He gestured to his trident in the corner to indicate that there was nothing resting on it, really!

The Mahant looked at Choudhury and asked after everyone at Harishchandra ghat before embarking on his account of the dead.

> Now, what is the probability theory? If you toss a coin, the probability of success is 50 per cent. Death is a reality for everyone. So the probability of death is 1. It has to come for each person. Banaras is the only place where death is celebrated. You will meet [people] here who have just come all the way to die in Banaras. When they leave their body, we celebrate that. Now, a Banarasi who isn't afraid of death, what else can he be scared of? He does not bother about NRC. Our makers are Brahma, Vishnu, Mahesh. Can you define their boundary? How can you then start finding people in your own country who are outsiders or insiders?

The excitement in the tea stall is now palpable. The Mahant is unforgiving. Shiv tells himself that this is what he meant when he said Banaras rests on his trident. The Mahant carries on.

> Now so much money has come, not for developing Banaras but to systematically ruin it. Everyone is afraid of Banaras. Sanatan dharam is the centre of Banaras. Muslims think Banaras is their place, Christian claim it [as] theirs. Buddhists came to Banaras finally, and Jain gurus have been born here. Banaras is a spiritual space for all people to flourish; it has given opportunities to all.

The Mahant finally turns towards Shiv, does a *pranam* and invokes him.

> This place is of the Shiva. Now the baraatis in Shiv's wedding were of all kinds. The message is that you have to walk taking

> everyone along. This is also the land of liberation. If you die here, if you step in Banaras, all your sins will burn away. Mukti is the ultimate goal. Who is the giver of mukti? The space of Banaras—the shetra-sanyas and the Ganga. We are part and parcel of almighty God. Will NRC work here? This is a city that accepts all without any conflict. The Mufti sahib tells me, I am his guardian. It is only possible in Banaras. If this model is spread across the country, then there will be no division in India.

A curious tea drinker who has been listening to this conversation looks around and asks the Mahant, 'Banaras has been the fountainhead of philosophy. In today's political climate, what can Banaras contribute to philosophy?'

> I met a political leader during a rally in 2013. He asked me to meet him for five minutes. Our meeting continued for forty minutes and we only talked about the Ganga. They won the election and then they dedicated a ministry to the Ganga. I thought that was serious work. But when they started working, I understood that nothing would happen. So they do not even mention it now. The Ganga has only become dirtier. But I say it again; Banaras is the place for maintaining equilibrium. It will see ups and downs, and then it will churn to balance everything. In Banaras ... people will realign and reorganise themselves. Only if Banaras survives will India survive. I have assigned it a word called *yug dharam*. It walks with the times, but if you rotate the wheel at some point, a part of it will point downwards. This is the down-time. When it comes up it will shape a new order.

Kashi is a city that has inherited temples and mosques, churches and monasteries. Sadiq Ali's ancestors were brought to Kashi following a *farmaan* by Aurangzeb in 1623 to look after the Dharhara mosque.

Ali, who is the custodian of the mosque, is at his eloquent best about the Ganga-Jamuni *tehzeeb*. After all, it was in Balaji Temple where for years Bismillah Khan and his family breathed into the *mangalvadya*, the shehnai. It was the same shehnai into which Khan would blow the delicate note of raag Kafi as the first Indian Prime Minister rose to speak on the morning of 15 August 1947. Ali entered the *adda* late, but as always, believed all was well because this is Banaras. He is a well-acknowledged Banarasi raconteur.

> I will narrate the story of Dharhara mosque from the Mughal period. During Aurangzeb's reign, the *kotwal* in any city was

like the owner of the entire territory. So the story begins when Ibrahim Khan was the kotwal. Most people living in a town that has a river spend their leisure time walking along the banks. Just like other people in the city, Ibrahim had gone to walk by the river when he saw a beautiful girl return from the river after a bath. He asked the man accompanying him to find out who the girl was. On the Panchganga ghat, there is the Bindo Madho mandir. Right behind that mandir was the house of a pandit. The young girl Khan fancied was Shakuntala Devi, the pandit's daughter. Now Ibrahim sent a farmaan to this girl's house, saying that he wanted to marry her. It was the Mughal rule; the kotwal was like a king of the city. Who would dare say no to such an order?

So it is believed that Shakuntala, along with her maternal uncle, walked to Delhi and stayed in a dharamshala. When asked why they were in Delhi, the uncle said that they wanted to meet Aurangzeb. Someone suggested that Aurangzeb would visit the Jama Masjid on Friday for jumma namaz. People line up near the stairs to present their requests and the king looks into those over the week. Shakuntala, on Friday evening, stood on the Masjid staircase disguised as a man. When the king passed by, she presented her request, and Aurangzeb immediately threw his robe over the girl's face and asked his men to present her in the court the next morning. The next day, around five in the evening, she was taken to the court. Aurangzeb asked what had bothered her so much that she had to come all the way from Banaras to Delhi disguised as a man. She cried and told him [about] the kotwal threatening to marry her against her wishes. Aurangzeb told her that a man from his court would go along with her to Banaras to protect her from the Kotwal. He added that when she got married, he himself would come for the wedding rituals. It is said that once the wedding date was decided, Aurangzeb, along with his soldiers, went to Banaras. The place where he stayed was a Mughal Sarai, it is called the Aurangabad Sarai. Even that locality has been renamed in honour of Aurangzeb, and that is known as Aurangabad Mohalla.

When he went for the wedding, he asked Ibrahim whether he [had been] sent to the city for wooing girls or for the maintenance of law and order? Some believe that he ordered Ibrahim's execution in the city centre. When it was time for namaz that day, Shakuntala requested Aurangzeb to leave a souvenir marking his attendance at her wedding. Aurangzeb then ordered the building of a small mosque. The Imam who conducted the namaz was selected from our family, and he became the keeper of the mosque as well. Our forefathers came from Delhi. He also issued a farmaan that stated that our family will receive 1 rupee daily from the royal treasury for the upkeep of the mosque.

Ali continued:

During the British period, when Warren Hastings was in India, they identified Banaras as a place where no rebellion or conflict has taken place. Taking that into consideration, they said that this mosque would be refurbished. The mosque is located in an entirely Hindu locality. They thought that if a mosque's reconstruction were to happen in a Hindu locality, it would disturb the peace within the space and the British would gain control of the situation.

When the minars were constructed, the people who wished to go all the way up from the staircase used to pay 1 anna. That money was used both for upkeep and the family expenses. Later, that minar crumbled and fell into the river, and the practice of allowing people to climb to the highest point of the minarets was stopped altogether. My father suggested that as the income from the mosque minarets was coming to an end, the children must be educated so they can earn [their living].

The Mahant nudged Ali, asking him to narrate how a Hindu became its caretaker.

I was in the services[32] and couldn't be there in Banaras all the time. That time, a person living behind the mosque, Balram, took charge of the cleaning and maintenance of the place. When my father died, Balram bhaiya took charge and till his death, he was the one looking after it. He had no appointment, we were the owners and custodians, but he was very kind to accept it as his own. There's not a single Muslim family in the vicinity, and the locals living around the mosque take care of it.

Another *addabaaj* asked, 'Ali saab, is this a true story? Because Aurangzeb is known for conquests and destruction more than anything else.'

Aurangzeb used to fight for territory. In his time, he took over the entire south. Aurangzeb also realised that the British were taking over, whereas [they claimed that] they have only come for trade. So he cancelled their permit, and this is the primary

> reason the British have written about Aurangzeb's reign as not a very pleasant one. So the Muslims were told that he was a very good king and the Hindus were told that Aurangzeb was brutal. These are useless [discussions meant] to incite communities.
>
> One last thing about Aurangzeb; it is said that he ordered the demolitions of temples. It is true. However, it is also true that he ordered mosque demolitions.

The addabaaj then asks him, 'But Ali saheb, what does it mean to be a Muslim in Banaras?'

> Banaras has a very high Muslim population. Many of these Muslim men are silk saree weavers. The saree business has both Hindus and Muslims in it. The ones who prepare the thread and make the sarees are Muslims. The sellers are Hindus. If there was to be any fight between Hindus and Muslims, the entire saree business would collapse. Even the pandits and maulanas sit together and talk. It is only the politicians who constantly make one community hate the other. In 1932, my father signed an agreement with the Archeological Survey of India for the maintenance of the mosque. I have met the director general of ASI many times, and they have ordered renovation. But nothing is being done.

No one noticed that Shiv had left. The Mahant had to leave too. More than two hours had passed. It is in such conversations that the present and the future can be situated. The Banarasi is not giving up yet. Shiv struts the samshan ghat; Dr Choudhury readies a pyre. Not far away, the Ganga Lahari can be heard, hymns created by Jagannatha, Shah Jahan's court poet, a Brahmin ostracised by his community for loving a Muslim girl. It is believed that the lovers sat on the ghats waiting for river Ganga to take them away forever.

GUWAHATI

The only way to experience the Brahmaputra is to sit by it and watch it flow as the sun goes down. The river here is the city, and its inhabitants are the river people. Aboard Sajida's cruise vessel during a summer sunset, I could only sit in awe of this city, perpetually moving since perhaps the beginning of time. A few minutes after the sun sets, the sky is full of colours and the shadowed hills descend into a primeval silence. Bats fly overhead. Birds have already settled in. Beneath the water, a world stays awake. It is by night that the boatmen set off in search of their livelihood: catching fish or transporting pottery and vegetables. By early morning, they return, weary, with whatever they have found.

On the banks of this river is Guwahati, divided by the water. Both the land and the water here have been witness to myths, folklore, and the rise and fall of dynasties and contested histories. It was the centre of an unlikely confluence of races and cultures, religion and languages. But its present is unkind to its past; a city that existed from the time of the Indus Valley Civilisation and stood as a bridge between South Asia and South East Asia, recording the migration of travellers and traders, pilgrims and spies, warriors and monks, is today confronted by the demons of chauvinism and xenophobia.

Whose city is it?

No one can claim the river. Miyahs, the inhabitants of the *chars* and *chaporis*,[33] and river people like the Mishings may know the river's language, but can they still claim it? When does a person start asserting their rights over land or water or mountains? If all of us have migrated, then what is this claim about?

You mad river
In a strange illusion you have trapped me
In our happy lives
You have drawn a ravine.

You have broken someone's land
You have broken someone's tin house
You have broken my new love.

You mad river
In a strange illusion you have trapped me
In our happy lives
You have drawn a ravine.

You have broken someone's land
You have broken someone's tin house
You have broken my new love.

You mad river
In a strange illusion you have trapped me
In our happy lives
You have drawn a ravine.

Some go to Mondira
Some go to Goruchar
Some go to Norikata reserve

You mad river
In a strange illusion you have trapped me
In our happy lives
You have drawn a ravine.[34]

As the boatmen hum *paargeet*,[35] they become stateless. The river does not know boundaries—it just flows. Through their songs and poetry, the Miyahs explore 'their relationship with the river, their struggle for survival and the larger issue of migration and identity' that has drowned out all other voices in the recent past.[36] They are as much outsiders as 'water is to land'.

As the river drives a wedge into land, divisions amongst people go deeper. Language becomes the little islands 'where ignorant armies clash by night'.[37]

An octogenarian born in the city—my mother—recalls how young girls in the old city would start their day plucking flowers: madhabilata, korobi, joba, aparajita, katgolap, atoshi. In the evening, they would walk into Jubilee Garden, which was known by the colloquial name, 'Julbi Garden'. The garden would be filled with fragrance from jui, malati and gondhoraj. Gandhi and other Congress leaders had come here to address 'citizens' before Independence. Today, the garden is dead. Flower sellers sit in rows before the Sukreshwar temple. To look back and describe one's home through flowers is a significant choice for someone who has lived through the changing hues of the city. Not the riots she witnessed, not losing her home, but a childhood nurtured by the river and its banks, the Kamakhya, institutions like Harisabha, festivals like Saraswati puja and Holi, the amazing Brahmaputra, and her wooden double-storeyed house in Panbazar—this can also be a citizen's autobiography. Most roads had trees on both sides, she remembers, and all roads led to the river. The city was small; everyone knew each other. Their little differences were buried under their love for the city. The Assamese and the Bengalis, the Marwaris and Biharis, the Hindus and Muslims, the tribals and the non-tribals—this was home to all. Then one day, the sky descended on the river and neighbours shut their doors on one another. Grounds where little girls picked flowers became battlefields. Fences came up in common courtyards where friends had once played.

Kulada also grew up in the same city and the same house. He is Shobhona's older brother, who was educated in Europe, but never quite left his favourite town. An actor, filmmaker, writer and theatre personality, he reminisces about his city and his journeys, and how he longed to return to his home. Despite his lifelong engagement with the Assamese language, literature, and films and television, he will still be a 'Bongal' (a pejorative term for Hindu Bengalis, just like 'Miyah' is for Muslim Bengalis).

> This is my city of birth and my most favourite city. But it is Panbazar with which I identified always. This house is where I live, but I know no one around [anymore]. In Panbazar, all my friends have now gone. At twelve years I acted as Amal in Tagore's *Dakghar*. At the age of 28, I left the city for Europe. I went to Leeds to study business management, but I didn't know higher mathematics, so dad suggested, 'why don't [you] study cinema instead?' When I reached London, I joined acting. I was always a topper and in acting, too, I fared well. Then I started working in a bookshop and the owners loved me. I started studying in the British Film Institute that operated out of a rented house. Then I moved to Hamburg, perhaps the wrong choice because I didn't even know the language.
>
> I was already in love with a girl in London, but she used to work in Hamburg. Every evening, we would meet in a restaurant near the Central Station. Suddenly, she declared that she wouldn't meet me till I married her. I wanted a year's time to find a job, and immediately wrote back home to my dad about the affair. Then I set sail back to India. I got at least five chances for a job, but missed all of them. At least in one case, I later realised that my brothers had conspired to block my travel so I wouldn't marry her. Then I started my firm in Calcutta, collaborating with the dancer Meenakshi Chaliha to launch our documentary venture, which did famously well—till one day, because of our accountant's lapses, we had to shut it down. We earned a lot of money making documentaries and through television coverage. I started moving between Calcutta and Assam and became known as an Assamese actor and director. From sixteen years of age, I cultivated [my interest in] the language and culture of Assam, and that continues even today. Even though I witnessed

> so much divisiveness between the Assamese and Bengalis, or even within Bengalis, the animosity towards Sylhetis has never affected my affinity and love towards the language and people. Not once have we as a family felt any different. Not just my city, my country is Assam and I am an Assamese with heart and soul.[38]

Nearly half-a-century of strife between communities has split open realities of ethnic identities and religious polarisation, with an undercurrent of caste and tribal affinities.

The city is thousands of years old. It was once called Pragjyotishpura, 'the city of eastern light'. Capital of the Kamarupa kingdom, it became the capital of the Pala dynasty in the tenth to the eleventh century CE. Later, it became an outpost of the Koch-Hajo and Ahom kingdoms.[39]

The architecture of this city of temples has an interesting element—water tanks or large *pukhuris*. According to historians, more than 300 tanks existed in Guwahati and north Guwahati for its citizens. Today, only a few survive. During the Ahom period,

> special officers called mati seleka bixoya (soil-testers) performed rituals and observed several factors such as the direction of the wind and tasted the soil to locate the natural aquifers underground for building these tanks. Such understanding of local geology may perhaps be the reason that many of these ponds still have water all round the year.[40]

According to the Department of Environment & Forests, Assam, there are an estimated 1,85,623 ponds and tanks in the state of Assam.[41] The city tanks are historical markers that indicate different stages in its evolution. They were built by kings near temples and served the community's needs, from drinking water to ritual bathing, and also served as groundwater recharge areas. If documented, they could well be used to trace the growth of the city, starting from the earliest known reservoir. The city is in many ways a congregation of water bodies and localities named after them, for example, Digholipukhuri, Jorpukhuri and Nagkata Pukhuri.

The river, however, remains the most dominant motif in the minds of its citizens. Yet, it is claimed by only a few. This ancient city is found across 'Indian' myth, folklore and legend. There is adequate historical data, inscriptions, coins and accounts about the city and its citizens, from the possible migration of the Zuh people in 2750 BCE to the arrival of Ahoms from South East Asia.

Here enters one of the most dramatic but underrated historical heroes, Sukapha, who may have come from the Shan state of Burma.[42] Rich folklore abounds around his decision to leave his kingdom to his stepbrother, the direct descendant and heir apparent of that kingdom. Sukapha then set out on a mission to conquer and subjugate every resistance as he marched towards the Paktai range. In 1228 CE, he reached the Brahmaputra Valley and set up his capital at Charaideo. It is from this point that record-keeping was practised in Assam, introduced by an 'outsider' who would lay the foundation of one of the longest reigning dynasties of the world. It was also the first non-Aryan conquest of the land; the dynasty took on Aryan domination but succumbed to its religious and linguistic hegemony.[43] After Sukapha's death in 1268 to about 1497 CE, the Ahoms did not pursue any further conquests and instead consolidated their gains. The powerful kingdoms to their east were the Chutiya, Kachari and Bhuyan kingdoms, which were either Hindus or under the influence of Hindusim, and could not be subjugated easily. So they turned to the Kamata kingdom in the west and after a long battle, brought home the Hindu princess in the first recorded Ahom-Hindu marriage. This alliance was the turning point that marked the Hinduisation of the Ahoms.[44]

Subsequently, Assam saw invasion by the Mughals and the decline of the Ahom kingdom; rebellions by Moamariyas and invasions by the Burmese; and then the arrival of the British and various communities from other parts of India.[45] The years following the Revolt of 1857 were a time of a deepening of what historians termed the 'national consciousness',[46] as well as the freedom movement. The Partition and the crossing over of 'refugees' led to the subsequent creation of an entirely new lexicon of identities. At the same time, it was also a time of awakening of new identities in the hills and the plains. People who had lived together for centuries were suddenly pitted against each other. Land became primary, territories were redrawn and animosities bred. After India's independence, Assam and the region as a whole was dotted with innumerable insurrections, and the violence assumed unimaginable proportions. Sub-national assertions gained momentum, metamorphosing to terrorist activities and widespread hatred. As the movements rose and fell, what deepened were the Hindu-Muslim polarisation and the Assamese-Bengali mistrust. The tribal and non-tribal relationship became irrevocably fraught. The sense of an 'outsider versus insider' question gained legitimacy, triggering decades of violence.

In 2019, I asked a young journalist, Tora Agarwala, who reported for *The Indian Express*, how she saw herself reporting the fresh spate of divisiveness and how she located herself in this city. She came from a family of 'outsiders', and her grand uncle, Jyoti Prasad Agarwala, is the acknowledged cultural icon of modern Assam. She began by narrating her experiences of covering the events around the implementation of the National Register of Citizens (NRC), and what citizenship and belonging means to her.

T. A.: I was the one who filled out my entire family's forms for the NRC. We are a big family. My dad was really confused about the entire process and I was on a break between jobs. While I knew something was happening around the NRC, I knew it very vaguely. I filled the forms mechanically, like I would a chore. I was not thinking of the larger picture at all. For maybe a moment in between, I thought, this may make big news later. But it was a fleeting thought.

Then I moved to Bombay. My new job was at a design magazine in South Bombay, far away from Assam, in a bubble of its own.

When I came back to Assam with *The Indian Express*, one of the first stories I did was an explainer on the citizenship bill. Obviously, nothing extraordinary, but that is when I started reading about this.

It was clear to me immediately that human error was inevitable in an exercise of this scale. Imagine going through piles and piles of paper. If things had been implemented right after the 1985 Assam Accord, it might have been easier—but forty years later, it's a different ballgame. As school-going children, while we knew about the ULFA and bandhs were a part of life, the Bangladeshi immigrant issue wasn't something we heard much about—perhaps my ignorance then was a byproduct of my sheltered upbringing in a city that was outgrowing its past. [Despite] whatever happened in the 1970s and 1980s with the language movement, the communities in Assam had chosen peace, delicate as it might have been. I'm not saying it was perfect, but it was a work in progress. Every election it would come up, and every political party would bring it up, but that did not cause disruption. But now you try to bring that up after so many years, [claiming that] you suddenly want to resolve this. It is like reopening old wounds. Everyone is so angry—you will see it on social media, across the dinner table—you will hardly find anyone who is able to speak dispassionately about it, irrespective of which side they are on. I am not speaking on behalf of any community, but having reported on it, it's clear to me that for a lot of people, the process is a punishment—especially for the poor who cannot afford lawyers, and across the country, lack basic documentation. My views may not sit well many in the region.

K. B.: This is more from a journalist's point of view that you say if you say something, the Assamese people will mind. But I have worked and lived here. I faced the same problem. If the story were in favour of Assamese people, I was one amongst them. Otherwise, I was the outcast; but that is a professional hazard anyway.

In the past one year, you have met people who were either sent to detention centres or came out of the detention centres. From that experience, give me a sense of who is a citizen here.

T. A.: All these [ideas] are generated by governments and politics. They are the ones who set up these borders. When I am reporting, I am very detached. I think it is very important to be. Whenever I speak to my subjects, I try to understand where they come from. I don't think the people living on either side of the border are 'illegal'. It is the border in between that brings in the sense of illegality. When I was reporting in Barak valley, it was about citizenship, NRC and what anxieties it triggered. I was there for four days in 2018, but till the third day I did not have a story because it was July, and it was raining the entire time. On the fourth day, I found this lady whose father was in the detention camp—he was 104! His photograph at a detention centre had already gone viral. One question I ask while doing NRC stories is: 'What do you mean by being Indian?' And the range of responses is very enlightening. [In this case, she] was a young woman, her father was about to die, her mother was unwell; they had a grim-looking tea shop. It was sad. She kept showing me documents, asking me what to do and saying that she has no idea. All these legislations and papers are confusing. She had no idea what the NRC was. I asked her and she said, I just know it is good if you are on the NRC list. So I asked her what it is to be an Indian. She said, I don't know much, but maybe the Sarkar will give us an Aadhaar card.

Later, I was interviewing two Gorkha women who used to meet in the Foreigners' Tribunal and became best friends when they found each other in the detention centre. Even there, I asked one of them what it is like in jail. She just told me that in jail, they called her Bangladeshi. So I asked her if she knew what that means. She said, 'I think it means someone who doesn't have papers'. I then asked her if she knew that Bangladesh is another country. She had no idea.

Growing up, I was sheltered from all this. My parents also took to the streets during the agitation [in 1979–85]. They would keep their gates open during lathi charge so people would come and hide. As a child, I never heard these stories. I only know now because I ask about them. Their generation had also fought the anti-foreigner movement. The AGP [Asom Gana Parishad] came in and they failed. Now when I ask my parents, they are indifferent to it. Many people also say that nothing was achieved in reality from the mass agitation. They lost work or academic years. But nothing happened. Maybe that's why it still has appeal for the older generation.

The upward trend for the city began around 2011–12. In 2004–05, we were still trying to get out of the shadow of ULFA violence.[47] So when Café Coffee Day opened in the town, I remember it was a thing in school to have gone there. Then a mall came up. Even when I was in school, everyone wanted to get out of here. After 11th grade, it was like—you knew this was the last year we were ever going to be in Guwahati. I have siblings, and all of them live elsewhere. At that point in time, it was ridiculous to think you would come back here.

K. B.: In my book *Che in Paona Bazar*, the semi-fictional protagonist is Eshei, a 28-year-old girl. It was a similar story, where she had come home after studying outside and was struggling to negotiate the distance. And Assam is still fine, Manipur is a different zone altogether. Things are much better there now. So when you decided to come back, what did you have in mind?

T. A.: I came back with a sort of anthropological interest. As a journalist, coming back to Assam to report on the Northeast was exciting — I didn't want to report from Delhi or Bombay or do the lifestyle writing I was at that time. I felt like I knew Assam, having grown up here, and I would get to know the rest of the Northeast. It's not like I was coming back for a job I could do anywhere else.

K. B.: Guwahati is an ancient city. How does the city speak to you?

T. A.: Growing up, you hardly appreciated the city for what it is. I did not have the sense to appreciate the massive river flowing here. There was a lot of negativity around how I saw the city. By the time I was eight or nine years old, all of my older siblings were like, 'get out of here and make your life elsewhere'. Ever since I have come back—and I don't know if it is because I am older, or the kind of work I do, or because I like to write and read—I know I appreciate the things now that I didn't notice earlier.

I know it sounds very clichéd, but when you come back, it is a moment of rediscovery. My job is to seek people out, hear the stories they have to tell. I don't know how I missed the cultural aspects of growing up here. We only listened to English songs [back then], but now I'm discovering Assamese pop culture and literature. I had a friend over once and I played Assamese songs. She asked me if I was listening to these because I had some work around it. I laughed and said, no, I listen to these. While I studied Assamese in school till Class 8, the written language in press releases still requires a dictionary—but I'm getting better.

K. B.: You come from an interesting family. Have you gone back and read their history?

T. A.: It is all very well-documented. There are books on my great-grandfather and they have diaries, so I know a good bit of the history.

K. B.: How do you then see yourself?

T. A.: My family is an example of assimilation in many ways. They chose to blend in—now, seven generations later, why they did so is anybody's guess. They came from Churu, Rajasthan. The story goes that there was a problem with the zamindars over there. The year 1826 is when the first of my Agarwala ancestors came to the banks of the Brahmaputra. People even now ask me, 'Don't you speak Hindi at home? You are not Assamese.' Maybe one reason the Assamese accept my family is because they wrote a lot of Assamese literature or made the first film.[48] Also, since they chose to marry into the Assamese community, generations later, we have retained nothing Rajasthani other than the surname—which if you think about it, would have been lost if ours was a matrilineal society —no one would then look at my name and ask how I speak Assamese so fluently.

But coming back to the question of being accepted as Assamese—is complete cultural assimilation or contributing to the growth of Assamese literature the only way? Can't you just be a regular person who chooses to make Assam home (and is as active in its cultural growth as the average Assamese) and still be accepted?

K. B.: You say they went out of [their] way to be Assamese. So why is it important for anyone to embrace Indianness? What is Indianness? We try to legitimise ourselves because there is a hegemonic identity.

T. A.: This is an interesting question—ideally there shouldn't be a need to blend in, in a country like ours where one has the right to live and work anywhere. But India is a complex country and while diversity is its strongest quality, some may think there is a need for an identity that unites us all. All I can say is that it should not come at the expense of one's own identity through any kind of forced homogenisation project.

K. B.: But who is an Assamese?

T. A.: Again, don't you think the political boundaries become a deciding factor in acceptance?

K. B.: I would be more acceptable to an Ahom than perhaps to a Naga. When do divisions come up? [It is] in that context [that] I'm asking the question, who is an Assamese?

Or do you think it is because the Assamese identity was exclusionary and the upper-caste Assamese Hindus controlled the narrative? Where did this hegemony come from? The caste Hindu people called the shots. Ahoms brought them here. So the tribals who were here earlier say, 'who are they to tell us what to do?'

Your identity is also subsumed or culturally assimilated. But you are conscious of your family's identity. Have you ever felt that you had to give up your identity to become a part of Assamese identity, because that blending in was so necessary?

T. A.: Maybe a few generations ago my family must have felt that, but I haven't. That is why coming back has been [an eye-opener]. I don't understand this militant need to protect the Assamese identity.

I didn't feel I have to prove Assamese-ness. I don't feel Othered. When I say this, I am aware that I come from a position of privilege.

K. B.: Have you felt the need to go back to your ancestral land?

T. A.: There is a curiosity to see if anyone is there in the village. It is a mild curiosity, [rather] than [a need] to reclaim identity. The world is a product of people moving for whatever reason.

K. B.: Are you an outcast for Marwaris here?

T. A.: Looking back, it is true that the Marwari kids would hang out with each other—a lot of them were neighbours and spoke the same language. I never thought of myself as Marwari so the question of feeling like an outcast didn't arise.

Tora went on to document several stories around identity and citizenship, and while her lineage is privileged and intriguing, I was left wondering whether she would blend in if she was a Bengali. Is it only the question of language here that legitimises a citizen?

An Evening in Guwahati with a Cat and Two Young Journalists

Makepeace Stilthou: There is an interesting thread going around on Twitter about how human a city is—[for example] Bangalore is described as a woman in a saree.

I moved in only last year [2018], and haven't adjusted to this city. I am still a stranger. I view the city as a haphazard place. I am an army kid who is used to living in Cantonments and have lived in a lot of places. But here, I don't have a defined narrative.

Sadiq Naqvi: I think of the city in parts. The place where I live is like my small hometown, Bijnor, though my town doesn't have a river. It's the most expensive part of the city, but you have all classes of people there, from the chief minister to a fisherman, but they are primarily Assamese. I have been coming to this city every year since 2014, so I have some background. In college, we had Assamese people, so I had a sense. The city is obsessed with identity.

Upper-caste Hindu Assamese set the narrative and others follow, including the Muslim Assamese. What disturbs me about this place is consensus. There is absolute consensus on NRC and as a civilised place, there should be healthy debate and criticism—and that's absent… [I have] not seen this anywhere… [I] tried to ask my friends here [about this] and there are no answers. My friends are still very reasonable and they blame it on circumstances. I ask, how do you claim ownership to this place when you have ancestrally migrated?

Makepeace Stilthou: My relationship with this city is intermittent. I am from Manipur—though I grew up outside this region—but one went back home every year and we passed by Guwahati, which was like a transit city for us. The inside joke amongst tribals is that Assamese are not considered Northeasterners. We refer to them as 'outsiders', just like other 'outsiders'. The Assamese don't have a name for outsiders like others have.

Sadiq Naqvi: The upper-caste Assamese have a sense of superiority that is amazing.

Today, even with NRC, it's not your Indianness that is being tested, but your Assamese-ness.

Gauhati has become Guwahati[49] and the river flows on. Kajaraat Ali sings along:

Nodir Kul Nai[50]

The river has no bank, no edge.
Which bank should I leave and where should I go
Who do I ask?

The big river's waters rock my boat

Now I see the face of beauty and now it's gone

The river has no bank, no edge.

The winds are roaring
And my boat is broken

How can I reach the bank?

Have mercy on me o merciful Allah
And take me to the bank.

The river has no bank, no edge.

Bhagnagar or Hyderabad

Mera shehar logan soon mamoor kar
Rakhya jyun tu darya mein min
Ya Sami

(O God fill up my city with people
Like you have the river with fish)

Sultan Mohd Quli Qutub

The Qutub Shahi dynasty ruled the Golconda Sultanate from 1518 to 1687 CE. On becoming the fifth ruler of the Sultanate, Mohd Quli Qutub Shah ordered the construction of a new city, and instructed that it be a 'replica of heaven'.[51] His prime minister, Mir Momin, came from the beautiful Iranian city of Isfahan. Momin chose a site on the banks of river Musi and the city was conceived. It was planned as an open city without walls and with an onion-shaped dome, the Charminar, the best of Qutub Shahi architecture, at its centre. Four roads radiated from the Charminar, separating the city into four quarters. The Mecca Masjid, one of the largest mosques in the city, stands next to the monument. North of Charminar, four arches on four sides enclosed a piazza. Inside, water flowed from four channels from an octagonal fountain. There were fourteen palaces in this area, guarded by a gate covered with a curtain of gold. The sultan named the new city Bhagnagar, after his beloved Bhagmati, and the city drew praise from travellers and visitors, who claimed that it surpassed even the glory of the Mughal cities.

In September 1687, Aurangzeb finally conquered Golconda. Abul Hasan, the last Qutub Shahi ruler, was captured and sent off to Daulatabad Fort. For the next four months, Aurangzeb would station himself in Hyderabad. The twenty districts of Golconda, north of the river Krishna, became Dar-ul-Jahad Hyderabad.

Intriguingly, of the nearly half-a-century of his reign over a vast empire, Aurangzeb spent a quarter of that time in the Deccan, running his dynasty into the ground. With his death, his three surviving sons were locked in a battle for the throne, and Prince Mu'azzam declared himself as Emperor Bahadur Shah Zafar in 1707. The Mughal dynasty had outlived its glory. 'By the time Bahadur Shah died in 1712,' writes Eaton, the nobles had gained in power. Within just one year, in 1719, 'four emperors had occupied the Peacock Throne'.[52] In 1722, Nizam al-Mulk, the governor of Deccan, Gujarat and Malwa, was appointed as the imperial vazir, but assessing the political chaos at the centre, he decided to strike out on his own and carved out Mughal Deccan as the state of Hyderabad. His descendants would simply be called the Nizams of Hyderabad. He, however, remained loyal to the Mughal viceroy in the Deccan, carrying the emperor's name on the currency he issued.[53]

It was during the Nizam's reign that north Indian kayastha accountants and Punjabi khatri bankers started moving southwards. The migrants included intellectuals, craftsmen, etc., as well, and Hyderabad soon became the centre of cosmopolitan activity.[54]

By the middle of the twentieth century, post-colonial nation-states suddenly began regulating 'migrants', marking a shift from the historically free-flowing movement of people within the Empire. Indians from Pakistan were accepted as refugees. Indians in South Africa lost their political rights. Indians in what was then Ceylon had neither Indian nor Ceylonese citizenship. Burmese Indians had to apply for permits to stay till they were forced to leave. Kenya cracked down on Indians and Uganda expelled them.[55] However, within India, another process of displacement was underway: for example, after Hyderabad's integration in 1948, Arab, Afghan and other Muslim origin groups were asked to return to their 'home countries'. People had to possess the correct documentation, and authorities demanded to know whether an individual 'belonged' to India. The home countries, however, refused to accept them, rendering a large number of undocumented people stateless.[56]

Sherman writes that in the late eighteenth century, Hyderabad had become a 'desirable destination…for Arabs from the Hadhramaut'.[57] In the nineteenth century, the Nizam of Hyderabad welcomed Arabs, Rohillas, Sikhs and Pathans, as well as north Indians who started working for the Nizam, adopting Urdu as their language and marrying locally. Hyderabad became a cosmopolis, with diverse groups living and working together. After Independence, the opinion in Delhi was that Hyderabad was a 'Muslim state' run by Muslims. The Majlis-i Ittehadul Muslimin and the Razakars wanted to stay out of India, and tried to raise a force of men, recruiting from the Muslim world to fight the 'invasion of the Hindus'.[58] Several hundred Muslims from other parts of India moved to Hyderabad, seeking protection. On 12 September 1948, India launched a 'Police Action' in Hyderabad, which was in reality a swift military invasion. By some estimates, 25,000 Arabs were jailed, 2,500 Afghans held and 6,225 Pakistanis detained. Some 21,000 people were to be deported and were kept in detention camps.[59] Even Indian-born wives and children were to be deported. Most of these families had been in Hyderabad for several generations. Yet, they were not seen as legitimate residents of the city:

> ...understandings of citizenship as a legal right gained by residency and established through written records contained within them conceptions of nationality that relied on ethnic origin as a marker of belonging and often directly conflicted with the requirements of the legal regime. When individuals self-identified in a way that did not match legal requirements, as in the case of the men who identified themselve as 'Arab Mohamadan', individuals could be left stateless. Indeed, the combination of documentary requirements for citizenship, and the failure of state borders to map perfectly onto imagined nations, had the potential to leave tens of thousands of migrants stateless.[60]

It was not until the Citizenship Act, 1955 that people of the princely states were accorded citizenship. Since then, many attempts have been made to deport or repatriate Arabs and Afghans, but with little success.

Hyderabad should have been different. The Telugu and Tamil rajas, Sahib Bahadurs, Patels and Patwaris blended with the Muslim Mirs, Mulks, Jungs, Daulas and Khans to create not just a distinct identity but a language—where the poetic phrases of Urdu touched the nasal vowel tones of Telugu.

But the curious subtext of citizenship is that while non-citizens can also be granted rights, the basic rights of the people who make up the heart of the city are very often denied, based on their ethnicity, caste and religion.

Yashoda Thakore: I was born here in Hyderabad. My schooling has been here, and I got married here. Everything is here. But my origins are not in Hyderabad. They are in the Godavari district, which is in Andhra Pradesh. It is very deep-rooted in the district, which is the coastal Andhra area. Both my parents hail from there. In fact, my parents are related. My father comes from a very modest background. He comes from [the kind of circumstances] where he had just two pairs of shorts and no shirt at all when he was a little boy. So, from there, he grew up and the caste reservation did help. We come from the Kalavanthulu, as it is called. Kalavanthulu is a term, which you will also have in Maharashtra, for the hereditary women singer and dancer families. We come from that family. That was the point where people wanted to break away, from the time of my father, or even grandfather, [from this tradition] and get into the mainstream. Both my mother and my father come from that community. They were in fact third cousins. Daddy studied engineering with scholarships and support from the government. He was a good student. He then got a job at APSRTC, the road transport corporation, and retired as the Additional Managing Director. He is very respectable, and we moved up to a very fairly comfortable position. By the time I was born, we were in a socially respectable position. We are three sisters; my sisters were born in the costal Andhra area in our ancestral house.

I was born in Hyderabad because by then, daddy had got a job here. Then we went to Pune for a short while.... Daddy had a posting there, and then we came back here. Despite that, my dialect has not changed. It is not the Telangana dialect at all. My mother was very particular that I don't get influenced. At home, we never had a Telangana dialect. We have a very strong hint of coastal Andhra. That is the lingo [*sic*]. My mother was also insistent that all three of us have Telugu as our first language. We know how to read, write and speak Telugu. At that time, the school I attended did not have Telugu. The only offered Hindi as the first language. I can read, write and speak Hindi because I am in Hyderabad. She would say, in any case, you couldn't compete with the north Indian Hindi. So, we took Telugu. I was very good at it, and I am still very passionate about the language. I am very passionate about all [four lingos of Telugu] and keep borrowing words from them. Telangana Telugu is the one which is not Sanskritised, and even though it is looked down upon, I like it... it is the non-Brahminic local Telugu. It is the common man's Telugu. Therefore, it has the native words in it. The Sanskritised version is what you'd find in the Krishna district, and to some extent the Godavari area. Again, in Rayalaseema and eastern Andhra, where we have Visakhapatnam and Srikakulam, the lingo is different. The Rayalaseema one is closer to Tamil Nadu and there is a Tamil mix there. There is that overlap and flow. On the eastern side, which is closer to Odisha, the lingo is different again. There again, it is not Sanskritised. It is a very beautiful singsong, just like the waves, and they call it the Turpu Andhra, which means East Andhra.

Dr Yashoda Thakore is a descendent of the Kalavanthulu or temple dancers, something she discovered only as a teenager. Trained in Kuchipudi, she decided to return to her roots, learn and establish herself as a Devadasi *nrityam* artiste, much to the chagrin of purists.

> My problem is when people say, 'All people are equal', or that 'Everybody is the same'. Why do they have to be the same? Each person is distinct. Suppose a person is different from you and not equal to you, why should you not love the person? Why can't you still accept the person? That is where you get unity. Yesterday, I was in this little village called Manepally where I wasn't even getting the telephone signal. I went to meet some of the ladies of my community to learn a little bit of those old songs. So, I was living in their house and talking to them. When they talk, they are so natural. I went with a student of mine, who is a Brahmin. This Brahmin girl learns all sorts of things: Dalit art, the Kalavanthulu art, and everything. They say, '*Idi Brahmin ammayi…*', meaning, she is a Brahmin girl and this house belongs to the Komatulu, they are the merchants…. But there is no malice amongst them. The conversation goes on very normally. They don't have this pseudo umbrella, which says 'everybody is the same'. They know their difference. They have their own culture. There are families that go to a certain function and take food there, but will not eat it there. They will go back to their house and eat it. There are things like that, which everybody respects. Even when I was talking to the ladies, the ladies were saying, 'just like our ancestors, now with us…the zamindar, our patron comes to visit. He comes, we cook for the zamindar, we maintain the house according to his likes and the house is maintained like that.' If the patron is a Brahmin, then they maintain a Brahminic house. If a patron is the king, the Kshatriya, then they prepare non-vegetarian food in the house. They cook for them and live by themselves. They live a respectable life and they are not [engaged in] prostitution. They are doing what their community is supposed to be doing.

There is a strange dichotomy of resistance and acceptance. Like in the language that Yashoda so emphatically explained.

K. B.: You said that your mother wanted all three of you to speak Telugu. That was the Brahminical, Sanskritised Telugu, isn't it?

Y. T.: No, it was whatever Telugu she was used to. Now I say that it is Sanskritised. You have poets who have [studied] Sanskrit [and] who started writing in Telugu. They started bringing the Sanskrit into Telugu. But then, that is the Telugu she is used to. If you go to the Godavari side and the coastal Andhra area, that is the Telugu that they speak....

In Hyderabad, they speak the Telangana dialect. That was the point she was making. The Telangana dialect is the one which doesn't have so much Sanskrit in it. Hyderabad is also interesting because there is an Urdu mix in it. Because of this Urdu mix, it is some Dakhini that they speak. It is neither Hindi, nor Urdu, nor Telugu, it is quite a mix of all the languages. But when you go to Mehboobnagar or Nizamabad, which is a little deeper in Telangana, there you have proper Telugu. They don't even speak Hindi, though it was Nizam-ruled.

K. B.: In Telangana, you have an Urdu mix, but they consider their language purer?

Y. T.: Absolutely. In Hyderabad, there is an Urdu. But that is proper Telugu, and this is not proper Telugu. Because of the Nizam's reign, there is a certain laziness that has set in in Telangana. Whereas coastal Andhra, which has three rivers—the Krishna, Godavari and Kaveri—is a rich place...the rest of Andhra is a very rich place. You have all the wealth there and because of the farming, there was a lot of physical work also.

I am a Kuchipudi dancer and Kuchipudi is a village in the Krishna District. In united Andhra, it was the dance form [that represented the state], like you have Sattriya in Assam. We had Kuchipudi for the united Andhra Pradesh. After [the bifurcation]— they said that Kuchipudi village is in Andhra, so Kuchipudi cannot be the dance form of Telangana. They disassociated with Kuchipudi for a while and started a new dance form called Perini Lasyam. This is based on a text that is written in Warangal. They studied the text and made the dance form.

K. B.: They created a new dance form completely?

Y. T.: They created a new dance form completely. And I have translated the text. When I translated the text in 2015, I didn't know this was coming. It is a very beautiful text...it is indeed very nice.

K. B.: This is like a non-violent way of sub-national assertion…that we'll have our own dance form, that we'll have our own text.

Y. T.: This is something that started with the nationalist movement when the states were formed. Each state had to do this—our state, our dance. That's how Kuchipudi came [into being], really. And now we have Perini Lasyam, which I am not very fond of.

When I got to know of my roots and my background….

K. B.: And when did you get to know about this?

Y. T.: When I was seventeen. I did not know before that. I started dancing very early, my parents were very happy to put me back to dance, despite a lot of resistance from relatives. They placed me with the best teacher of Kuchipudi, Vempati Chinna Satyam Garu. For fourteen years I did Kuchipudi. I was an established artist in Kuchipudi. When I was seventeen and got to know about it, I was told that I belong to the prostitutes' community.

K. B.: In so many words?

Y. T.: Yes, my parents told me this. Why don't we talk about it, is what I asked them. It is like, you won't know your community, but everyone else around you will know your community. See, what happened is that we were going with a troupe. There was this singer who would keep saying that I am very goodlooking, and that ladies in [my] family are very goodlooking. That people of my 'families' are very devoted. Once or twice, I took family [to mean] my parents…my mother. I went and told my mother that someone said I am very good-looking because you are very good-looking. I repeated the entire sentence to her. That is when my mother understood. She sat me down and explained to me that that is not what he is saying. She told me about the whole thing. She told me that we belong to this class called Kalavanthulu, who were the temple dancers. At one time, [our ancestors] used to dance in the temples, and that we don't know anything about it. They fell into bad times and [some of them] got into sex work. The minute she said that, I questioned [her], saying that I have been observing [my family] and none of my buas, mausis and chachis are in it. For three generations, nothing of that sort has been seen by me. They told me that it is a stigma that has come upon the community. But not all of them are married. Marriages in our community have just started a generation ago. They may not have been married, but they were dedicated to one person. The patron would be taking care of them, or rather, in reality, the lady would be taking care of the patron. That is a completely different take.

Then I asked them about the dance part. I was interested in that because I was dancing by then. They said they don't know anything about that, or whether anyone is dancing anymore. They were not into the history or anything, and I was only seventeen. I didn't know where to go. I asked them if there is anyone who is still dancing. I told them I would like to go and speak to them. They said, 'No way are you going back and meeting any of them. We don't know ourselves.' So, it went on…life went on like that, but it was lingering in my mind that I have a lineage. I have a lineage of artists, dancers. Knowingly or unknowingly, I have gone back to that. I am a dancer…six generations after the last singer-dancer, about whom poetry has been written and it is all published, I am the one who started dancing again.

K. B.: And you are directly from that lineage?

Y. T.: Yes, directly from that lineage. That lady, Kotipalli Madhuravani—her son's daughter is my mother's mother. I was very excited. She, of course, was not alive. The only one alive was my grandmother, who was living with me. She was in our house all the time. She was happy seeing me dance and she had taken the Gaudiya Namam…she was a part of the Hare Krishna cult. Therefore, all of us followed the Hare Krishna cult and we still do. Much later, after a point, the caste thing was used against me. Even in this society, where nobody talks about it openly [to one's] face.

K. B.: You said you wanted to go back and learn. Your great-grandmother was Kotipalli Madhuravani. But your parents were against it. Then how did you learn?

Y. T.: I have only started going now—since the past four or five years. I did my Masters in dance and we had Dr Nataraj Ramakrishna as our professor. He was one person who [had done] extensive research on the Devadasis of Andhra, Telangana and everywhere. He was a typical Hyderabadi. He was not born here, and we do not know where he was born, but he knew Hyderabad completely. He would ask me to get married and stop dancing. But he would also keep correcting my dance and my expressions. That is when I really wanted to go back and start dancing. And Swapnasundari at that time was teaching Vilasini Natyam classes. I started learning Vilasini Natyam from her and after a while, I realised there is more to it than just Vilasini Natyam. That is when I met Professor Davesh Soneji. He is from Canada and he had come down to give a lecture. His whole lifetime's work has been on the Devadasis of south India. When he gave the lecture, I went to him and told him that I belonged to this community and that I would like to know more and learn from the actual people there. It was actually he who took me back to them.

K. B.: How many people are there in that community? Is it still a large community?

Y. T.: It is still a large community. Not all of them sing and dance any more.

I met this lady [from the community] yesterday after learning that she was still alive, and I returned this morning. Therefore, I can't really say for sure how many there are. If you see my position, by virtue of my birth, my education, my marriage and everything else, I am very connected to Hyderabad. I was married into a Khatri family. The family is very hardcore Hyderabadi-speaking. They have this dialect, the Hindi in Hyderabad. I found it difficult when I got married because for one, I could not speak any Hindi, despite having been born and brought up here. We live in a joint family, and that didn't make it easier. I had to speak Hindi there, which I am grateful for because today I can speak Hindi easily. When I was doing my Masters in Dance, he was doing his Masters in Theatre, which is where we met. He eventually got into Telugu films and became a director.

Hyderabad is a nice place. When you go to the cities or the little villages in the Krishna District, they do address you by your caste, but there is no discrimination based on it. But when you go to the cities in the Andhra side, they first ask your surname. Immediately, your family name gives away your caste. That isn't there in Hyderabad. There is no caste differentiation, not openly at least. If you go to Vijayawada, it is very clear and in your face. Hyderabad is by no means a Brahminic place. It is not a place of the elite class, and I am comfortable here. It is a very cosmopolitan place and it has people from all states coming in and settling here. It is not like Bengaluru, where the identity has been lost. The two dance forms I practice are from Andhra, both Kuchipudi and the Devadasi one.

K. B.: What is the Devadasi dance called?

Y. T.: I call it the Courtesan Repertoire. I have not given it any Sanskrit name. It is Kalavanthula Nrityam.

K. B.: You mentioned that when you first performed the Kalavanthula Nrityam, your Kuchipudi peers were disappointed with you …?

Y. T.: Very much. They came and asked me why I am doing it. I was considered a good dancer and they were very nice to me too. But then, they didn't want me to do this. I told them that I really wanted to and went ahead. [Their objection] wasn't about me, but more about not wanting that style to come back.

K. B.: Why is that?

Y. T.: Because it is not the dance of the elite. That dance form belongs to the 'fallen women'. There is a difference here. The patrons really understood the art and were intellectual and magnanimous. The patrons at that time were the Kshatriyas and the learned Brahmins. There is another community called the Kamma community, and a certain section of that community also patronised the ladies with a lot of respect. The Kamma community comes under the merchant class. Now, the Kuchipudi Brahmins are also artists. The Kuchipudi dance form is supposed to belong to the men of the Kuchipudi Brahmins. The men were the ones who were dancing at one time. Even the female roles were done by them. Ideologically and even psychologically, there is a lot of difference between the Kuchipudi Brahmins and the others. The Kuchipudi Bhagavathulu, they say. The other Brahmins don't accept them in marriage. Kuchipudi is a place, and the Brahmins of that place, who are artists, were not and are still not considered equal to the other Brahmins. The family would say that they as Brahmins or as Kshatriyas should be patronising art and giving them intellectual inputs—that they shouldn't be the ones dancing on the stage as the main dancers. As they are not accepted by their community they often don't get married. That is the Kuchipudi part of it.

I am living in Hyderabad and I was being provoked by the Andhra government to prove whether I belonged to Andhra Pradesh or Telangana. I was born here, did my schooling and got married here…even my doctorate was here, but my art forms are from Andhra Pradesh. My roots are from there. I never thought I would be in this position, where I have to choose between two places where I belong equally.

K. B.: So, did people have to give proof to be part of Hyderabad?

Y. T.: People had to choose between the two. If they were in the government, and fortunately I am not, they had to declare whether they are from Telangana or from Andhra Pradesh. They had to choose which side they are on. Kuchipudi Brahmins who got a job here in the university and were dance teachers there had to declare that they are from Telangana to keep their jobs, even if [their] roots were in Andhra Pradesh. At that time, I was being encouraged by the Andhra Pradesh government because my art is from there. I was also awarded by the Andhra government for the Devadasi art form. I was asked by one or two people, though not seriously, and I said if I had to choose as an artist, I would choose Andhra because my art forms are from there. But I am dancing here and giving so much more here [in Telangana], if they didn't want me, it was their loss because there is only so much that I can contribute. What happened eventually is that the Department of Culture saw wisdom. They understood that they couldn't completely do away with Kuchipudi. It has been there for so long and they just can't do away with artists. They relaxed it a bit because all the senior artists are from Kuchipudi. I translated *Nritta Ratnavali*, as I mentioned before, which is from Telangana, and when I did it, there was no question about all this. There was no discussion about the division of Telangana and Andhra Pradesh when I started doing that translation. That worked to my benefit, because I translated a Telangana text into English.

K. B.: Hyderabad is a partially cosmopolitan city. I wouldn't call it completely cosmopolitan, but yes, people from other parts can survive pretty well in Hyderabad. They can comfortably speak Hindi and English. It became a software city, thanks to Mr Naidu. He lost his stronghold eventually, but he did introduce a lot of things. It was a progressive city. It has a wonderful mix of traditions. As a woman first, and then in terms of the discovery of your lineage, did you start looking at the city differently? In all the cities that I have visited, I find this sort of invisible spatial segregation based on caste or religion. Is this city also segregated in a way?

Y. T.: No, we don't have that here. The only segregation is in the Old City area, which is predominantly Muslim, and in the Mehdipatnam area. They are spread out, but the Charminar area is predominantly Muslim. My in-laws' family came to Hyderabad with the Nizams. They worked for the Nizams. Large landholdings in the Dilshuk Nagar and Lakdi ka Pul belonged to them, which unfortunately they lost.

I wish I didn't have to do this thing of identifying with one state, because I didn't grow up like that. For me, this whole state is one. It broke my heart. They say that 2 June is Telangana Day celebrations, but it is a [day of] mourning for me. There is one thing about this place, though. When I get off the train at a railway station, I look for a Muslim rickshaw driver. I consciously avoid auto drivers with a bottu or a bindi on. I very consciously look for a Muslim driver, because I think I am safe then.

K. B.: Why do you say so?

Y. T.: I say so because of something that happened when I was younger. I don't travel so much by auto rickshaws. I don't know so much about the younger drivers, but the older Muslim drivers don't overcharge and don't exploit you. They drop you exactly where you need to be dropped. There is a certain culture about them. I was very fond of the old Muslim chachas I knew. So, I connect with that culture. We had a Muslim neighbour who was very nice. I do miss that kind of camaraderie. There is a certain kind of guilt in me when I must send my son to the old city if he wants to go there, because I wouldn't go to the old city too much. I only saw the Charminar properly after getting married, because whatever that property is, is meant to be 'there'. We grew up very happily. My father's PA was Shuban Uncle, who was Muslim…my driver was Khurshid, who was Muslim, and we were very happy. I miss the sheermal and the meat during Ramzan. I don't eat meat now, but I used to at that time. They used to send kheer then… and they don't do that any longer today. I feel very sad about it now.

K. B.: Is there a visible divide?

Y. T.: There is a very visible divide.

K. B.: In states like Andhra Pradesh and Telangana, there is a caste division in the villages, but they don't make a big deal out of it. In the cities, the division is more discriminatory, except in Hyderabad. Is this division increasing, both in the villages and cities?

Y. T.: I don't think it is increasing in the villages, because I don't think it affects their life. They are all aware of their lifestyle, and they are happy to be doing what they are doing and are growing professionally. In the cities, on the other hand, it does affect you. When you belong to a 'lesser' or a 'lower' community, you can feel it in the city. Not so much in Hyderabad. The Madhapur and the Gachibowli side is totally not Hyderabad. Hyderabad is whatever developed around Husain Sagar. Everything around it is the real Hyderabad. The extension is all an add-on because the city is spreading. We don't even talk about that side. There is more crime there than in the Old City. I feel very safe here. It could also be because I know the place and I know which places to avoid, but I couldn't think of a place to avoid.

But I will tell you a curious tale about Hyderabad's syncretic past, which is of course in the realm of lore, but is true to some extent. Abul Hasan Tana Shah was the last ruler we had. There is a story; Golconda, from the Hindu perspective, is a very holy place because that is where you find Ramadas from Bhadrachalam. The story is this. There was this devotee called Kancharla Gopanna, who was a devotee of Rama. He was made the Tehsildar of the Bhadrachalam area (now in Telangana) during Abul Hasan Tana Shah's time, around the sixteenth century CE. [The area features] a small hill with [idols of] Sita, Lakshmana and Rama. It is believed that this is the place where Rama wanted to settle down. Anyway, that place has a story of its own. This Tehsildar gave a lot of money and developed the temple and was accused of swindling government money. He was jailed in Golconda by the Nizam. When the Nizam ordered his execution, Abul Hasan Tana Shah saw Rama and Lakshmana in his room in the palace in Golconda itself. They brought bags of gold and told him that it was what Ramadas had sent for him. Even though he used government money for the temple, it was returned, and this is recorded because Tana Shah revoked the execution. This is the place where Rama and Lakshmana set foot. These things happen in India. Ramadas, till he died, never saw Rama and Lakshmana, but Abul Hasan Tana Shah, despite being a Muslim, saw them in the flesh.

K. B.: In the language of dance, how would you describe Hyderabad? Have you ever created a dance for the city of Hyderabad? If the city were a living organism, what would be your relationship with it?

Y. T.: Did you know that Bhagyanagara was named after a dancer? Bhagamati and Taramati were two Kalavanthulu dancers from the coastal Andhra area. A Nizam, whose name I can't recollect right now (but you will find out easily if you read), fell in love with Bhagamati. She walked and danced on a string across the river Musi when it was in spate to meet him and keep their rendezvous. At that time, he called the city Bhagyanagara. I don't know if there is another city that is based on a dancer. There is more dance here than anywhere else. It is just unfortunate that consciousness towards dance is not so strong in the citizens. Yet, it is the dancers who are to blame because it is they who must create that consciousness. I do my bit.

Hampi

'A Dancer Long Lost – Chinnama Devi, Queen of Vijayanagara'[61]

The Tungabhadra was in spate,
the rains better than ever.
The breeze from the river, now habitual visitor –
At ten each night, the curtains would lift on a precious
Zenana,[62]
lover of the queen, the river sang.
Chinna Devi sat in abstract silence,
the red dot that adorned her hand, bordered an enriched
terracotta wall -
She was Sita in decadent unsettledness,
prisoner of her own accord -
queen of Vijayanagara, dancer at heart.

Soon it would be time for Mahanavami –
Durga would be worshipped in every possible human form,
memory brought bheebatsa![63]
Twenty dancers would dance on the dusty road -
with her mighty lover, this dancer would watch,
alone –
hands moving from Trishula, to Anjali to Swastikam.
The Dasara Dibba would come alive -

nine days and nine nights,
the poor would rejoice, alms be given,
kindness thrust upon, Sultans unknown.
Her legs spread, the queen sat,
a courtesan in every thigh.
The hair soaked in blood,
curled -
beggars in every papilla.

The breeze tonight sang of yesterday,
of a far away Matunga[64] asleep.
All summer she had danced on those stones,
bare feet burnt,
as her lover in disguise,
(a future king) watched.
Purandaradasa had sung,
while the rain poured,
a hundred fifty year old Champa
in Vittala temple blossomed.
Tonight her old friend slept
with the Vijayanagara jyoti[65] as its crown.

The Andhra Bhoja,[66] third ruler of the Tuluva
Kṛṣṇa Deva Rāya would be awake still,
and yet he had not called her.
Just beyond the dot on her hand,
a red dirt road stretched -
The Neem had turned yellow.
From another unadorned street on another wall,
another queen sat, and then another –
Like prisoners of time,
dolls of passion gone mute,
bereft of dance, laughter and shringar –[67]
they held court, over his highness's groins.
The Varaha,[68] sun, moon and dagger -
flew strong on every temple pillar,
how they mocked her tonight.

In the corridors of courtesans,
sleep is uneasy—frightening even.
Growing placid, almighty and a queen—became a morning bath, soon.
She had shrunk her feet and grown three breasts.

Fine silks moulded her thighs,
in the corner of a tiny foot,
an anklet, somehow survived –
every night, the curtains sang Raag Biraha,[69]
the price of a crown too high.
The right thigh twitched,
desire ran down empty halls of a stone empire.
Nimble shadows ran on dusty roads,
down to the courtesan's lane—of familiarity and songs.
Her home lay empty and lit every night, somewhere there -
the smell of Jasmine had poured into her lover's vein,
crystallized her anklets,
kings and queens, they had become.

The Sultans came,
an empire looted, Vijayanagara died.

On moonlight nights, near empty and broken
Saalumantaps,[70]
a courtesan still dances with the Tungabhadra.
Matunga echoes her call,
a lone Krishna weeps on Shaivaite land.

Maitreyee B. Chowdhury

Hampi is officially described as the 'last capital of the last Hindu kingdom of Vijaynagar'.[71] What one can see today is the incredible intensity of destruction witnessed by the region, and yet what remains is an able testament to its magnificence. With more than 1,600 monuments in ruins, spread over 24 hectares of the Tungabhadra basin, this ancient city is, in many ways, an introduction to why 'India' was seen as a place of splendours by the rest of the world. Located in a craggy, rocky landscape with open plains, the sophisticated urban planning and architecture of the city is sufficient proof of a highly developed society. The ruins and excavations indicate a large number of religious, yet secular structures, and a diverse population that included Hindus, Muslims and Jains. The architecture shows that each community lived separately, and had their own places of worship. But human habitation began in the region around 3,000 years ago, long before the Vijayanagara kingdom came into being. Even today, one can see prehistoric rock shelters, paintings and megalithic burial chambers.[72]

I drove into Hampi from Hyderabad on a monsoon afternoon. The urban Indian city is missing here and every turn of the road brings us to a ruin, a temple, a few pillars—standing like milestones to an empire that once reigned supreme. The only modern monument in the town square is a badly sculpted figure of B. R. Ambedkar. Massive rocks almost seem to tip over, having stood here for centuries. Granite boulders of various shapes and sizes take us back to the primeval age. This is considered a highly ancient and stable earth surface, created not by earthquakes, but 3,000 years of erosion. Like its almost lost heritage, the rocks are precariously balanced on each other. The Tungabhadra flows through this granite landscape.

Hampi assumed importance in the present Hindu-India position because of the way it was founded, and subsequently, how it was destroyed. Its foundation resulted from invasions into southern India by Delhi sultans at the beginning of the fourteenth century. Despite having overrun the Hindu kingdoms here, Delhi failed to exert control and hold onto its conquests. This led to the rise of autonomous satraps like Kampila and Sangamas in the Tungabhadra region. It was the two Sangama brothers, Harihara and Bukka, who gained control over major parts of south India at the same time as the Bahmani kingdom of the Deccan began its expansion.

The next morning, my first stop was the Vittala Temple, an exquisitely ornate structure that exemplifies Vijayanagara's temple architecture. Dravidian in style, it has the 'Kalyana Mandapa and Utsava Mandapa within a cloistered enclosure with three entrance Gopurams'. The 'Garuda shrine is fashioned as a granite *ratha* and a grand bazaar street' stands in the quadrangle. The wells and a network of water channels are said to be the finest examples of waterworks anywhere in the world during that age. The small but imposing stone chariot in front of the temple is now imprinted on Indian currency notes. Hampi temples were 'constructed from local granite, burnt bricks and lime mortar'.[73]

The fifty-six pillars of of the Ranga Mantapa of the Vittala Temple, considered a masterpiece of temple architecture, still carry the strains of those evenings when perhaps Chinnamma Devi had danced for the king. Each pillar has cut-out colonnettes that emit tones when tapped lightly. The music is over, what remains is just rock art and folklore.

Existing literature states that 'Vijayanagara architecture is also known for its adoption of elements of Indo Islamic Architecture in secular buildings like the Queen's Bath and the Elephant Stables, representing a highly evolved multi-religious and multi-ethnic society.'[74] Two hundred years of glory and power are palpable in Vijayanagara, which was easily the largest for any city in India. It is as if the city was designed to showcase artistic evolution, wealth as well as religious and political thought. The city achieved metropolitan proportions in the accounts of foreign travellers, who described it as one of the most beautiful cities in the world, only comparable to Rome, as Portuguese traveller Domingo Paes recounts:

> What I saw... seemed as large as Rome, and very beautiful to the sight; there are many groves of trees within it... many orchards and gardens with fine trees... many conduits of water which flow in the midst of it, and in places there are lakes.

He concluded, 'This is the best provided city in the world.'[75]

Thirumaladevi, Chinna Devi and the Kalinga Princess Jaganmohini were the three principal wives of Krishnadevaraya. But it was Chinna Devi, a devadasi, with whom the King was deeply in love. Historians are divided on whether Chinna Devi was a commoner, a courtesan or a princess. But the fascination with Deva Raya's wives remains a central chapter in Hampi's historiography. Domingo Paes says Krishnadevaraya had some 'three to five hundred wives', and his account shows that close to 'twelve hundred women' lived there

> as dancers, singers, musicians and astrologers. Each wife, [Paes] says, 'has her own house to herself, with her maidens and her women of the chamber, and women guards and all other women servants necessary; all of these are women, and no man enters where they are, save only the eunuchs who guard them.'[76]

Women in general played an important role in the society. Sculptures and carvings of women are seen in every temple complex across Hampi. Their contributions extended to law and order, literature, commerce and astrology. Many of them were bailiffs, accountants and even astronomers.[77] The king himself was a celebrated poet. His epic, the *Amuktamalyada*, or *The Giver of the Worn Garland*, survives to tell the tale.

An inscription dating back to 1540 CE shows donations provided by 'Chinnamamba, sister of a Chief Minister, for the construction of a water-tank'. A later inscription tells us about a certain 'Kuppayani, who contributed to the building of irrigation channels in Tirumala.'[78]

An inscription dating back to 1542 CE indicates that women ruled entire regions.[79] Women artists were patronised. Tirumala Devi herself wrote and hosted poetry sessions. Even courtesans could mingle freely with the queens; perhaps Chinna Devi's royal status demanded that.

According to sources, the Hemakuta Hill in the northern part of the city dates back to pre-Vijayanagara times: 'It became a pilgrimage by the 8th century CE. One of the earliest temples that came up on the spot is the shrine to Goddess Pampa, another name for Tungabhadra.'[80] This is probably the source of the name 'Hampi'. The Kishkinda mountains, home to the mythic half-human, half-monkey *vanara* (monkey), is believed to have been the home of Sugriva, Hanuman and Bali, divine figures who helped Rama fight Ravana and rescue Sita. The Hajara Rama temple, still standing with exquisitely carved reliefs depicting tales from the epic, makes the city quite the Ayodhya of the south.

In 1443 CE, Abdur Razzak Samarqandi arrived in Vijayanagara to establish diplomatic relations between the Timurid Empire and the 'Hindu City of Victory' that controlled peninsula India. He came from as far as Herat in West Afghanistan by a circuitous route and left rich accounts that help us piece together the history of this kingdom. Of the town of Belour, Razzak wrote, 'the houses were like palaces and the beauty of the women reminded me of the houris of paradise'.

> The city of Vijayanagara simply has no equal in the world.... It is such that the pupil of the eye has never seen a place like it, and the ear of intelligence has never been informed that there existed anything to equal it in the whole world.... It is a city of enormous magnitude and population, with a king of perfect rule and hegemony, whose kingdom stretches more than a thousand leagues. Most of his regions are flourishing, and he possesses three hundred ports. He has a thousand elephants with bodies like mountains and miens like demons.... The Empire contains so great a population that it would be impossible to give an idea of it....[81]

Even the ruins today suggest the extraordinary use of precious metal, gems, gold and silver that attracted travellers and traders, diplomats and conquerers. As Razzak arrived at Deva Raya's palace, he found him

> ...seated in a hall, surrounded by the most imposing attributes of state. Right and left of him stood a numerous crowd of men

> ranged in a circle. The king was dressed in a robe of green satin; around his neck he wore a collar composed of pearls of beautiful water and other splendid gems... on which a jeweller's intellect would have found it difficult to put a price. He had an olive complexion, his frame was thin and he was rather tall; on his cheeks might be seen a slight down, but there was no beard on his chin. The throne, he wrote, 'was of an extraordinary size, made of gold inlay encrusted with beautiful jewels and ornaments with exceeding delicacy, dexterity and artistic refinement... It is probable that in all the kingdoms of the world, the art in inlaying precious stones is nowhere better understood than in this country'.[82]

Vijayanagara dazzled anyone who visited the city. The Kohinoor came from this very land.

However, historical narratives can be a slippery slope. As the novelist V. S. Naipaul enters the ruined city, he recasts the story as a tale of defeat and destruction. His India is a 'wounded civilisation', mortally hurt by 'invasions' and still impacted by its effect. The rise and fall of Vijayanagara, as understood by British historians like Robert Sewell, is problematic. Sewell, in *A Forgotten Empire: Vijayanagar*, describes the kingdom as 'a Hindu bulwark against Muhammadan conquests'.[83] For many, Indian nationalism meant and still means Hindu nationalism. Sewell's characterisation was timely and found a sizeable audience. Other historians, like Richard Eaton, have not only debunked Sewell, but have contradicted his evidence:

> Peninsular India in the fifteenth and sixteenth centuries was not so much a sacred realm, far less a zone of two mutually exclusive sacred realms, as it was a crossroads. As in contemporary north India, peoples in the fifteenth- to the seventeenth-century Deccan circulated through overlapping religious, political and commercial networks. Long-distance merchants such as Mahmud Gawan brought horses, precious metals and other goods from the coasts inland and textiles and spices from the interior to the coasts. Jain, Hindu, Muslim pilgrims moved in all directions. Sufis, ascetics and lay seekers circulated from place to place, or from person to person, pursuing salvation, wisdom or more mundane goals.[84]

Eaton cites that Deva Raya II recruited 10,000 Turkish archers for Vijayanagara.[85] He provides several examples of how peninsular

India was an interconnected zone, rather than a Hindu domain. The Qutub Shahi prince Ibrahim, for example, fled Golconda to escape to Rama Raya's court, and Raya himself was patron to Qutub Quli Shah. Vijayanagara currency was in circulation across the Deccan, and the Bahmani kingdom traded in Vijayanagara currency as well as their own, which indicates that for the citizens of these kingdoms, the entire region was a single economic zone.

What V. S. Naipaul's history ignored was that Vijayanagara had 'nearly two centuries of intense and creative interaction with the Islamic world',[86] to the extent that the costume of the royalty changed from the Dravidian sartorial tradition of bare-chested kings to Islamic court attire. It adopted several attributes of warfare, commerce and technology from the Islamic world. Deva Raya II is said to have employed 10,000 Muslim horsemen.[87] The kingdom was part of the alliance of Muslim armies that defeated the Sultanate of Ahmadnagar, but later fell prey to the shifting Deccan politics—this was the reason for its downfall, rather than a 'Muslim' invasion of a 'Hindu' kingdom. Revisiting Vijayanagara's history would confront us with a sensual hybridity and syncretism that challenges the notion of an immutable Hindu identity. Archaeology, inscriptions and history only reinforce the fact that the line between Hindu and Muslim faith was blurred here.

So much has been lost, yet Hampi is widely documented and is still being excavated and studied. What, however, intrigues me about the city is how its citizens may have related to the state—the recurring idea and question running through this book.

It may well be in the realm of speculation, but in archaeology and anthropology, the study of ceramics is believed to throw adequate light on the lifestyle, social organisation and economy of cities. The city quarters of Hampi were spatially segregated by caste, and their cooking and serving vessels were different, underlining social group identity. However, they lived next to each other and the residential patterns suggest that the caste system was perhaps less rigid than in other parts during that time. The 'heuristic division of the site into discrete zones on the basis of architectural and topograophic features is supported by ceramic analysis'.[88] There was a distinct East Valley and a Noblemen's Quarter and Islamic Quarters. It was certainly a well-developed city and the citizens had freedom and rights.

Today, Hampi stands deserted, and the contours of legend and lore seem to have consumed a kingdom that was once rich and powerful beyond measure. The rocks still threaten to tip over. Lush green banana plantations are everywhere. The city is today a collection of villages, and the villagers, although aware of their rich history, are not enthused about being citizens of a fairytale past.

Mohamed Roshan Jameer lives in Ramsagar.

Mohamed Roshan: We are farmers. We grow bananas and rice. We sell these in Hosapete. For the past forty years, we have been growing bananas. Before that, we were growing wheat. My father and grandfather were also farmers. I have around 7 acres of land. When my grandfather or great-grandfather were engaged in farming, they owned around 50 acres of land. Then, it kept getting divided among brothers of the next generation.

K. B.: So where are you from?

M. R.: I am from India!

K. B.: But most of us have never seen the entire country. What do you mean when you utter the word 'India'?

M. R.: It is impossible to know the meaning. I cannot think about it. We come to know about the number of languages, number of people from the media, from books… but cannot say what is the meaning of India. But when something happens in the country and the media reports it, I do think about why it is happening or what is happening. Because I am an Indian, I have to think why such a thing is happening in my country.

K. B.: What is your relationship with Hampi? When you think about the historic significance of the place that you live in, do you feel good?

M. R.: My relationship with Hampi is…is good. Nothing to complain about. It feels good to think that I am the citizen of a place which was under such a great king and whose empire was huge.

K. B.: Has your family always been in Hampi?

M. R.: Yes, since the time this place was a kingdom, they have been here. We have always been told about the glorious past of our city. They used to say that the king used to lay gold on the ground, he was so rich. Whenever the king conquered a new territory, he used to bring gold from there. People from other countries still come here to search for the gold. No one till date has been able to find Krishnadevaraya's *mahal*. People around the place say once the mahal is found, India can be free of all its debt.

K. B.: Krishnadevaraya was a Hindu king and the invaders who destroyed the temples or stole gold were Muslims. Has that caused any differences between the Hindu and the Muslims in this place?

M. R.: There is no such difference. Everyone treats each other well. In the raja's court also, both Hindus and Muslims were there. At that time, the population of Muslims in this area was less. So temples are more in number here. There is hardly any Muslim population here. But we get everything…water, ration, etc.

K. B.: After this place became a world heritage site, did it make things easy for the residents?

M. R.: See, we have agricultural lands. For us, farming means eating. Now these people come here, they want to dig up and check in places. They pay some money to take up that land and we suffer because of that. So, I can't say that the heritage tag has made our lives any better.

K. B.: Hasn't tourism benefitted the citizens/residents?

M. R.: No, not at all. To benefit from tourism, one has to work with the world heritage sites. Tourists come, see and go. We do not derive anything from this. For acquiring a site, they take up 10–12 kilometres of land. People lose land because of that.

K. B.: Do you visit the ruins in Hampi?

M. R.: Yes, if a relative or a friend visits Hampi, I go and show them the place. I explain it to those people. You won't find art like this in any other place. It is very different. See the Virupaksha temple, it is different.

K. B.: Do you have any proof of Indian citizenship?

M. R.: Aadhaar card, Ration card… *pata nahi kya hota hai* (don't know what those are).

Hampi is still untouched by the noise and the rhetoric across the country. In an India that would rather emphasise Hampi's long tale of defeat and destruction than its history of Hindu-Muslim hybridity, the people living there, who claim lineage to the once-eminent city, are neither proud of it nor despondent. Life in Hampi flows on like the Tungabhadra. Dusty red earth and banana plantations are situated where the ruins of another world stand firm—a multi-faith and multi-ethnic world that India may well prefer to ignore, because it challenges the idea of a monolithic identity.

Identity and Citizenship

Former Vice-President Hamid Ansari's pithy and powerful lecture on identity and citizenship, delivered at the University of Oxford in 2013,[89] sums up the problems inherent in the ways we study these notions.

'Instead of a narrow concept of a singular identity implied by the classical concept of citizenship,' Ansari says, 'the need is to recognize and accommodate the existence of a plurality of social identities.'

The citizens' narratives recorded here from across the various cities they inhabit clearly demonstrate the tension between a sense of belonging on the one hand, and a sense of 'othering', often by the majority communities, on the other. The intersection is difficult to miss: a Dalit activist in Jalandhar or a dancer with roots in a devadasi community in Hyderabad are both proud of their cities and are legitimate citizens, but at the same time, they are acutely aware of their peripheral status in society.

The section on identity and citizenship demonstrates the manifold conceptions of pedigreed identities and citizenship that have developed over time, including the sub-national, supra-national, meta-national and the transnational.[90] The changing spatial coordinates of citizenship shift the focus to legal citizenship or nationality. Strangely enough, it is the state that determines who its citizens are, rather than the other way around.

It is useful to understand the evolution of the concept of citizenship based not on Western doctrines, but as a citizen perceives it. This section began with the earliest known city and its citizens, and then travelled to a cross-section of today's cities, described from the point of view of citizens who come from its fringes. It encompasses a worldview that juxtaposes marginal identities and the history of the city to illustrate how we often view identity and citizenship through a very narrow and shallow understanding of these concepts, and the emotions they evoke. These are not merely words and ideas laid out in the book of law, but deep emotions that make up who we are and where we are.

Chapter 3 includes a set of case studies of certain communities, spread across the geography of the nation. The experiences of these communities drive home the tension and the contestations around identity, and the subsequent prejudice and discrimination based on race, religion and ethnicity. While this chapter narrated the citizens' personal stories against the backdrop of their city, Chapter 3 studies communities as a whole from within as well as the outside.

Endnotes

1. See Oxford Languages definitions, s.v. 'citizenship'.
2. Ibid., 'stateless'.
3. Warschawski, Michael. 2002. *On the Border*, trans. Levi Laub. London: Pluto Press.
4. Swati, K. S. 2022. 'Recent Excavations in Haryana's Rakhigarhi Throw New Light on Indus Valley Civilisation.' *Outlook*, 10 May. Available at https://www.outlookindia.com/travel/recent-excavations-in-haryana-s-rakhigarhi-throw-new-light-on-indus-valley-civilisation-news-195971 (accessed August 2022).
5. Shinde, Vasant et al. 2019. 'An Ancient Harappan Genome Lacks Ancestry from Steppe Pastoralists or Iranian Farmers.' *Cell* 179 (3), 5 September: 729–735.e10. Available at https://www.cell.com/cell/fulltext/S0092-8674(19)30967-5. (accessed August 2022).
6. Vahia, Mayank. 2007. 'The Harappan Question.' *Annals of the Bhandarkar Oriental Research Institute* 88 (2007): 43–59, especially p. 44. Available at http://www.jstor.org/stable/41692084 (accessed August 2022).
7. Wheeler, M. 1968. *The Indus Civilisation*, p. 137. Cambridge: Cambridge University Press.
8. Possehl, Greggory L. 2002. *The Indus Civilization: A Contemporary Perspective*. Walnut Creek, CA: Rowman and Littlefield Publishers, Altamira Press.
9. Joseph, Tony. 2018. *Early Indians: The Story of Our Ancestors and Where We Came From*, p. 117. New Delhi: Juggernaut Books.
10. Possehl, Gregory L. 1990. 'Revolution in the Urban Revolution: The Emergence of Indus Urbanization.' *Annual Review of Anthropology* 19: 261–82. Available at http://www.jstor.org/stable/2155966 (accessed August 2022).
11. 'Because race science has always been innately political, it shouldn't surprise us that prominent thinkers used science to defend slavery,

colonialism, segregation and genocide.' Saini, Angela. 2019. 'Why Race Science is on the Rise Again.' *Guardian*, 18 May. Available at https://www.theguardian.com/books/2019/may/18/race-science-on-the-rise-angela-saini (accessed August 2022).

12. Joseph, Tony. 2019. 'New reports clearly confirm "Arya" migration into India', *The Hindu*. 14 September. Available at https://www.thehindu.com/society/history-and-culture/theres-no-confusion-the-new-reports-clearly-confirm-arya-migration-into-india/article29409611.ece (accessed August 2022)

13. Habib, Irfan and Faiz Habib. 1995. 'A Map of India 600–320 B.C.' *Proceedings of the Indian History Congress*, 56: 95–104, especially p. 96. Available at https://www.jstor.org/stable/44158590 (accessed August 2022).

14. Ibid.

15. Ibid., 96.

16. Habib, Irfan. 1999. 'The Envisioning of a Nation: A Defence of the Idea of India.' *Social Scientist* 27 (9/10): 18–29. Available at https://doi.org/10.2307/3518100 (accessed August 2022)

17. Here, Balley refers to the *Bheem Patrika*. See Anand, S. 2015. 'May 15: It was 79 Years Ago Today that Ambedkar's "Annihilation of Caste" was Published'. *Scroll.in*, 15 May. Available at https://scroll.in/article/727548/may-15-it-was-79-years-ago-today-that-ambedkars-annihilation-of-caste-was-published (accessed August 2022). See also http://www.upkaar.com/News/News_2014/498-journalism-award-for-balli-06112014.htm (accessed August 2022).

18. See Government of India. 1950. 'The Constitution (Scheduled Castes) Order, 1950'. *The Gazette of India, Extraordinary*: 163–172. Available at https://socialjustice.gov.in/writereaddata/UploadFile/CONSTITUTION%20(SC)%20ORDER%201950%20dated%2010081950.pdf (accessed August 2022).

19. See *Constituent Assembly of India Debates (Proceedings), Vol. 2*. Available at http://loksabhaph.nic.in/writereaddata/cadebatefiles/C24011947.html (accessed August 2022).

20. Balley produced condensed versions of these texts.

21. See https://www.unicef.org/india/what-we-do/clean-drinking-water (accessed August 2022).

22. Harjinder, Dilgeer Singh. 2004. *Encyclopedia of Jalandhar*. Belgium: Sikh University Press.

23. See http://www.royalkangra.com/intro.html (accessed August 2022).

24. Originally appeared in Cunningham, Alexander. 1882. *Archeological Survey of India Reports, Vol. XIV*. Available at https://www.bl.uk/onlinegallery/onlineex/apac/photocoll/p/019pho000001003u00924000.html (accessed August 2022).

25. Sardarilal Sharma passed away in 2021, a few days after celebrating his 102nd birthday.

26. See Sadiq. 2019. 'Gained in Translation: Ghalib in Banaras'. *The Indian Express*, 19 May. Available at https://indianexpress.com/article/opinion/columns/narendra-modi-varanasi-elections-mirza-ghalib-in-banaras-5735383/ (accessed August 2022).

27. Singh, Harmeet Shah. 2018. 'How Kabir's Maghar Defies Modi's Constituency Kashi.' *DailyO*, 30 June. Available at https://www.dailyo.in/politics/narendra-modi-maghar-kabir-varanasi-dalits-2019-general-elections/story/1/25208.html (accessed August 2022).

28. Varanasi, also called Benares, Banaras, or Kashi, has been used in this book interchangeably.

29. While Banaras makes for a fascinating space for inclusivity, the spatial associations based on caste and religion allow for exclusionary habitation or segmentation in many areas within the city.

30. The speaker is not a doctor by profession, but is referred to with the prefix.

31. According to mythological accounts, Raja Harishchandra, having given away all his possessions to appease the sage Vishwamitra, eventually sold himself to Kalua Dom and was employed in collecting fees at the cremation ground. The clan of Doms traces its genealogy to Kalua.

32. A reference to government employment.

33. 'Chars and chaporis are shifting riverine islands of the Brahmaputra and are primarily inhabited by the Muslims of Bengali-origin (pejoratively referred to as 'Miyas')…A char is a floating island while chaporis are low-lying flood-prone riverbanks… "They are used interchangeably or with a hyphen… They keep changing shapes—a char can become a chapori, or vice versa, depending on the push and pull of the Brahmaputra."' Agarwala, Tora. 2020. 'Explained: The Miyas of Assam, and their Char-Chapori Culture.' *The Indian Express*, 6 November. Available at https://indianexpress.com/article/explained/explained-the-miyas-of-assam-and-their-char-chapori-culture-6943279/ (accessed August 2022).

34. Translation of a song sung by Kurajat Ali in the film *Nodir Kul Nai* by Parasher Baruah, commissioned by ArtEast 2019, New Delhi. Translation courtesy of Shalim M. Hussain.

35. *Paargeet* is a genre of music that comes under the Bhatiali tradition followed by the river-folk of Bengal.

36. Chakraborty, Proma. 2019. 'Hear the River Sing its Song.' *patriot.in*, 14 March. Available at https://thepatriot.in/2019/03/14/hear-the-river-sing-its-song/ (accessed August 2022).

37. From the famous poem 'Dover Beach', by Matthew Arnold.

38. As narrated to the author by Kulada Kumar Bhattacharjee.

39. Dewani, Usha. 2016. 'Forgotten Water Bearers of Guwahati.' *India Water Portal*, 19 September. Available at https://www.indiawaterportal.org/articles/forgotten-water-bearers-guwahati. (accessed August 2022).

40. Ibid.

41. See https://environmentandforest.assam.gov.in/portlets/biodiversity-of-assam-0 (accessed August 2022).

42. For more details on Sukapha, see Dutta, Arup Kumar. 2016. *The Ahoms*. Guwahati: AJB Trust.

43. See Guha, Amalendu. 1984. 'Pre-Ahom Roots and the Medieval State in Assam: A Reply'. *Social Scientist* 12 (6): 70–77. Available at https://doi.org/10.2307/3517005 (accessed August 2022).

44. See Sarma, Diganta Kumar. 2010. 'Religious Transformation of the Ahom Rulers in the Crossroad of Making a Unified Society'. *Proceedings of the Indian History Congress* 71: 243–47. Available at http://www.jstor.org/stable/44147491 (accessed August 2022). See also Baruah, Chandan. 2004. 'Hinduisation of the Ahom Court in the Medieval Assam'. *Proceedings of the Indian History Congress* 65: 357–61. Available at http://www.jstor.org/stable/44144751 (accessed August 2022).

45. Guha, Amalendu. 1986. 'The Decline of the Ahom Kingdom of Assam: 1765–1826'. Centre for Studies in Social Sciences (CSSSC), Occasional Paper No. 84. Calcutta: CSSSC.

46. Baruah, S. L. 2005. *A Comprehensive History of Assam*. New Delhi: Munshiram Manoharlal Publishers.

47. For an overview of ULFA violence, see Misra, Udayon. 2009. 'ULFA: The Beginning of the End'. *Economic and Political Weekly* 44 (52): 13–16. Available at http://www.jstor.org/stable/25663932 (accessed August 2022).

48. See Das, Radha. 2020. 'Jyotiprasad Agarwala: Creativity and Context'. *Sahapedia.org*, 16 April. Available at https://www.sahapedia.org/jyotiprasad-agarwala-creativity-and-context (accessed August 2022).

49. The change of name was made official in 2006. See *The Telegraph*. 2006. 'Assam Sheds British-Era Skin', 27 February. Available at https://www.telegraphindia.com/india/assam-sheds-british-era-skin/cid/817637 (accessed August 2022).

50. Lyrics from the film *Nodir Kul Nai* by Parasher Baruah, commissioned by ArtEast 2019, New Delhi (excerpted with permission). Translated by Shalim M. Hussain.

51. See Former Vice-President Hamid Ansari's lecture about Qutub Shah in 2017, available in *Business Standard*. 2017. 'Hyderabad's Founder Quli Qutub Shah was Secular Ruler', 13 April. Available at https://www.business-standard.com/article/news-ians/hyderabad-s-founder-quli-qutub-shah-was-secular-ruler-117041300897_1.html (accessed August 2022).

The full lecture has been made available by the Press Information Bureau. 2017, 'Vice President Delivers the First Mohammad Quli Qutub Shah Memorial Lecture', 13 April. Available at https://pib.gov.in/PressReleasePage.aspx?PRID=1487830 (accessed August 2022). Narendra Luther has written a book on the historical figure, available in Urdu. 1998. *Muhammad Quli Qutub Shah*. New Delhi: Publication Divisions, Government of India.

52. Eaton, Richard M. 2019. *India in the Persianate Age 1000-1765*. London: Allen Lane.

53. Ibid., 383.

54. Ibid., 385.

55. Sherman, Taylor C. 2011. 'Migration, Citizenship and Belonging in Hyderabad (Deccan), 1946–1956'. *Modern Asian Studies* 45 (1): 88–107. Available at http://eprints.lse.ac.uk/32791/1/Sherman_Migration_citizenship_belonging_2011.pdf (accessed August 2022).

56. Ibid.

57. Ibid., 85.

58. Ibid.

59. Ibid.

60. Ibid., 101.

61. Poem, including glossary, published online in 2019. Available at https://writinginawomansvoice.blogspot.com/2019/07/a-dancer-long-lost-chinnama-devi-queen.html (accessed August 2022).

62. Persian word for women (has reference to the Zenana Mahal in Hampi).

63. An expression in Bharatnatyam signifying disgust.

64. A hill in Hampi.

65. Fire (here, a reference to the royal torch that was lit every night on Matunga Hill).

66. A title given to Krishnadevaraya, meaning the king of the Andhra land.

67. 'Shringar' is to dress up.

68. Boar (refers to the sign on the Vijayanagara flag).

69. A *raaga* in Indian classical music. Biraha denotes a sense of longing.

70. Shops from the Vijayanagara era, still present in Hampi.

71. See https://whc.unesco.org/en/list/241/ (accessed August 2022).

72. Ibid. See also Fritz, John M. and George Michell. 2019. *Hampi Vijaynagara*. Mumbai: Jaico Publishing House.

73. *Historical India*. 'Hampi.' Available at https://historicalindia.org/article/hampi (accessed August 2022).

74. Ibid.

75. Fritz and Michell, *Hampi Vijaynagara*: 33, 27.

76. Dalrymple, William. 2018. 'The Untold History of Hampi.' *Open*, 26 July. Available at https://openthemagazine.com/essay/the-untold-history-of-hampi/ (accessed August 2022).

77. See the *Chronicle of Fernao Nuniz*, probably written in 1535–37. In Sewell, Robert. 1991. *The Vijayanagara Empire: Chronicle of Paes Nuniz*, p. 382. New Delhi/Madras: Asian Educational Services.

78. Rixon, Nicholas. 2018. 'The Women of Ancient Hampi.' *Evolve Back*, 20 August. Available at https://www.evolveback.com/hampi/fr/women-hampi/ (accessed August 2022).

79. Nagaveni, A. 2018. 'Tanks of Kamalpura'. *Aayushi International Interdisciplinary Research Journal* 5 (4): 300–305. Available at http://aiirjournal.com/uploads/Articles/2018/04/3193_61.Dr.%20Nagaveni%20A..pdf (accessed August 2022).

80. Srinivasan, Sharada. 2016. 'Hampi: Splendours of a World Heritage Site.' *BRICS Young Scientist Forum*. Available at http://docplayer.net/52356580-Hampi-splendours-of-a-world-heritage-site.html (accessed August 2022).

81. Sewell, Robert. 1924. *A Forgotten Empire: Vijaynagara*, p. 124. London: Allen & Unwin.

82. Ibid.

83. Ibid., 1.

84. Eaton, Richard M. 2019. *India in the Persianate Age 1000-1765*, pp. 190–91. New Delhi: Allen Lane.

85. Ibid., 149

86. Wagoner, cited in Dalrymple, 'The Untold History of Hampi.'

87. See ibid.

88. Carla, Sinopoli M. 1993. *Pots and Palaces: The Earthenware Ceramics of the Noblemen's Quarter of Vijaynagara*, p. 128. New Delhi: American Institute of Indian Studies.

89. Ansari, Hamid. 2013. 'Identity and Citizenship: An Indian Perspective'. Oxford Centre for Islamic Studies, University of Oxford, 1 November, London.

90. Here, sub-national refers to an area within a nation that has its own cultural identity. Supra-national is an area of influence that goes beyond the territorial borders of a nation. Meta-national is a concept used in business and economics, but I use the word to explain asymmetry in dislocation, and at the same time receptiveness to newer identities. Trans-national refers to people who belong to one country but live their lives in some other country.

3 WHERE THE MADNESS ACTUALLY LIES

Kayas, Manipuris, Gorkhas, Indian Chinese, Coolies, Chakmas

Refugee[1]
/rɛfjʊˈdʒiː/

noun
1. a person who has been forced to leave their country in order to escape war, persecution, or natural disaster.

Nationality[2]
/naʃəˈnalɪti/

noun
1. the status of belonging to a particular nation.
2. an ethnic group forming a part of one or more political nations.

MIGRATION, REFUGEES AND CITIZENSHIP

How the law transacts inconsistently with the insider, outsider, guest and stranger.

Law transacts even if invisibly so with affective figures such as the insider, the outsider, the guest and the stranger. How does the law produce, visibilize or invisibilize these relational figures, and what would it mean to legally foreground these figures and the conceptual universes they inhabit at a time when there could not be a greater demand for legal hospitality even as we are witness to the greatest forms of legal inhospitality. The Muslim ban promulgated by the Trump administration and the stance of the Indian government towards the Rohingyas are kindred instances of the challenge we face. If the law has been inherently spatial and territorial, where then do we turn to if we are to articulate a radical politics of belonging—Is the Kantian ideal of a cosmopolitan right to hospitality a solution or only a bigger problem in neo liberal times?[3]

Case Studies: Kayas, Manipuri Gorkhas, Indian Chinese, Coolies, Chakmas

Kayas

Colonial Assam's most prosperous newcomers were the Kaya traders, who are known to us as Marwaris. During the Mughal era, many Rajasthani traders migrated out of Rajasthan and settled in various parts of the country. Amongst the most well-known were the Jagat Seth bankers of the Oswal caste, who settled in Murshidabad, Bengal. In the absence of banks during the period of British economic expansion, these traders, after having consolidated themselves in the United Provinces, Bihar and Bengal, decided to enter Assam. Within a very short span of time, they had made their presence felt in almost every town of Assam with their *golas* (warehouses).[4]

After the abolition of slavery in 1843, peasants and sharecroppers started growing rice in small landholdings, but had no market in which to sell rice to pay the colonial tax. The Kayas stepped in and offered cash to farmers, who agreed to grow opium. *Kanee* or opium was not unknown to the locals, but now it was being cultivated on an industrial scale. While the opium market was expanding, tea had also become an important commodity. Commerce in Assam virtually passed into Kaya hands.

The Kaya moneylender and trader, who obviously profited at the expense of the people, soon became a target of abuse. The first visible protests against them took place in 1894 in rural Assam, when the colonial state increased the share of revenue. Instead of state authorities, the Kayas were attacked. During the 1896 food shortage in Assam, the state had to call in the army to quell a riot against Kaya traders.[5] Even the British, who benefitted from them, saw the Marwaris as upper-country exploiters of the hill tribes and distanced themselves from them, even withdrawing their protection. Rajasthan was a princely state at the time, and not a British subject.

During the anti-foreigners' agitation of the 1970s, the Marwaris, along with many other groups, became the target of Assamese nationalists; they were seen as outsiders, much as the others.[6] However, they continued their trade and retained financial control despite the fast-changing political machinations of the state. While other ethnic communities were displaced after clashes and encounters with the Assamese, the Marwaris consolidated their already established financial control.[7] For all groups operating in the state, the Marwari could never be ignored. During the last phase of terrorist violence in the state, beginning roughly around the year 2000, many Marwaris relocated to other states but have not given up their businesses or financial linkages.

In the 1850s, Guwahati's main market was Fancy (or Phasi) Bazaar, the epicentre of Kaya business and residence. In the bazaars of Jorhat, Upper Assam, Kayas owned the main business establishments and plantations. Even today, Fancy Bazaar is dominated by Marwaris, and urban folklore states that the cash flow of the entire region of Assam is operated from these *gaddis*. In many of these families, successive generations have adopted an assimilative tradition and have a hybridised cultural life. One of the finest examples of this is the early entrepreneur Navrangram Agarwala of Churu, Rajasthan, who joined ranks with the Ramdayal Poddar firm on the Assam-Bengal border in 1829. He soon struck out on his own and traded in elephants, rubber, mustard seeds, cane, rice and military rations. He rose in financial power and even became a *mouzadaar*.[8] He married a high-caste Assamese woman, who died early. His second marriage was again to a woman from yet another Assamese high-caste family, and he also became a disciple of a local Vaishnavaite Gosain. While his identity remained that of a Kaya, his family members were bona fide Assamese. For example, his son Haribilas married an Assamese woman and ate fish, unlike his father (who was a vegetarian, in keeping with Marwari tradition); yet he followed the Kaya business tradition and maintained accounts in the Nagari script. Assam's cultural icon, Jyotiprasad Agarwala (mentioned in Chapter 2), was the grandnephew of Haribilas. Jyotiprasad and his genre of music, 'Jyoti sangeet', became nationalist anthems for the Assamese. The family carries the Agarwala surname, but is Assamese in every respect.

The rise of the political right-wing and the coming of the BJP to power, which is partly attributed to Marwari heft, have reinforced the influential position of this community. However, they continue to be the targets of pejoratives and slurs. Nevertheless, their north Indian Hindu ancestry has ensured their citizenship. This is a 'migrant' community that Assam cannot do without. They may hate them, but they cannot ignore them. The Marwari stranglehold over affairs of the state makes them serious stakeholders in Assamese society, but they remain 'outsiders'.

Manipuri Gorkhas

Nepali Gorkhas—a group of people who earned their fame and reputation through their valour and the battles they fought and won for other countries—are the stuff that legends are made of. During the latter half of the nineteenth century, British military officers developed the 'ethnographic state' based on the merits of races, which were derived from anecdotes of heroism or martial ideologies.[9] After the Revolt of 1857, the British handpicked Punjabi Sikhs, Jats, Rajputs, Gorkhas and Pathans for the British army. By 1875, Gorkhas and Punjabis formed the bulk of the infantry brigades, and through recommendations, they later secured their entry at a senior level into the reorganised Indian Army. By 1908, there were ten Gorkha Regiments.

'Gorkha' is actually a loose term used for the hill people of east and west Nepal. Assam had a significant number of Nepali settlers, as the British granted land in the region to retired Gorkha soldiers.

Although residents from Nepal joined the Kayas as migrants to Assam in the ninenteenth century, here we shall restrict ourselves to Manipuri Gorkha soldiers, who reportedly arrived in Manipur in 1824 during Maharaja Gambhir Singh's reign. The attempt by the Manipur government in 2015 to introduce the colonial Inner Line Permit (applicable in some other states) triggered a narrative from the Gorkha diaspora in Manipur claiming indigenous rights. There were several articles that reproduced the story of the Gorkha migration to Manipur.

In 1817, a corps of 'Hindustanis and Gurkhas' fought on behalf of the British in an army operation in Sylhet. Recruiting Gorkhas from Sylhet in 1825, the Manipuri king called this unit Victoria Paltan for the regiment's reputation in the British Indian army. This was done to secure Manipur from Burmese troop intrusions. As part of colonial policy by the end of the nineteenth century, the Gorkha/Nepali *gwalla* (cowherd community) had already settled in the Manipur valley. With the arrival of the British and the Anglo Burmese War, they were given grazing grounds in the northern part of the state and issued land ownership documents or *pattas*. But since the Meitei community were not major users of milk or ghee, and land was becoming scarce in the valley, the government decided to shift the populace to the northern parts by creating a Gorkha/Nepali reserve between Sekmai and Kangkokpi and partially extending it later to include other parts of the state. The Manipur State Administrative Report 1915–16 in Chapter V[10] confirms this.

The Gorkha contribution to Manipur was marked with blood; Major Subedar Niranjan Singh Chhetry was 'hanged…alongside Bir Tikendrajit and General Thangal by the British' on 13 August 1891.[11]

The paramilitary force 4 Assam Rifles finds its origins in what had earlier been the Cachar Levy, raised by Mr Grange in Nowgong district of Assam in 1835. From this point, the Gorkhas were a major ethnic group within the British army and the frontier police. The duties of this force were to guard Assam, from the Brahmaputra to Cachar. It is only in 1917 that 'titles of all the Assam Military Police Battalions were changed to "Assam Rifles" by order of the Government of India, in recognition of the excellent services rendered by its men in various theatres of the Great War'. The composition of this battalion, formed in Manipur, was dominated by the Gorkhas. When World War-II reached Kanglatongbi-Kangpokpi, the Gorkha community was evicted by the Manipuris because they were fighting for the British. Interestingly, the king of Manipur supported the British during World War I, but while he had tacit support in World War II, Manipuris were in support of Netaji Subhash Chandra Bose's Indian National Army (INA), which was fighting alongside the Japanese in a bid to win Imphal. Netaji believed the Gurkhas would rebel within the ranks in the British army, but that did not quite happen.[12] Meitei nationalism was gaining ground against the feudal system. The Gorkha/Nepali Reserve had been entirely seized during the period of 26 August–1 December 1946. Though many left, several families returned to claim their land.[13]

Of the state's total population of 27 lakh, the Gorkhas are fewer than a lakh in number.[14] Until recently, they were considered a part of Manipuri society.

In 1977–83, close to one lakh Gorkhas were forced to leave the Northeast due to relentless targeting and being booked as foreigners.[15] While Nepalis were domiciled in some parts of the region, including

Manipur, the anti-foreigner agitation of the 1970s in Assam included the Gorkhas and the Nepali-speaking population. They were seen as foreign immigrants and the same sentiment spread across other states. State governments started restricting entry of Nepalis. In Manipur, there were violent attacks in 1980, forcing several families to flee. Meghalaya witnessed violence against this community in 1987. Soon Mizoram and Nagaland too started evicting Nepali-speaking people.[16]

Once invited to settle in Manipur by the king, this community is now no longer wanted in their place of birth and belonging.

Coolies

Once the British realised that tea can be grown in Assam on an industrial scale, they were on the lookout for cheap labour. The first uprisings against the British by the Kols in 1831–33, followed by Santhals in 1855–56, and their subsequent suppression, provided the Empire with a reserve of bonded labour. Following the rebellion, the Santhals were relocated to permanent settlement zones to clear jungles for cultivation. There emerged forms of bonded labour, and by the end of the nineteenth century, the 'coolie'[17] labourer moved out of Chotanagpur and assumed a migratory identity. They supplied labour to sugar planters from Mauritius to Trinidad. Colonial race theorists considered them industrious and loyal. They worked in indigo plantations and on railroads, and were swiftly inducted into the Empire's favourite gardens. By the late 1860s, the British had passed numerous laws like the Transport of Native Labourers Act (1863) to move the coolies into the tea plantations of Assam. By 1901, 13 per cent of Assam's population were from outside the state, like the coolies from Central India. They alone numbered 645,000.[18]

Over a period of 150 years, these plantation workers became part of Assam's secure vote bank,[19] but continued to provide labour for the gardens even as the ownership patterns changed. Despite the pretence of reforms within the garden labour force, the coolie remained a coolie, totally segregated in terms of physical and cultural space, inside as well as outside the garden. The maternal mortality, infant mortality, social security measures and development indicators are abysmally low amongst them. They were used like contract labourers and the colonial-era policy continued in the plantations. With a substantial population,[20] they remained on the fringes in Upper Assam. In Lower Assam, they were the first targets of the violent Bodo movement, killed and displaced from their land and source of occupation.[21] Two Adivasi armed guerilla groups subsequently emerged, but in the absence of resources and support from any other armed group, could not sustain themselves for too long. The erstwhile coolies became the most vulnerable target of ethnic cleansing. While the Kols and Santhals have Scheduled Tribe status elsewhere in the country, in Assam they remain outside that fold.

It was a Saturday afternoon in the high-security capital complex of Guwahati in 2007. A large Adivasi protest march demanding Scheduled Tribe status took an ugly turn when the protesters—who were allegedly inebriated—started damaging public property. Stunned urban residents, mostly middle-class Assamese, launched a counter-attack on the protesters. In the midst of this riot, an Adivasi woman was beaten and stripped naked. Photos of her running through the street, chased by men, instantly made the national headlines.[22] In one of the pictures, she could be seen pinned against the gate of a house and being assaulted by some men, with one man kicking her in her genitals, even as an elderly lady looked on. The news went viral, and the Assamese people, embarrassed by what had happened, reacted angrily to the coverage. I had witnessed it all, and while we reported this news, which mounted tremendous pressure on the government to make arrests and order an enquiry, we were socially ostracised. I had to personally meet with citizens and local journalists to clarify my position. For the next six months, my network was blacked out from the state. I was accused of being an 'outsider' who shamed the state by misrepresenting facts. The facts, however, were for everyone to see.

The Adivasi coolie could never become an Assamese.

Deoli, 1962

> 19 November 1962, at midnight, we heard knocks at our door. The war would end that day. We were picked, huddled into a jeep and put on a train. We had no idea where we were going and why. That night changed our lives forever.
>
> Michael Cheng, in his late fifties

Michael Cheng was just two years old when he became one of an over 3,000-strong group from the Indian-Chinese community—'men, women and children including infants'—who were

> summarily arrested without trial and placed in a disused World War II POW camp in Deoli, Rajasthan.... [T]hey were incarcerated for periods ranging from a few months to over four years, and much of their property was confiscated, auctioned or simply allowed to be vandalised.[23]

The Indian government never gave an official reason for its actions, but sources indicate that these people were perceived as a threat to national security following India's humiliating defeat to China in the 1962 war. India has never expressed regret or made the official documents public, so this shameful history remains virtually unknown to most Indians.

However, just after the war ended, Indians recalled how their Chinese classmates did not return to school. Chinese schools, newspapers and establishments shut down overnight.[24] For instance, Shillong's popular New China Restaurant became the New India Restaurant. Yin Marsh, a teenager then, was forced to leave her school, the Loreto Convent, Darjeeling, and, together with her 8-year-old brother, her father (who had been arrested and jailed a month earlier) and grandmother, sent to Deoli, a seven-day train journey away.

She recalls: 'As I walked down the staircase to board the police jeep waiting to arrest us, what I felt in me that moment is something I can never forget: we are different and I am a Chinese, not Indian'.[25]

Yin, who now lives in the USA, is the author of *Doing Time with Nehru*. She returned to India in 2015 to tell the tale. 'We are a group of Chinese Indians, ethnic Chinese who were born in India. We started this campaign because no one knows our story. We want everyone to know who we are and what happened to us.'[26]

She is one among many Deoli inmates who became outsiders overnight, and whose travails have now been captured in a documentary film, *Beyond Barbed Wires* (2015). One of them, Joy Ma, who also lives in the USA now, was born in the Deoli POW camp. Her '[pregnant] mother...along with her father and two brothers,' writes Ellias, 'were picked up from their home in the Dooars near Siliguri, well after the war ended'.[27]

Ironically, they were taken to Deoli on the day of the Chinese New Year. Ellias informs us that 'Joy's family was among the last batch to be released, more than 4 years after their internment. When they returned to Calcutta, Joy's father was abruptly re-arrested. Again without trial and put in Alipur jail for another year.'[28]

Piecing together family history from the POW camp also means accounting for the dead. More than twenty Indian-Chinese people are said to have died in the camps, and are believed to be buried in a cemetery in Deoli. Whole families were broken up, since individual members were released in batches. Even after they returned, fear, intimidation and harassment remained part of their everyday life. Sadly, no records are available of precisely how many people were arrested, how long they were held and when they were released.

Yin hopes for real closure, saying,

> We have been silent for fifty years because of a multitude of emotions: fear, humiliation, sadness, not wanting to relive the loss of dignity and loss of identity. We want new generations who have never heard our story to know what happened. We realise the healing process may be a long one, but we have started the journey and hope for peace and eventual closure.

The Indian-Chinese continue to live, not as Indians, but somewhere in between.

Chakmas

The Chittagong Hill Tracts were made part of Pakistan in 1947, against the will of the Chakmas, who inhabit the region. While there was a referendum in Sylhet, no one really cared to ask the Chakmas where they would like to go, India or Pakistan. On 15 August the Indian tricolour went up in Rangamati, in the Chittagong Hill Tracts. A few days later it was replaced by the Pakistani flag, raised by the new army of Pakistan. Even today, the Chakmas insist on joining India, and it was their stated position in 1947.[29] Yet, strangely enough, during the 1971 war between East and West Pakistan, the Chakmas decided to support West Pakistan instead of the Awami League. The Chakma king, Raja Tridib Roy, remained loyal to the idea of a united Pakistan, alleging discrimination by the Bengalis in East Pakistan. When he realised that Pakistan was losing the war, he moved to West Pakistan and even served as Pakistan's Ambassador to Argentina.[30]

Meanwhile, in 1964, the Kaptai Dam Project in East Pakistan submerged 54,000 acres of agricultural land in the Chittagong Hill Tracts, and the Chakmas became climate refugees. Almost 100,000 of them were displaced.[31] The Chakmas, already oppressed under an Islamic Pakistan, now fled to India. Over the next few decades, alleged acts of genocide by the Bangladesh Army[32] forced the Chakmas to migrate in phases to Tripura and Mizoram, where they are still discriminated against.

In Arunachal Pradesh, India's farthest state in the east which is also the most sparsely populated (with just thirteen persons per square km), reside some 60,000 people of the Chakma tribe.[33] They are distinctly identified as 'non-natives'.

However, political mobilisation in Arunachal Pradesh, which included student movements, unleashed a systematic and violent campaign to drive Chakmas out of the state. For years, Chakma children were denied education in government schools, their books burnt; Chakma youth were targeted in stray but repeated incidents of violence; the granaries and fresh harvests were often destroyed by mobs; and health centres refused to treat Chakma patients, even children.[34]

In 2015, the Supreme Court directed the state government to ensure that the Chakmas enjoy citizenship rights. However, despite court orders, Chakmas remained outsiders. The government even challenged the order. Sinister as it may sound, Chakma areas are quite deliberately devoid of any governance structures. Panchayat elections have not been held even once in these villages, despite the state having accepted the Panchayati Raj Act in 1993. Not holding elections for local governments also meant not allowing the Chakmas to govern themselves, or allowing them access to direct power and resources. Giving Chakmas leadership roles in elected tiers of the Panchayati Raj system would have required acknowledging them as bona fide citizens, which the state has successfully avoided so far. Chakmas are India's stateless people.[35] Despite the Right to Education (RTE) Act being in place for thirteen years now, the literacy rate for Chakmas is way below the national average.[36]

The BJP government has been treading a middle path with Chakmas since the Citizenship (Amendment) Act includes Buddhists. At the same time, to assuage other groups in Arunachal Pradesh, they deny land rights and ST status to them, even though Chakmas are categorised as a Scheduled Tribe in Tripura and Mizoram.

The Chakma is simultaneously a guest and a refugee, a citizen and a stateless subject.

The 'Coolies', Gorkhas, Chakmas and Kayas are not representative of any broad categories, but are a diverse set of communities. Some, like the Kayas, have agency, while others are vulnerable to exploitation and often victims of discrimination. They are all citizens who must enjoy the same rights, and they are all members of the same nation—except some are accepted while others are not.

Citizenship to Nationality

In Chapter 4, nationality is the recurrent theme; personal stories and historical narratives raise questions about the core notion of nationality and the relationship between a citizen and the state.

Why is it that in 2020, the Indian state, which insisted on creating a citizenship register, did not consider a document like the passport (that verifies nationality) adequate? Why are legacy and lineage important, and how far does one go to prove them? Given the criteria set to establish the bond between the state and the citizen, one is curious about the intent and outcome of a very expensive exercise like a population register.

Can citizenship and nationality be interchanged? While citizenship refers to the citizen's relation with the state, the right to a nationality is a fundamental human right under international law.[37] Citizenship also extends to individuals' membership in society or a commune. A citizen is a member of the community who enjoys rights and assumes duties of membership. While notions of citizenship can be traced back to a very long time ago, the idea of nationality has its origins in the modern nation-state. The notion of the loyal, committed citizen grew out of this new nation-state.

The first nationality laws were codified only in the early nineteenth century. Nationality laws became necessary when territories marked sovereignty. Till two centuries ago, international law had nothing to do with nationality, but as the movement of people from different countries increased and nations were created, problems and conflicting claims increased. The codification of nationality laws was stressed only at the League of Nations' Committee of Experts and the Nationality Committee at the First Codification Conference in 1924. However, one must examine the notion of the decolonised citizen when studying Indian nationality. Besides, the expanding scope of human rights can no longer detach rights from nationality. There is the possibility of multiple citizenships that intersect with nationality and the nation-state has to accommodate such arrangements if the need arises. For example, the Chakmas were refugees but they were granted citizenship in India. They are also naturalised citizens of Bangladesh. Finally, migration and statelessness will continue to challenge the legal boundaries of citizenship and nationality. India is among the top ten nations to offer asylum,[38] yet its policies around migration are fuzzy and discriminatory, to say the least. Citizenship and nationality in India have gained agency through their politicisation—when untenable anti-minority laws collide with the majority's resentment against 'minority appeasement'.

The first fifty years of Indian nationhood were witness to some of its toughest challenges, from armed insurrections to ideological opposition. Over the next twenty-three years, some of these challenges dissipated, while new ones replaced them. But at the heart of these challenges lie the hyper-sensitive but confusing issues of identity, citizenship and nationality. For example, the Nagas, having fought the fiercest and most protracted armed movement in India, cannot see themselves as part of the Indian nation, even while participating in the Indian electoral process. The Adivasis rebel against the formal institutions that conveniently trample upon their rights. The Dravidian opposition to Hindi imposition has been well-documented. Kashmiri nationalism has been at loggerheads with mainstream Indian attempts at setting right the 'historical wrongs' in the valley and beyond. Nationality should perhaps only be defined by the limitations that the notion has acquired. There will always be contestations to rigid majoritarian ideas around this concept.

Endnotes

1. See definition provided online by Oxford Languages, s.v. 'refugee'.

2. *Shorter Oxford English Dictionary on Historical Principles*, 6th ed., volume 2: s.v. 'nationality'.

3. This is the abstract of a talk by Lawrence Liang as part of a series, *Beyond Borders*, curated by the author in 2017. The lecture was never delivered due to unforeseen circumstances.

4. See Sharma, Jayeeta. 2011. *Empire's Garden: Assam and the Making of India*, 87. Durham and London: Duke University Press.

5. Ibid., 92.

6. Here, 'others' refers to communities other than Assamese and plains tribals from Assam, such as Biharis, Bengalis, Nepalis, Punjabis. etc.

7. Weiner, Myron. 1983. 'The Political Demography of Assam's Anti-Immigrant Movement'. *Population and Development Review* 9 (2): 279–92. Available at https://doi.org/10.2307/1973053 (accessed August 2022).

8. A mouzadaar is a revenue officer in Assam. See *Assam Tribune*. 2010. 'State Mouzadars Deprives of their Due Status', 15 September. Available at https://assamtribune.com/state-mouzadars-deprived-of-their-due-status (accessed August 2022).

9. See Dirks, Nicholas B. 2011. 'Three: The Ethnographic State'. In *Castes of Mind: Colonialism and the Making of Modern India*: 43–60. Princeton, NJ: Princeton University Press. Available at https://doi.org/10.1515/9781400840946-005 (accessed August 2022). See also Gurung, Tejimala. 2014. 'The Making of Gurkhas as a "Martial Race" in Colonial India: Theory and Practice'. *Proceedings of the Indian History Congress* 75: 520–29.

10. See Huxford, H. J. 1952. *History of the 8th Gurkha Rifles, 1824–1949*. Aldershot: Gale and Polden Limited.

11. *Darjeeling Chronicle*. 2019. 'Ask Me How I Feel About Inner Line Permit.' 8 August. Available at https://thedarjeelingchronicle.com/ask-me-how-i-feel-about-inner-line-permit/ (accessed August 2022).

12. The theatre of war in this region is subject to detailed discussion. See Chakravarty, Ipsita. 'As Manipur Recovers its World War II Past, it Digs into Both Japanese and British Version of Events'. *Scroll.in*, 3 December. Available at https://scroll.in/article/859171/as-manipur-recovers-its-world-war-ii-past-it-digs-into-both-japanese-and-british-version-of-events (accessed August 2022). See also https://www.nam.ac.uk/explore/battle-imphal (accessed August 2022).

13. This history is available through archival sources, including Shakespear, L. W. 1977. *History of Assam Rifles*. Tribal Research Institute,

Mizoram. See also https://www.battleofimphal.com/manipur-and-wwii/the-world-visits (accessed August 2022).

14. See Government of India. 2011. Census of India. Available at https://www.census2011.co.in/census/state/manipur.html (accessed August 2022).

15. See Subba, Tanka. 1992. 'To Be or Not To Be "Nepali"'. *Himal Southasian*, 1 May. Available at https://www.himalmag.com/to-be-or-not-to-be-nepali/ (accessed August 2022). See also Nath, Lopita. 2005. 'Migrants in Flight: Conflict-Induced Internal Displacement of Nepalis in Northeast India'. *Peace and Democracy in South Asia* 1 (1): 57–72. Available at https://core.ac.uk/download/pdf/1325224.pdf (accessed August 2022).

16. Nath, 'Migrants in Flight'.

17. While this term is viewed as a pejorative now, it is a specific term that the group in question itself uses. The term originated from the Tamil 'kuli', used for low-level labourers in the Indian Ocean labour force. Some accounts suggest it may have been derived from the word 'Kol'.

18. For a detailed discussion, see Sharma, *Empire's Garden*: 80–81.

19. They are a secure vote bank because they are thought to vote en-masse, they live in ghettoes and are stereotyped as a community that can be easily wooed by political parties with liquor and money. They dominate the vote in forty of the 126 seats in the state assembly and are seen as a single community that can change the electoral fate. See Saikia, Arunabh. 2021. 'Assam's Large Tea Worker Community Has Always Lacked a Political Voice. Could This Be Changing?' *Scroll.in*, 26 March. Available at https://scroll.in/article/990446/assams-large-tea-worker-community-has-always-lacked-a-political-voice-could-this-be-changing (accessed August 2022).

20. For instance, Indrajit Sharma writes that as per the 2011 census, 'Demographically, the tea tribes form around 20% (approximately 5 million) of the total population of Assam'. 2018. 'Tea Tribes of Assam'. *Economic and Political Weekly* 53 (9). Available at https://www.epw.in/journal/2018/9/notes/tea-tribes-assam.html (accessed August 2022).

21. See Bhattacharjee, Kishalay. 2016. 'The Recent Killing of 14 People is Yet Another Marker in Kokrajhar's Long and Bloody History'. *Scroll.in*, 9 August. Available at https://scroll.in/article/813511/the-recent-killing-of-14-people-is-yet-another-marker-in-kokrajhars-long-and-bloody-history (accessed August 2022). See also Das, Diganta. 2016. 'The Itinerary of Genocide on Adivasi in Assam'. *International Journal of Humanities & Social Science Studies* 3 (2): 305–310. Available at https://www.ijhsss.com/old/files/29.Diganta-Das.pdf (accessed August 2022).

22. For example, see *The Times of India*. 2007. 'Mob Strips Woman Protester in Guwahati', 27 November. Available at https://timesofindia.indiatimes.com/india/mob-strips-woman-protester-in-guwahati/articleshow/2573606.

cms (accessed August 2022). See also *Hindustan Times*. 2007. 'Assam Simmers over Woman's Stripping', 27 November. Available at https://www.hindustantimes.com/india/assam-simmers-over-woman-s-stripping/story-OG3PIzw2MXe8RL5L1X0U7L.html (accessed August 2022). For a more detailed commentary, see Misra, Udayon. 2007. 'Adivasi Struggle in Assam'. *Economic and Political Weekly* 42 (51): 11–14. Available at https://www.epw.in/journal/2007/51/commentary/adivasi-struggle-assam.html (accessed August 2022).

23. Ellias, Rafeeq. 2015. 'The Chinese-Indian Prisoners of Deoli are Here and Their Voices Need to be Heard'. *The Wire*, 5 October. Available at https://thewire.in/rights/the-chinese-indian-prisoners-of-deoli-are-here-and-their-voices-need-to-be-heard (accessed August 2022). 'POW' here refers to 'Prisoner of War'.

24. Based on the author's conversation at 'The Brown Bag Seminar', National Foundation for India India Habitat Centre, 1 October 2015.

25. Ibid.

26. Ibid.

27. Ellias, 'The Chinese-Indian Prisoners of Deoli are Here'.

28. Ibid.

29. Deb, Debraj. 2020. 'Chakma National Council Observes "Black Day" Against Inclusion of Chittagong Hill Tract in East Pakistan during Partition'. *The Indian Express*, 17 August. Available at https://indianexpress.com/article/north-east-india/tripura/chakma-community-black-day-chittagong-hill-tract-partition-east-pakistan-6558465/ (accessed August 2022).

30. See Subramanian, Nirupama. 2009. 'A Chakma in Pakistan'. *The Hindu*, 16 December. Available at https://www.thehindu.com/opinion/op-ed//article59879052.ece (accessed August 2022).

31. For details on the submerged area and number of displaced persons, see Chakravarty, Ipsita. 2017. '50 Years On, Chakma Refugees from Bangladesh are Still Denied Citizenship Rights in Arunachal'. *Scroll.in*, 30 July. Available at https://scroll.in/article/845129/50-years-on-chakma-refugees-from-bangladesh-are-still-denied-citizenship-rights-in-arunachal (accessed August 2022). See also Chakma, Nalori. 2021. 'One Dam, Six Decades of Disenfrachisement: The Story of the Jumma Indigeneous Peoples'. *Internationalrivers.org*, 1 November. Available at https://www.internationalrivers.org/news/the-kaptai-dam-a-story-of-disenfranchisement-displacement-and-destruction/ (accessed August 2022). The impact of the Kaptai dam is also detailed in Parveen, Saila and I. M. Faisal. 2002. 'People versus Power: The Geopolitics of Kaptai Dam in Bangladesh'. *Water Resources Development* 18 (1): 197–208. Available at https://theasiadialogue.com/wp-content/uploads/2018/03/

People-versus-Power_-The-Geopolitics-of-Kaptai-Dam-in-Bangladesh.pdf (accessed August 2022).

32. See Chakma, P. J. 1989. 'The Genocide in the Chittagong Hill Tracts'. *Seeds of Peace* 5 (3): 4–6. Available at https://www.cwis.org/document/the-genocide-in-the-chittagong-hill-tracts/ (accessed August 2022).

33. See *The Hindu*. 2021. 'Bid to Deport 60,000 Chakmas from Arunachal Slammed', 23 August. Available at https://www.thehindu.com/news/national/other-states/bid-to-deport-60000-chakmas-from-arunachal-slammed/article36055227.ece (accessed August 2022).

34. See Gogoi, Suraj and Shyamal Chakma. 2016. 'State of Exclusion'. *Himal Southasian*, 13 May. Available at https://www.himalmag.com/state-of-exclusion/ (accessed August 2022).

35. See Ghosh, Aparajita. 2022. '57 Years After India Gave Them Refuge, Former Refugees From East Pakistan Threatened By Indian Xenophobia'. *Article 14*, 2 February. Available at https://www.article-14.com/post/57-years-after-india-gave-them-refuge-former-refugees-from-east-pakistan-threatened-by-indian-xenophobia-61f9f4b18da1f (accessed August 2022).

36. For instance, see Chakma, Premanand. 2022. 'Literacy and Educational Conditions of Chakmas in Arunachal Pradesh, India'. *Chakmalibrary.net*, 1 March. Available at https://chakmalibrary.net/2022/03/01/literacy-and-educational-conditions-of-chakmas-in-arunachal-pradesh-india/ (accessed August 2022).

37. See The Office of the High Commissioner for Human Rights (UN Human Rights), which states that this right 'implies the right of each individual to acquire, change and retain a nationality'. Available at https://www.ohchr.org/en/nationality-and-statelessness (accessed August 2022).

38. See Connor, Phillip. 2017. 'India is a Top Source and Destination for World's Migrants'. *Pew Research Center*, 3 March. Available at https://www.pewresearch.org/fact-tank/2017/03/03/india-is-a-top-source-and-destination-for-worlds-migrants/ (accessed August 2022).

4 The Notion of a Nation
Citizen Imaginaries

Nation[1]
/ˈneɪʃ(ə)n/

noun
1. a large body of people united by common descent, history, culture, or language, inhabiting a particular country or territory.

Nationalism[2]
/ˈnaʃ(ə)n(ə)lɪz(ə)m/

noun
1. identification with one's own nation and support for its interests, especially to the exclusion or detriment of the interests of other nations.

Dissent[3]
/dɪˈsɛnt/

noun
1. Think differently; have a different opinion, disagree.

Anti-national[4]

adjective
1. opposed to or hostile to a nation.

This is an old fashioned book. It does not claim to contribute to theory. It deals rather too much with human beings.[5]

Iconisations

One of the most authentic ways of studying nationalism is through art. A growing vogue of salon art in nineteenth-century Europe was imported to Indian art societies such as the Brush Club of Calcutta and the Bombay Art Society, first formed by Europeans and then taken over by Indians, which radically changed art from the personal to the institutional. The politics of such societies is said to have helped the rise of the Indian National Congress. The printing press became instrumental in the proliferation of a kind of visual journalism through art. Art could now be reproduced. One of the earliest graphic artists in India, Ramananda Chatterjee, seized the opportunity to edit and publish the *Modern Review* in English and *Prabasi* in Bengali. Chatterjee's interests were dominated by art and nationalism. Born a Brahmin, he became a Brahmo after joining the Brahmo Samaj and engaged with the issue of women's education early in his life.[6] As a teacher at Kyastha College in Allahabad, he started the first illustrated magazine, *Pradip* (1897). He was then asked to edit the English edition of *Kyastha Samachar* in 1899, where he tried to foster nationalism through art.

However, it was Chatterjee's *Modern Review* that caught the attention of the colonial administration as well as Indians educated in the modern colonial system in India. Having a friend in Upendrakishore Raychauduri[7] (the founder of the Ray Tint Process and widely acknowledged then by the Western world) helped Chatterjee reach liberal Brahmos and personalities like Tagore and Jagdish Chandra Bose. By 1907, Dhurandhar, who was already a famous Bombay artist, had also become a regular contributor to *Prabasi*.

This was followed by a huge growth in children's literature in Bengal, which made liberal use of Hindu mythology and folktales. The evolution of popular writings for children, from *Balak* (first published in 1855) to *Tuntunir Boi* (1911), *Sandesh* (1913), and *Basumati* (1922), saw engaging and simple language slowly take over to make these books more accessible to urban children. Illustration took the form of new literature and Sukumar Ray's *Abol Tabol* (*Nonsense Rhymes*, first published in 1923) became a milestone in children's literature. Then came a period of multilingual 'punches', cartoons and satire.

However, it was really Raja Ravi Varma (whose biography Chatterjee wrote in 1907) who stood tall in the world of Indian salon art as an acknowledged master. Despite this, an interesting article by Sister Nivedita, published in 1907 in *Prabasi*, denounced Varma's paintings as debased art. His art was problematic to the newly awakened Indian nationalism, and Varma was sacrificed at the altar of Hindu political consciousness. Varma's paintings were perceived as 'indecorous, imitative, and simply not real art—they belonged on the cheap calendars where Varma himself apparently doomed them forever'. Aurobindo too saw Varma as 'the grand debaser of Indian taste and artistic culture'. Ananda Coomaraswamy said Varma's 'fatal flaws' were 'theatrical conceptions, want of imagination, and lack of Indian feeling'.[8] With the proposed partition of Bengal in 1905, art flew headlong into the political arena. Sister Nivedita wrote in the *Modern Review*: 'Art's rebirth in India today can only take place, if it be consciously made the servant and poet of the mighty dream of an Indian Nationality.'[9]

Ramananda Chatterjee imagined visual imagery as the only way to speak in a common language, due to the lack of translation of literary texts across different regions of the nation. This was realised by Varma's paintings and Mhatre's sculptures. But it was a slim volume by Shyamacharan Srimani, *The Rise of Fine Arts and the Artistic Skills of the Aryans* (1874), which marked the development of cultural nationalism. Like in other parts of the world, this new-found nationalism was almost entirely a product of European nationalism. While the new national identity that emerged followed Westernisation, its adherents turned their gaze towards linguistic and cultural revivalism. For example, in Bengal, they harked back to a Sanskritic and Aryan culture that had been conceptualised by Europeans but fed the national pride, an image of a glorious 'Hindu' past. The myth of the common Aryan descent of people who spoke the Indo-Aryan languages was being nurtured.[10] The Hindu Mela was a product of a Hindu revival movement in Bengal. The first congregation of the Hindus, it took place in 1867, organised by playwright and poet Nabagopal Mitra. The idea was to instil national pride. Tagore's first published poem was 'Hindu melar Upahar' ('The Gift of the Hindu Mela'). As a battle cry against British barbs about the 'effeminate nature' of Bengali men, the Mela hosted national gymnastic exercises, wrestling and stick fighting. In 1876, Bankim Chandra Chatterjee wrote 'Bande Mataram', which became the Hindu anthem and heralded the beginning of an era.[11] The nationalist Surendranath Banerjea called upon the people: 'miserable and degraded as we are, our degradation has followed upon a chain of sequences, but history demonstrated that there are still relics of past greatness, that the Hindus were not only great in literature and science but in war as well.'[12]

Hindu self-confidence had been restored since Max Muller's translation of the *Rig Veda* (1845–79). It was only getting stronger now. Edwin Arnold's biography of the Buddha as the founder of a spiritual empire found currency with Indian nationalists. Thus, colonialism in a sense created and handed over the Orientalist image of a Hindu community. Partha Mitter writes that the swadeshi ideology imagined the Hindus as the exclusive inheritors of the past.[13] In one stroke, the Muslims were disinherited from the Indian ancient past. The term 'Hindutva' was apparently first used by Chadranath Basu in his book *Hindur Prakrita Itishash* (*Actual History of Hindus*). He believed in the idea of the 'Hindu Rashtra' or a homeland for Hindus where other religious groups will not find a home. Hindu nationalism found another spokesperson in Rajnarayan Basu, who established the Jatiya Gaurab Sampadani (Association for Achieving National Glory) in Medinipore and the Savjibani Sabha in Calcutta. His book, *Hindu Dharmera Srestha*, spoke about the superiority of the Hindu religion. At the same time, an organisation was created to stop religious conversions. It was named the Dharma Rakshini Sabha.[14] Bankim Chandra Chatterjee started writing about Muslim invaders, from whom Hindus had to be saved. For example, in his novel *Anandamath*, the Muslims are represented as invaders responsible for the cultural degeneration of the Hindus. It attempts to re-establish the Sanatan dharma against the disastrous consequences of Muslim rule, resulting in the decay of the Hindus. In *Sitaram*, his last novel, the polarisation between Hindus and Muslims is complete, and the war must be fought with the divine intervention of Sree, who transforms the Hindus into an army to take over.[15]

In many ways, the nationalist art movement was thought to be led by Abanindranath Tagore, who was a member of the Tagore family in Bengal. His meeting with the English art teacher Havell prompted a series of nationalist art based on indigenous styles seen in Mughal art. But Abanindranath was more influenced by the soft tones of Japanese art, and it was his collaboration with two Japanese artists, Yokoyama Taikan and Shunso Hishida, that led to the creation of Bharat Mata in 1905. The year coincided with British viceroy Lord Curzon's unpopular decision to partition Bengal, in order to reorganise the imperial contours of the eastern and northeastern regions of British India. This partition resulted in the division of the Muslim peasantry in eastern Bengal and Hindu landowners in the west. The Muslim League was formed in 1906 in Dhaka, in eastern Bengal, to protect the interests of the Muslims. The Swadeshi movement also emerged during the resistance to this partition, and these years witnessed a surge of nationalist art tied to the idea of India. The familiarity of the mother cult and the worship of the devi in Bengal helped Abanindranath's mythographical depiction of the nation as a (Hindu) mother.[16]

On 16 October 1905, when Bengal was partitioned, Rabindranath Tagore was at the forefront of the protests. Abanindranath had initially dismissed the emotional outbursts against the partition. He had benefitted from the promotion and patronage of both British Orientalists and Indian nationalism. But he was tied to his discipline in art, even as his iconic painting was appropriated to represent the ideal of India.[17] Sister Nivedita introduced this work in *Prabasi*:

> We have here a picture which bids fair to prove the beginning of a new age in Indian art. Using all the added means of expression which the modern period has bestowed upon him, the artist here has given expression nevertheless to a purely Indian idea, in Indian form. The curving line of lotuses and the white radiance of the halo are beautiful additions to the Asiatically-conceived figure with its four arms. This is the first masterpiece, in which the Indian artist has actually succeeded in disengaging, as it were the spirit of the motherland…. If nationality, and the civic ideal…are to be distinguishing marks of the new era, then it is clear that we must have definite symbols under which to think of them….[18]

The objects held by the deity were the nationalist aspirations towards self-sufficiency: *anna* (food), *vastra* (clothing), *siksa* (secular learning) and *diksa* (spiritual knowledge). This was a visual representation of Bankim's 'Bande Mataram', introduced in his famous novel, *Anandamath* (1882). Nivedita wrote, 'I would reprint it if I could, by tens of thousands, and scatter it broadcast over the land, till there was not a peasant's cottage nor a craftsman's hut…that had not the presentement of Bharat-Mata somewhere on its walls'.[19]

In a paper titled 'Icon-ising national identity: France and India in comparative perspective', Subrata K. Mitra and Lion König state that '[i]t is curious how one cannot resist the tendency to give an anthropomorphic form to a country'.[20] Mitra and Konig argue, '"icon-ising"—the act of transforming an idea to an image that the nation as an imagined community can identify with—is an integral part of nation-building'.[21] Comparing France and India, they discuss how Marianne and Bharat Mata, in their manifestations, provide what nationalists need, but question why Marianne remains a true icon in France while Bharat Mata has receded into the 'contested space of partisan politics'. France adopted 'Marianne—an image with pre-revolutionary origins—as a "secular saint" to be revered by the masses with the aim of instilling the new Republican-secular spirit in the citoyens'.[22] In that sense, Marianne is supra-political while Bharat Mata lingers only in the margins.

Mitra and König argue that national icons legitimise the state and help in mass mobilisation. They create an idealised past, which in turn becomes the driver for future nationalist assertions, thereby forging a national identity. Unlike Bharat Mata's single depiction, Marianne has diverse manifestations, ranging from the martial, as in Delacroix's painting, *La Liberté Guidant Le Peuple*, to the maternal Marianne of Daumier's *La République*. Marianne became the post-revolution icon of the government and could be found in every aspect of life in France, from coins to business cards. Her portraits have been modelled after French celebrities like Brigitte Bardot, Catherine Deneuve, and even Laetita Casta. A new face of Marianne emerged in 2002: a woman of North African descent, signalling a 'modern, plural and diverse France'. The country has over five million citizens of Muslim faith. Barring this exception, depictions of Marianne usually contain undertones of a white ethnic identity, as exemplified by the French far-right wing's use of the Marianne imagery in an election campaign in 2009.

While the French Revolution was led by dissidents and was against the church and the king, the Indian freedom movement 'drew on the religiosity of the masses'.[23] The religious icons of Ganesh and Kali were used as figures of power. In France, religion and politics were kept apart, whereas in India the two fed on each other.

Mitra and König refer to what Sumathi Ramaswamy terms 'bodyscapes' to explain Bharat Mata's body and apparel. Bharat Mata's apparel, and especially her sari, helps in a significant way in producing and claiming national space.

> The sari invariably extends to cover pre-partition India—*Akhand Bharat*, the undivided and indivisible India—even in

> those 'bodyscapes' produced after 1947, and certainly in Hindu nationalist iconography. Bharat Mata covers the entire territory, her feet stand firmly on the southern tip of the subcontinent and her body reaches up to Kashmir and beyond, thus blurring the geopolitical boundaries. Such is the power of this 'bodyscape' that an anonymous interviewee stated that 'India giving away Kashmir would be equal to beheading Bharat Mata'.[24]

In independent India, painters like Shobha Singh and K. K. Rajaram invoked the militant Bharat Mata in terms of either her 'holy' spirit, or as the image of Shakti protecting the nation. The Ashoka Pillar, the official 'Marianne' for India, is too static to evoke emotion, and that is why Rajaram has the four lions descend from the pillar to confront the dragon in his 1962 depiction of the Indo-China war. Bharat Mata is always calm and controlled, but her religious identity and the saffron flag she carries has pushed her towards the Hindu right. More than the image, it is the war cry, 'Bharat Mata ki Jai', that has resuscitated the mother goddess. Much like Vande Mataram's Hindu overtones, Bharat Mata is overtly Hindu, and thereby not a secular Marianne. It is seen as a divisive ideological symbol, whose role in Indian independence or post-independence history has not been hugely significant. Mitra and König end their paper with a sentence that is relevant in today's India:

> ...even when at a given point of time they do not fulfil their desired function and become meaningless shibboleths, iconised national identities do not just disappear into nothingness; they bide their time in the entrails of collective memory, re-emerging when the context makes space for it.[25]

Imagi(nation)

There are other ways of imagining a nation.

For the sake of a cartoon, R. K. Laxman created the Common Man. The cartoonist has limited space and lines and words with which to present his daily quip. Laxman invented this man who would play the role of an everyday Indian: 'He was bald and bespectacled.... He had a permanently bewildered look and was dressed in a dhoti and a checked coat. This man finally minimized my deadline agonies and took over the strenuous task of representing the mute millions of the country.'[26]

He bears witness to an India that was promised but never delivered. Laxman always employed 'controlled distortion' for his characters, and the Common Man is not exactly a caricature, but rather someone who embodies the caricature that the 'nation' has made of the everyday Indian. He observes everyday situations, but not without his silent and often bewildered disapproval.

Laxman did not name his character 'Indian Man', perhaps because there is no one Indian look, and that is why it is the benign Common Man, wearing a dhoti and a jacket and mostly sporting a confused, but stoically resigned look.

> Today he is found hanging around a cabinet room where a high-powered meeting is in progress. Tomorrow he is among slum dwellers listening to their woes, or marching along with protestors as they demand the abolition of the nuclear bomb. That, of course, doesn't preclude him from being present at a banquet hosted by the prime minister for a visiting dignitary. This man has survived all sorts of domestic crises....[27]

Laxman's portrait of the Common Man holding a photo frame of his bust, a few droplets of perspiration breaking out on his forehead, and the familiar, bespectacled, not-knowing-what-to-say look is another representation of the nation.

The Common Man's observations on the elections are as sharp as those on education. Laxman sarcastically and literally thanks the political class and citizens for privileging the cartoonist. He remarks that had the nation functioned as its founding fathers had envisioned, the cartoonist would have died long ago. As one leafs through the pages of the Common Man's daily observations, one realises that nothing has changed. The language of politics has become more vitriolic, but the essence of a failed community and a failed nation is disturbingly constant: from water scarcity to the demand for separate states, politicians wearing traditional headgear in remote outposts to the incongruity of a protest fast alongside a starving, homeless family.

Czeslaw Milosz, in the Author's Note in his extraordinary work, *The Captive Mind*, describes the book thus: 'Its subject is the vulnerability of the twentieth century mind to seduction by socio-political doctrines and its readiness to accept totalitarian terror for the sake of a hypothetic future.'[28] The common man today, irrespective of place and time, is a victim of such a vulnerability. In the 1985 edition of the book, Milosz stated that what he had described thirty years ago as 'a classical phase' in the history of totalitarianism has not elapsed yet. We can say the same in 2022.

> The world of today is torn asunder by a great dispute; and not only a dispute, but a ruthless battle for world domination. Many people still refuse to believe that there are only two sides, that the only choice lies between absolute conformity to the one system or absolute conformity to the other.[29]

However, there are compelling stories of everyday people who defy the idea of binaries. The state must respect the citizen's right to disagree. The citizen has duties, but conformity is certainly not one of the Directive Principles of the Constitution.

To Die in India

Zarina Husain was actually born Zaiteii Sailo. She grew up in a village about 60 kilometres beyond Lunglei in south Mizoram, and was the daughter of a chieftain.

She became an auxiliary nurse and worked with the erstwhile British Indian Army before the Partition, and was posted in the army hospital in Dhaka during the Second World War. That is where Zaiteii met Dr Altaf Husain, who came from Lucknow's King George's Medical College. An early cataract had made her blind in one eye.

They met and fell in love. He proposed to her, and when she asked, 'Why would you want to marry a one-eyed woman from a tribal village in Lushai Hills?', he told her that he would be her second eye. She agreed, but one of her conditions was that she would not convert from her faith and that if they had children, they would be brought up to choose the faith they wished to follow. And that is a promise he kept till the end. During the Partition, he decided that it would be safer for them to live in the newly created Pakistan, since they were an interfaith couple, rather than return to Lucknow where he had a family: he had earlier married his cousin, and they had two sons. All of them migrated to Karachi, where they stayed in a housing colony comprising primarily of Mohajirs.

When they went to Pakistan, Altaf felt that it would be easier for her if she were to be given a Muslim name. They had a court marriage there, and she became Zarina. The two boys came to live with them. She raised them to be staunch Muslims, even as she remained a practising Christian herself. She was allowed to practice her faith. Altaf then left for England to do a super-specialisation in psychiatry. For about ten years, she lived alone in Karachi and brought up the two boys. On his return, he set up his own practice and ran a hospital.

For ten years until 1971, her only contact with her home in Lushai Hills was through sporadic letters. She would write in English. In 1971, with the fall of Dhaka, when the Mizo National Front had to find new headquarters, they fled to West Pakistan and contacted her. She gave them shelter, funds, and food.

She only sheltered them because her nephew Sangliana, who was the Mizo rebel chief Laldenga's right-hand man, was amongst them. And because she had sheltered rebels, she was always denied a visa to India. For her family back in Mizoram, she was someone whom the elders would mention with fondness: this nebulous, slightly exotic great-aunt somewhere in the wilderness of Pakistan, whom the children in the large family had never met. In 1980 or 1981, a grandniece wrote to her. That is when she found out that her niece had had all these children. She had not known they existed!

Brigadier Sailo, her younger brother and Sangliana's father, became the Chief Minister of Mizoram in 1978. It was then that they managed to get a visa to come to India.

> I remember we all went to Palam airport to receive them. It was quite surprising because we were expecting a 'chinky' lady and out comes this really Pakistani couple. She was tiny…they were both really small…barely five foot each. She was in a full Pakistani salwar kameez and covered. You know those billowing salwars that they wear? The thing that I remember was that even in the 1980s, women of a certain class [in India] never wore synthetics. Pakistanis did, and it is something we noticed… I also realised that she is blind. She couldn't see in both eyes. When she met us, she couldn't speak a word of Mizo. So, what came out was English and Urdu. I still remember she would say 'He Khuda' and all kinds of things. [Altaf] never addressed her by her name. He called her 'Busybody'.… What happened was

> that they stayed in Delhi and Dr Madan Mohan from AIIMS operated on her eyes. And she got her sight back.
>
> It was quite miraculous, actually. She could finally see her family members. When we had first met, she felt our faces and try to sense them, because she had been blind for a long time.[30]

While in Delhi, she managed to pick up, or perhaps remember, some Mizo. Some words would come back to her, and the family could then converse with her. She spent long hours sitting and chatting with her grandchildren, just to catch up on the years she had been away. She had spent very exciting years in Pakistan, organising the Christian Women's Movement in Karachi, and getting her two stepsons married to Muslim-Siamese women.

They went up to Mizoram several times and stayed there. While Brigadier Sailo was Chief Minister, it was easy.

The family knew nothing of Altaf's first wife, who had faded into the background.

They never had children of their own. In the 1990s, the two of them decided that they were becoming too old and infirm, and that she would come back to India to spend her last remaining years.

> Both decided that she would return to India so that when she died, she would get a Christian burial. He did not have the confidence to give her a Christian burial in Pakistan. The last years were very sad because of the separation.... And she lived on for another five years, waiting to die in India!

They spoke to each other every day. He did not come with her because he wanted a Muslim burial.

She was so lost and lonely in Aizawl. Her visa had expired, but the government did not throw her out.

After her death, Altaf was informed. There was no further news from him subsequently.

> We assumed he died soon after. We don't know anything. We were never able to get [in touch with] them.... Either [his sons] did not allow him to remain in touch with us or, as we suspect, he died soon after. They were quite inseparable. When they were together, they fought like a quarrelsome couple. But it was quite interesting: anything he said, she would argue against. Anything she said, he would do the same thing! His family was very accepting of her.

Altaf was a thorough Lakhnavi—Lucknow was home for him. Karachi did not fit his notion of home. He loved Delhi because it reminded him of all the people and places that he had left behind. In a sense, he regretted going to Pakistan. His sons, however, were Pakistani, even though his nephews and nieces here were not. He found it very sad that he himself did not belong, and that the children were growing up during the Zia times.

Here was a woman who was born in a tribal chief's home in a British colony, far removed from colonial or anti-colonial notions. But she left the love of her life and returned to an 'India' where she wanted to die. Maybe it was her idea of a homeland, rather than a nation.

Body in Two Nations

Ian Cardozo was still at Wellington Staff College when his unit, the 4th Battalion of the 5th Gorkha Rifles, moved to the international border in East Pakistan. He left his family back home to join the units. Pakistan had launched an offensive against India on 3 December 1971. By 4 December, the Indian Army, Navy and Air Force had launched counter-offensives.

The war was inevitable. The Pakistan army had unleashed one of the worst genocides in history on the innocent people of East Pakistan. India was overwhelmed by the flow of refugees; ten million had crossed over, forcing India to intervene to ensure its own security. That war continues to haunt the collective memories of all three countries.

Satyabrata Pal, who was a young probationer on the Bangladesh desk in 1971, spoke to me in 2010 and put the events in perspective.

> We said that war was just because the terrible human rights violations committed by Pakistan's Army had robbed its rule of all legitimacy and the huge exodus of refugees into India, fleeing the pogroms, placed an intolerable burden on our own security. The UN recognises now that 'masses in flight', escaping from a breakdown of security and grave human rights violations, can cause exactly the same problems in the sanctuaries they seek. For instance, the meltdown of the Democratic Republic of Congo started with the huge influx of refugees after the genocide in Burundi and Rwanda in 1994. So our cause was just in 1971, but

> we also thought that breaking Pakistan into two would at least halve the threats to our security.[31]

That was the Indian justification for military intervention.

Pakistan, of course, had their own rationale for what they considered a justified operation to protect the nation. Not too long before 1971, on 5 March 1966 four fighter jets of the Indian Air Force—French-built Dassault Ouragan fighters (nicknamed Toofanis), and British Hunters—were deployed to bomb the Indian city of Aizawl.[32] India defended the strafing of its own citizens in the name of protecting the nation.

> In the Pakistani narrative, even thirty-five years later, when I was posted in Islamabad, Pakistani Bengalis were traitors; very few Pakistanis acknowledged that systematic political and economic discrimination had driven them to desperation. The Pakistan Army claimed they were defending the unity of Pakistan, but they thought the East Pakistanis were alien in appearance and culture, not entirely Pakistani. What they were defending therefore was the territory of Pakistan, perhaps an idea of Pakistan, not its citizens. The local militias they raised to commit the worst outrages—the Al Shams and the Al Badr—were vigilantes turned against their own people. There are uncomfortable parallels to the attitude of our own armed forces in the North-East and in J&K; in the anti-Naxal operations, General Niazi might be considered the godfather of the Salwa Judum.[33]

On the evening of 3 December 1971, the Pakistan Air Force attacked Indian airfields at Srinagar, Jaisalmer and Uttarlai. Cardozo was on the Frontier Mail heading for Delhi. They were scheduled to catch a special flight, the Assam Courier, the next morning, which would take them to Guwahati, from where they would have to find their way to their units. But Pakistan's air raids posed a threat to air transport, so instead they took the train. The officers and men were expected to arrange their own transit. Ian barely made it on the Assam Mail, which had left the New Delhi platform by the time he arrived.

The Pakistani submarine PNS Gazi had been sunk off the port of Visakhapatnam by then; the Indian Navy was attacking Karachi and the Indian Army was attacking Pakistani defences on the Eastern and Western fronts.

On the morning of 6 December 1971, Ian reached Dharmanagar railway station in Tripura.

Ian's battalion had already launched two attacks at Atgram and Gazipur. They had lost three officers and four were wounded. The only way for him to reach his men was by road. He would have to replace the Second-in-Command, a jinxed position in the regiment. Much later, Ian would recall an astrologer telling him that he would face accidents, but stay alive.

A forty-hour drive to a place called Kala Shehr. Four helicopters were on the ground. 'The moon was in its third quarter and sinking slowly into the horizon, and by its pale light I could see groups of soldiers lying asleep on the ground.'

The Battalion had been tasked to capture the airfield at Sylhet, along with a road junction and the broadcasting station, in the Indian Army's first ever helicopter-borne operation. Part of the battalion had been lifted via helicopter the previous day and the others were in the process of being moved. Ian and his reduced battalion strength of 584 men had to capture Sylhet. They had food and water for only forty-eight hours.

On the evening of 8 December 1971, Ian became a 'Vazir' on the insistence of a subedar who persuaded the Commanding Officer to change his designation because '2i/c' in the regiment was cursed, and many of his predecessors had died.

Ian recalls:

> The soil beneath the top layer was soft and moist and I can in my imagination still smell the soft earth of Bangladesh—not that the soil of India was any different, but it was into this soil of mother earth that we would finally be consigned, except that we were now alive and breathing her strong aroma.

A day later, the BBC wrongly reported that a Gorkha Brigade had landed in Sylhet. This piece of disinformation may have changed the course of the war, with half a battalion on the ground facing almost an entire division of Pakistani forces in Sylhet. Neither side really knew the other's strength.

On 12 December, four Pakistani artillery rounds destroyed their medical post. Nothing was left of the facility, not even body parts.

On 15 December, at around 5.45 PM, the Pakistani forces at Sylhet wished to surrender. The surrendering force included 202

Pakistan Infantry Brigade, 313 Pakistani Infantry Brigade and the Sylhet Garrison. A total of 3 brigadiers, 2 Colonels, 173 Officers, 290 JCOs and 8,000 troops surrendered to a mere handful of Gorkhas. The Gorkha strength had been reduced to 532 due to casualties.

18 December 1971. Ian went across to a BSF platoon in a state of panic, having spotted Pakistani armed soldiers who had been allowed to retain their arms for self-defence. After walking for some distance, Ian stepped on a Pakistani P2 mine, which blew up. His leg was in a mess. A Bangladeshi man who witnessed the incident entered the minefield, lifted him up and carried him to a jeep that was standing close by.

After that, it was all a blur. There was not even any morphine since the medical post had been destroyed. Ian called Balbahadur, his batman, and asked him to fetch the *khukri*.[34] Then he told him to strike off his leg.

'*Saab mo garnu saak daina*,' he said—I cannot do it. '*Doctorsaab lai intezar garnoos*,' he continued, asking Ian to wait for the doctor.

Ian was impatient and chopped off his own leg. The severed part of the leg fell to the ground. He then asked Balbahadur to bury it. The poor chap did as he was ordered.

Ian was subsequently forced to go to the Sylhet Garrison Military Hospital. He initially resisted, refusing to be touched by an enemy doctor or receive Pakistani blood. Later, he was evacuated, wrapped in a Pakistani blanket etched with a soldier's name on it. He still carries the blanket.

Ian's leg remains buried in Sylhet. He has not revisited the site. He laughs, saying that he owns a square foot of Bangladeshi earth.

When asked for his thoughts on what is happening around us today in the name of nationality and religion, Ian paused and said:

> In the 1971 war, we had Field Marshal Sam Manekshaw, a Parsi Army Chief, Lt. General J. S. Arora, a Sikh Eastern Army Commander, and General Jacob, a Jewish Chief of Staff and the brains behind the operation. Of the divisional commanders, three were Christian: General D'souza, General Gonsalves and General Pinto. So we have always fought wars shoulder to shoulder with people practising different faiths.

Exceptionalism: Nagaland, Kashmir and Manipur

> The majority community in India believes these lands are part of India, but does not quite see those who live there as Indians; in the popular belief, the tribes of the North-East are much too much like the Chinese, the Kashmiri Muslims are all closet Pakistanis. The fact that we use the Army, whose primary mission is to fight enemy soldiers, against only these citizens of India deepens their conviction that the rest of India sees them as foreigners. And the fact that we give the Army an impunity to act against them that it would not enjoy in a war against a foreign force only deepens their alienation.[35]

Nehru and the Nagas

> Then came the case of that lady, Rani Gindalo, who after suffering long period of imprisonment was released some years ago.... It was a story of young women of their tribe belonging to the Koboi (Kabui) clan in the Naga Hills.... Gindalo was her name and she was about nineteen six months ago when civil disobedience blazed over the length and breadth of India. News of Gandhi and Congress reached her in her hill abode and found an echo in her heart. She dreamed of freedom for her people and an ending of the galling restrictions they suffered from, and she raised the banner of independence and called her people to rally around it. Perhaps she thought rather prematurely, that the British Empire was fading out. But [the British] Empire still functioned effectively and aggressively and it took vengeance on her and her people. Many villages were burnt and destroyed, this heroic girl was captured and sentenced to transportation for life. And now she lies in some prison in Assam wasting her bright young womanhood in dark cells and solitude.... But her own people remember their Gindalo Rani and think of her with love and pride. And a day will come when India also will remember her and cherish her and bring her out of her prison cell. [On his way back] I thought of Gindalo, the Rani, sitting in her prison.[36]

During his trip to Assam in 1937, Jawaharlal Nehru, who observed the Nagas as a distinct tribe, wrote this when he heard of Guidiliu, the otherwise unknown Naga freedom fighter. The Naga Hills (in what was then Assam) presented the Indian state's first and immediate challenge to nation-building. Nehru's romanticism on the subject of the tribes soon gave way to a hardened stance. He recognised that

> ...the problem in these areas is to make the people feel that they have perfect freedom to live their lives and to develop according to their wishes and genius. India to them should signify not only a protecting force but a liberating one. Any conception that India is ruling them and that they are the ruled or that the custom and habits with which they are unfamiliar are going to be imposed on them, will alienate them and make our frontier problem more difficult... [37]

Nehru agreed to grant autonomy to the Nagas and the Naga question made him reflect upon the different aspects of minority nationalism. He, however, anticipated the secessionist mood amongst the Nagas, and warned that it was too small to exist as a sovereign state between two giants, India and China. The letter he wrote to the Naga National Council, explaining why autonomy is better than sovereignty, became the basis for the Fifth and Sixth Schedules of the Indian Constitution:

> It is obvious that the Naga territory in eastern Assam is much too small to stand by itself, politically or economically. It lay between two huge countries India and China and part of it consists of rather backward people who require considerable help. When India is independent, as it is bound to be soon, it will not be possible for the British government to hold on the Naga territory. It must form part of India and of Assam with which it has developed much close association. At the same time it is our policy that tribal areas should have as much freedom and autonomy as possible so that they can live their own lives according to their own customs and desires.... The whole Naga territory should go together and should be controlled in a large measure by an elected Naga National Council.... I agree entirely with your decision that the Naga Hills should constitutionally be included in an autonomous Assam in a free India, with local autonomy and due safeguards for the interest of the Nagas.... I see no reason whatever why an extraneous judicial system should be enforced upon the Naga Hills. They should have perfect freedom to continue their village panchayats, tribal courts, etc, according to their own wishes. Certainly the people of the Naga Hills should not be exploited by others and their right to own and work on the soil should remain with them. I do not want them to be swamped by people from other parts

> of the country who might go there to exploit them to their own advantage.[38]

Angami Zapu Phizo had by then moved ahead with an assertion of Naga nationhood akin to the princely states, and now that the British were departing, the Nagas were expected to return to their imagined nation-state. By 1952, Nehru had categorically stated that the demand for Naga independence was 'absurd'. Sajal Nag writes that the 'thrust of his Naga policy was to grant them the fullest autonomy', a policy that created unending satraps in the eastern frontier.[39]

Then followed a well-known incident that is worth remembering as a metaphor for the Naga challenge to the Indian nation. Nehru visited Kohima with the Burmese Prime Minister, U Nu, and Indira Gandhi. While a crowd had gathered at the proposed venue, his delay in arriving there prompted the people to believe that India was not interested in talking to them. When his convoy arrived, the Nagas reportedly signalled their displeasure by flashing their bare bottoms at Nehru and the guests, before leaving the venue. Nehru was deeply embarrassed. For some reason, the NNC members were held responsible, hounded and arrested. Many were forced underground and took up arms.

The same Nehru who had been so taken with the idea of freedom in the Naga Hills had by now agreed to send in the army. That would be the beginning of the end of Nehru's nation-building in the North East. Nehru, in a speech in the Lok Sabha during the debate on the Naga Hills situation on 23 August 1956, clarified the incident:

> ...the facts are somewhat different. I went to Kohima. The prime minister of Burma had also come over flying across the border. We met at Manipur and were going to Burma a day or two later. I thought I might utilise that opportunity to visit Kohima. We went to Kohima and we relaxed. I suggested to the authorities there... that some kind of welcome might be given to the Burmese prime minister. He was our guest and people gathered to say a few words. It was not a normal visit of mine to that place. What I found later was that [the] Nagas there wanted to read out an address to me. The deputy commissioner told them you can hand it over to the Prime Minister afterward. I cannot allow your reading it out to him at a time when the prime minister of Burma and others have come. It is therefore not correct to say that I refused to take the address. As a matter of fact, on

> a previous occasion at Kohima I had actually met the Naga leaders, discussed the matter with them and had taken a long document from them. That was just a year earlier and so it is not true to say that I refused to receive an address or that the Deputy Commissioner came in the way. But he did come in the way of an address being read at the meeting. I did not know it at that time; I know it later. [*sic*] Then when U Nu and I arrived at the meeting place, the Nagas who were present got up and walked away. I was distressed, not on my own account but because the prime minister of Burma, an honoured guest of ours had been treated so discourteously.[40]

He was still cautious, and asked the army general to supervise and use only moderate force. But he was obsessed with 'winning them over', even as the Nagas continued to battle it out. Seventy-five years later, Nehru's dream is somewhat realised, not because the Indian state won the Naga people over, but because half-a-century of bloodshed has left the people fatigued and eager to move on. Minority nationalism has since been countered only with force, and some measure of autonomy for the privileged.

Kashmir Blinded

How does one write about Kashmir in 2022? I struggled to imagine a narrative, a story, or a journey, like you do while tossing and turning on a sleepless night, shrouded in darkness. Too many things have happened in the now bifurcated state and in the country since I began writing this book.

Ellen Berry's 'dead eyes' still haunt:

> The surgeon's knife slides into an eyeball as if it were a soft fruit.
>
> The patient's eyelids have been stretched back with a metal clamp, so his eyeball bulges out of glistening pink tissue. The surgeon sits with his back very straight, cutting with tiny movements of his fingers. Every now and then, a thread of blood appears in the patient's eye socket. The patient is 8 years old.[41]

In another 2016 article, novelist Waheed Mirza suddenly breaks down:

> How did India get here? How is it all right for a constitutionally democratic and secular, modern nation to blind scores of civilians in a region it controls? Not an authoritarian state, not a

> crackpot dictatorship, not a rogue nation or warlord outside of legal and ethical commitments to international statutes, but a democratic country, a member of the comity of nations. How are India's leaders, thinkers and its thundering televised custodians of public and private morality, all untroubled by the sight of a child whose heart has been penetrated by metal pellets? This is the kind of cruelty we expect from Assad's Syria, not the world's largest democracy.[42]

Farzan Sheikh is in his early twenties, exactly my daughter's age. He was in the ninth grade when a pellet gun hit him. He lost his left eye. On the day he returned home, hoping to soon write his examination, he was again shot with pellets when he stepped out on the verandah to switch off an outdoor light that was hurting his eyes. This time, it was the right eye. 'I recognize people by their voices. I just see shadows,' says Farzan.[43] His memory of the layout and furniture helps him to move around the house. His father runs a small store from a room in their home, while his mother is a babysitter and a caretaker. Farzan wanted to be a professional cricketer.

How does the nation appear when you are blinded by it for no reason?

For months in 2019, I tried to speak to Kashmiri youth and see what they see, but the indefinite communication blockade and repression frustrated all attempts to reach them. They tried to speak, but found their words muffled. I then turned to historian Siddiq Wahid for a more academic understanding of Kashmiri nationalism vis-à-vis the Indian state.

K. B.: Is Kashmiriyat equal to Kashmiri nationalism? What does it constitute as of today?

S. W.: No. 'Kashmiriyat' is a term that was invented as recently as sixty or so years ago by Sheikh Mohammad Abdullah and the National Conference to legitimise its 'struggle' for, successively, the right to referendum in the interests of autonomy, independence and accession—not necessarily in that order. So it is a purely 'invented tradition', as [Eric] Hobsbawm would say, for instrumentalist purposes.

As to what the term 'nationalism' constitutes for Kashmir: it is fraught with problems when considering the J&K question. This because the erstwhile state of J&K, prior to October 1947, was an independent, sovereign state. In that frame, the question was one to be settled between the state of J&K versus the state of India. However, soon after 1947, the state of J&K was stripped of its 'statehood', by implicit acts and practical steps, and became known merely as a bone of contention between India and Pakistan. This then devolved into the peoples of the state, in its entirety, being unable to independently determine their own future and, *a priori*, being made subservient to the states of India and Pakistan with the region being militarised and occupied under a deferred referendum.

In the above context, the J&K dispute was not a 'nationalist' dispute but a state-to-state territorial and political dispute. The latter was subsumed because of the lack of statesmanship and clarity of intent on the part of the primary states following the British withdrawal from South Asia in 1947.

K. B.: The semantics of 'sub-nationalism' as opposed to 'nationalism', you said, is deeply problematic. But academicians have popularised the idea of sub-national assertions. How would you articulate this notion?

S. W.: The [prefix] 'sub' privileges the majority 'nation', depending on how one identifies the entity: ethnically, religiously, linguistically and culturally. In this sense, it may be acceptable to talk about 'sub' nations in the US or Australia, because of the idiosyncrasies of their histories as a state, which is recent and involves the virtual decimation of the continents' autochthonous populations. The problem with such populations is that the authochthons who have survived to modern times in Asia, Latin America and Europe can each claim an historical heritage of at least a thousand years or more. That makes it a difficult proposition to 'melt' these groups into a homogeneous whole, as several present-day states would want. So, no nation would want to be a 'sub' nation. 'Democracy', be it capitalist or socialist, has promised this, but finds it difficult to practise it, which is how the problem asserts itself.

As for 'popularising' the term 'sub-nationalism', I think it is less 'academics' who popularise it, and more practitioners, politicians or wielders of state power who popularise it by privileging 'majorities' because of representative politics and the utility of vote-bank influences in less than perfect electoral politics. Academics perhaps use the term as an empirical comment on practice.

K. B.: Patel had indeed agreed to let go of Kashmir when Hyderabad and Junagadh decided to merge with Pakistan. History seems to have forgotten that. When Kashmir utters 'Azadi' now, it seems like treason, but the idea of that existed even then. How did it become so convoluted?

S. W.: This is an important historical question which cannot be answered in brief. Suffice it to say that the answer lies in the acceptance of the idea of the state, lock, stock and barrel, by the protagonists of the South Asian independence movement, which has resulted in a schizophrenic (between 'tradition' and 'modern') South Asia that is not understood by 'the peoples' of the region, and is dangerously exploited by the state leaderships of the region.

K. B.: You invoked Perry Anderson and he clearly points at Nehru for the incarcerated existence of people there, where the Indian state is seen as occupational since the creation of the nation. Do you share his view?

S. W.: Yes, I do.

K. B.: Anderson also points out—and rightly so—that the politics of nationalism of both Gandhi and Nehru were very Hindu-centric. The far-right only took off from there and is without any inhibitions [today]. Where is this politics headed now?

S. W.: I cannot remember exactly how Anderson put it, but I think my view may be slightly different. In my estimation, Gandhi and Nehru were not advocates of a Hindu state or Hindutva politics. But they engaged in populist politics through their espousal of the ideology of liberal democracy.

With that caveat in mind, to comment on the first part of your question: it would not be wrong to say that the needs of Indian electoral politics enabled far-right politics of both the Hindu and the Muslim variety. It took India forty-five years (if we were to use 1992 as the 'start date') to forsake secularism overtly.

As for your question in the second part, I do not mean to be glib, but the politics of India, if it maintains the current course, is headed towards no less than a dismantling of what we have known since 1947, a further [sense of] dysfunction in South Asia, and a very complex economic and political problematic for the world at large, in a region that is home to two billion human souls.

K. B.: I understand what you say about Kashmiri nationalism being subsumed, but is there a brand of 'Kashmiri nationalism' or nationalism for all which constitutes the same elements?

S. W.: It is difficult to answer this question for a variety of reasons: (*a*) The question seems to assume that the Kashmir conundrum is a dispute over identity rather than a political [dispute] that has become one about identity. The two approaches are different and will result in different responses. (*b*) You cannot have a subjective definition of 'nationalism' because it ends up creating an internal logic which makes the discussion not one about justice (truth), but of mere validity (logic). And (*c*) it is difficult to tell from the arguments of any of the parties (India, Pakistan and Kashmir) to the dispute whether by 'Kashmir' they mean the valley or the erstwhile undivided (on both sides of the Line of Control [LoC]) state of J&K.

My point of departure has been to respond to the dispute from the historical location of 1946, when a collective of nations was made a state by a combination of conquest, political bargaining and administrative convenience—which is how most states are made. It is the convergence of these acts that makes the dispute a political and territorial one. It has been my argument that identity, or nationalism, emerged as an instrumentalist argument by opportunist argumentation on the part of politicians among all the three parties to the dispute.

K. B.: Given Kashmir's Hindu and Buddhist history, which the current regime routinely invokes, what do Kashmiris think of Indian nationalism or the idea of India?

S. W.: States, whether they are large (such as the former Soviet Union formed after Tsarist Russia, India formed after British India or Communist China formed after Qing China) or small (such as Nepal, Sikkim or J&K) are artificial territorial entities that come into being from time to time, given the ups and downs of political power and brute force. The Kashmir valley has had Buddhist, Hindu, Muslim, Sikh, Hindu and secular (in that chronological order) governments ruling it. In such a scenario, the present must respond both to 'the pastness of the past, and its presence', to cite the poet and philosopher, T. S. Eliot.

As to what Kashmiris think of Indian nationalism, that depends on what 'nationalism' means at any given point. It would be fair to say that today, Kashmiris see Indian 'nationalism' as an aspiring Hindu majoritarian nationalism that has prevailed over other ideas of India.

K. B.: Is there an overarching idea of Kashmir?

S. W.: I am sure there is, but it would be difficult for me to define its articulations immediately and briefly.

K. B.: The sub-national narrative is also a favourite of fringe organisations and armed militias, who assert themselves without realising that [their plank] could have been simply nationalism and not sub-nationalism.

S. W.: This question is moot if you make a distinction between 'sub' and 'non-sub' nationalism. But nationalism is nationalism. If you have an argument that is predicated upon the importance of identity first in political life, then nationalism will have a role. So 'fringe' and 'armed' organisations are born because of this real or perceived threat to blood and soil.

K. B.: Is it semantics, then, in a sense that allows governments to negotiate to their advantage? How has semantics played out in the Kashmiri nationality/nationalism rhetoric?

S. W.: Governments are able to dictate—not negotiate—their advantage because of power, not semantics. Governments have it and people do not. So people use rhetoric to mobilise and governments use power to stop them. Semantics—such as the Camp David Accord and the Delhi Agreement—are the outcome of meek hope and bold hypocrisy on the part of peoples and government, respectively.[44]

K. B.: The far right Hindu and Muslim politics have, in a way, subsumed all the other voices. Even the Kashmiri common person's voice is lost in the din. How does one go beyond the right or left voices?

S. W.: I truly wish I had the answer to that question. It would go a long way in solving much of South Asia's problems!

K. B.: Have the last few months broken the Kashmiri will, or is it a matter of time before they raise their voice?

S. W.: The Kashmiri is resisting suppression and oppression. Resistance is like water; it finds its own level and keeps moving forward in one way or another. So no; the last few months will not break them if the last thirty years, the last seventy years and the last 400-plus years have not broken them. Nor have they fallen silent. They do and will continue to raise their voices.

K. B.: Is a balkanised India a more prudent way to move ahead?

S. W.: The word 'balkanisation' implies the dismembering or the disintegration of a state, society or other entity. I do not advocate it because balkanisation augurs a chaotic, inchoate and dangerous precedent for this region and for the world. Besides, the etymology of the word has a very negative connotation. That said, we cannot also deny that almost three centuries ago, colonisation dismantled huge tracts of traditional territorial, economic, social and political entities in Latin America, Africa and Asia. Starting in the mid-twentieth century, the process of decolonisation did not address this historical injustice and the political inheritors of colonial power did not address the injustices to the traditional set-up either. As a result, there have been historical injustices on all the four continents mentioned above. These need to be addressed in the light of both past and present. It applies to decolonisation in India too. In this context, if by balkanise you mean degrees of decentralisation so that India can move ahead, then I would agree with you. India will move ahead only if it looks ahead; it cannot do this by pursuing a purist past for the modern Indian state, as it is doing today.

A Kashmiri Pandit in Jammu[45]

When you go to the Teen Murti Bhavan, you see a *kalam* written, 'We were Kashmiri Pandatas from the Himalayas of Kashmir'. Nehru has signed it. That means we have a relationship and commonality with our ancestors. Nationally we may be Indians, but culturally we are Kashmiris. It is about a belief that whichever country you belong to, you are a national of that country. The rest is all a documentary proof. If I am an Indian citizen, but I do not feel I belong there, then what is the purpose served? I will be a traitor then. Nationality is where you feel you belong, what your mind has accepted. So you don't think about what your nation has been able to give you. You think in terms of what you can give back to the land that nurtures you.

The ones who made me leave my city were the citizens of this country. Why did I not go to Pakistan, Bangladesh or Nepal? Why did I tell my children that you go to Hindustan and study in Bangalore or Mumbai? Because we accept this nation as ours. It is a different thing to say that I have my problems with the government. Government and nation are two different entities. Governments change. When teachers teach a student, they don't think about whether the child is a Kashmiri or Haryanvi, they think these children are the future of our country. If someone hates my children, then I feel this nation is not mine.

When it comes to talking about the good of my country, it is patriotism. In the *Mahabharata*, in the *Bhishma Purana*, the following is written. When Bhishma Pitama is lying on a bed of arrows, he tells Yudhisthir that there are many widows and they need a son to take care of them, be it from the Kauravas or the Pandavas so that they have food, clothing, etc. Draupadi suddenly laughed. Bhishma says he knows why she laughed. He tells her, whenever something unwanted is happening, we must raise our voice. If we do not have the courage, then we must leave from there. When you (Draupadi) were being disrobed in front of the entire court, despite being the eldest, I could not raise my voice. But it was my duty that I leave the room, so I did. There is a lesson in here. In Kashmir, when slogans of azadi and merger with Pakistan were being raised, it was my duty to revolt. The same fear was there in the Muslims as well. That when wrong will happen, it will be [resisted]. As I was not in favour of what was happening, I left Kashmir. I was in line with my Rashtradharma. Deshbhakti does not mean I will only be happy when Kapil Dev will win a World Cup. It means that even when he doesn't, I will maintain the same respect. Deshbhakti is not just the flag or the national anthem.

Culturally, I am a Kashmiri. When you say Kashmiriyat, it stems from the traditions of Kashmir. Say in the month of *Maagh*, the tradition in our house was that more rice will be cooked, so that some is left over. Why should it be left? So that the daughter-in-law of the house can feed it to the animals. Why only in the month of Maagh? It is the coldest month of the year. The entire land is covered with snow. Where will the animals get food? In this weather, you'd not want to cook it in the morning either, so save it for them from the previous meal. During *Sawan* in Kashmir, no one would eat fish. Why? Sawan is the breeding month for fish. Eating one fish would mean we are stopping the birth of 1,000 others. On *Amavasya*, we would prepare khichdi with a lot of spices and keep it under a tree. Why? These spices and rice protect the wild animals in severe cold conditions. Our culture is different. We don't follow what Hindustanis do. You celebrate your birthdays according to the British traditions. Till date in our tradition, yellow rice is prepared, the devis and devatas are offered rice, the *janeyu* is changed. We follow the lunar calendar, not the solar one. Our tradition and cultures are different from what other Indians follow.

Nationality is about being [part of] the nation. We have no control over it. But language, culture and traditions distinguish us.

We celebrate Shivratri with splendour, not Diwali. While the rest of India celebrate Janmashtami, we celebrate Saptami. This is to signify that we must fast for the protector who is to come. It is the time of the labour pains that is pious for us.

I was so scared when we initially arrived. I was a complete outsider. But then slowly, while I stayed with my brother-in-law in Chandigarh for some time, I got used to it. They also started seeming human then.

Northeast of river Jhelum—give that territory to us, the Kashmiri Pandits. Declare it a Union Territory. Then we do not have to run. We cannot face a cultural death because there is no scope for revival. I don't want to see Kashmiriyat die.

Sajik Tampak

Agha Shahid Ali's *The Country without a Post Office* could well have been set in Sajik Tampak.

I arrived here sometime in 2004 when a massive military operation was being carried out in the area, referred to locally as the 'valley of death'. We had travelled there on the Indian Army's assurance that they would facilitate our movement to this place. However, the defence ministry decided otherwise, and we were asked to either return or try and reach Sajik Tampak on our own and, of course, at our own risk. Obviously, we chose the latter, and hired a Tata Sumo vehicle in curfew-bound Imphal. A stout middle-aged man was the only person willing to risk this journey and drive us there. I was tentative about our odds, but it was worth taking a chance. At several bends of the journey, I was almost certain that we would be ambushed. The only hurdles were army *nakas* (barricades), but curiously enough, each post let us pass, asking only that we not reveal we were allowed to go through. That was amusing because one could not reach the forward posts without negotiating the previous ones, and it would be apparent that we had been provided passage. However, the journey was not without its risks.

We finally reached the destination, the town of Sajik Tampak, and met with the commandant, a Sikh army officer. He made me coffee and sat down to convince me that the army has been empathetic to the villagers. He told me how he had once been humiliated as a young officer returning home to Punjab in a bus during the years of Khalistan terrorism, and how his approach as a commanding officer had therefore changed. He was sitting in a half-built concrete office that he said was the adam-base for all valley-based UG (underground) groups to collect ransom and extortion money. It is here that the groups summoned 'culprits' from the valley for trials and to mete out punishment—often a bullet shot at the knee. He was a jolly good man who, like his other colleagues, made me promise that no one should know he had met me. There was a strange game being played here, but I did not mind.

As I entered the village, the only landmark that caught my attention was a huddle of people on the staircase of a wooden cottage that needed urgent repairs. There was a postbox tied to one of the pillars on the verandah. I was told that this was the post office. Except, in the past twenty years or so, not a single letter had ever arrived or been posted here. No Indian administrative officer or personnel had visited them in recent memory.

The village was readied with artillery guns and helicopter gunships and villagers were being evacuated for a final onslaught on any possible militant hideouts. It was a complete warzone without any gunfire. This was one of Manipur's many 'liberated zones', which in many ways lie outside the control of the Indian state. The irony of it all is that the state has finally decided to liberate the place from stranglehold of armed militias.[46]

Now no one writes letters any more. That postbox may still be there, waiting for its first letter.

Manipur has been the eastern outpost challenging the limits of Indian democracy. The year 2019 marked seventy-five years since the most decisive battle of the Second World War, fought here at the Red Hill and won by the Allied Forces.[47] Since then, this kingdom, later annexed controversially by India,[48] has been witness to the most violent and non-violent resistance against the Indian state. The narrative of Partition and nation-building does not fit here. None of the security and academic templates is applicable to its reality. Although it was the neighbouring Naga Hills that first raised the question of nationality, it is Manipur that has stood its ground against the notion of nationalism.

Chhits Nationality

In April 2001, I set off for the Indian border with Bangladesh at Pyrdiwah, Dawki, not far from where I had grown up, but an altogether unfamiliar place. We arrived late one morning and witnessed the Indian Border Security Force (BSF) taking positions for what appeared to be an imminent war: bunkers, mortars, heavy troop deployment. We jumped into an Indian security jeep to enter what is Bangladesh territory, and within a few metres, again entered Indian territory, where a battalion of Indian soldiers were being held hostage. Let me explain: the Bangladesh Rifles (BDR) had encircled this plot of Indian land and asked the soldiers to vacate. It was like conquering India inside Bangladesh. It was an eyeball-to-eyeball confrontation, and both sides were waiting for the other to open fire. A day later, at another part of the border, sixteen BSF soldiers were abducted, tortured and killed. I was there on that summer afternoon to witness the Indian state receiving the mutilated bodies. India decided not to go to war with Bangladesh, and the issue was diplomatically resolved.

This 4,090 kilometre-long border is unlike any other international border. Partially fenced, it has stretches of jungle, rivers, streams, and a bizarre number of enclaves or 'chhits' that exist in isolation within another nation. Some are as small as 50 square metres, the size of a small apartment in an Indian city. Some are even enclaves within enclaves, like a little India within Bangladesh and then another Bangladesh within that as well. Now go figure out your nationality! Identity was blurred; students, for example, had to register under false names. Medical facilities were not available, nor could the residents cast their votes in their chosen country. The movement of people was complicated. They were bona fide citizens, yet not acknowledged by the state. The bitter relationship between India and Pakistan—and later India and Bangladesh—did not help the residents. In both countries, the people of the 'chitt mahals' were looked upon with suspicion.

It is popularly believed that three centuries ago, the Raja of Cooch Behar and the *faujdaar* of a district in Mughal Bengal played chess with local villages as the wager.[49] As a result, with each game of chess, one village was lost to the winning side. Another theory is that in the war between the Mughals and Cooch Behar, the Mughals could not evict some of the zamindars, despite their win. Under feudal law, as long as these zamindars paid the tax, Delhi was happy and so the land was never given up. Given that Cooch Behar was a princely state, Sir Cyril Radcliffe did not run his pencil through this kingdom, and this was passed on to India and Pakistan to resolve. These enclaves became the flashpoint of many skirmishes, and any effort to resolve the issue failed till May 2015, when the NDA-II government pushed through the truly historic 119th Amendment which facilitated the swapping of enclaves to redraw the border.

I search for my field notes, but I am not sure the people I met then are even alive. I come across an article I had asked my colleague Sudeep Mukhia to write on his visit just after the swap had taken place. It was for a website[50] I tried to run (I had to shut it down for paucity of funds), and he called his piece 'Fake Fathers of Mashaldanga.' The following is a telling excerpt from the article:

> At Ground Zero though, for those whom it mattered the most, things were far more subdued even though for them, Independence Day came two weeks early. It couldn't have come a day sooner, deprived of schools, hospitals, police—every facility that administration provides, because neither state can technically enter the other's territory. For these people, the struggle was to prove their very existence, because they really were no-where people, neither Indians nor Bangladeshis, without an identity or a nationality.
>
> Inside the enclaves, what people went through was beyond these abstractions. It wasn't a matter of material survival: I saw no apparent poverty, homelessness, beggars or destitutes. The struggle for these people was a very basic one, that tore apart and laid bare in public even the most personal; like who [is] the father of Anu Ara's children?
>
> He is standing right next to her, Muzamil, slight and shorter than her, in an oversized shirt and pants. So why did she say her children had four different fathers? Both of them look away in silence before a neighbour pitches in. 'Inside the chhiths we have no schools or colleges and we can't leave the chhitths because we have no papers, so....' By now, Anu Ara has taken over the conversation. 'So we have to name an Indian man as the father so that our children get some kind of identification papers and attend schools outside.' Who are these men? They could be relatives or just random friends of friends who were paid for pretend paternity.

Every day for sixty-eight years, a large number of citizens were excluded from legal rights and exploited in every way on a daily basis as they occupied an absent space. They were only the subjects of academic case studies on theories of 'statelessness'.

Mapping a Crown Colony

Since the departure of the British, various ideas about establishing hill polities have been in circulation in today's Northeast India. The British tried for some time to interest the hill people in the idea of a Crown Colony, which also comprised parts of what became Burma and Bangladesh. The Naga leaders, who were by then already mobilising for their own sovereign state, dodged the plan, and it was soon dropped.

The Khasi leader and educationist Rev. B. M. Pugh provides an interesting account of the demand for a separate homeland in his autobiography:

> So we agitated for the separation from Assam.... We felt then that the [State Reorganisation] Commission did not want to create a State for the hill areas only, as they feared...that it would be a Christian State.... [W]e felt that this prejudice was the real reason for not giving us a separate State.... A hill State comprising, as we envisaged then, of the present Meghalaya, Nagaland, Arunachal, Mizoram, and the two districts of Mikir and North Cachar Hills, would have been a much bigger State and a much more viable State than the present individual mini-States.... The only advantage which might accrue to the Centre from the creation of these small States is what comes from the oft-quoted policy of 'divide and rule.'[51]

The balkanisation of the region was a result of similar schemes. In the 1950s, the Nagas reacted against the Assam government's decision to make Assamese the state language. Ironically, in the nineteenth century, Assam had fought against the British imposition of Bengali as the language for administrative convenience. Later, the Mizo National Front waged an almost decisive guerilla war against the Indian state after the latter's failure to provide aid during the disastrous famine of 1958–59. As recently as 2010, R. K. Meghen, the chief of the United National Liberation Front (UNLF) in Manipur, was in discussion with other separatist leaders for an autonomous homeland. But therein lies a contradiction of sorts; most insurgent organisations across these seven states were founded on the conviction that the Indian state had failed to deliver development. In that sense, the separatists in Northeast India seem to 'straddle between a kind of longing for the state and the opposite, that is, a rejection of it'.[52]

The study of the Northeast over the last seventy-five years, since the Second World War and the first hoisting of the national flag of India in Moirang, Manipur, by the Indian National Army in 1944, is a study in contested nationalisms.

Some are of the opinion that India's 'Northeast' is an invention of post-independence India. 'But this geographical expression appears to have an older root,' write Zou and Kumar.

> For instance, a British military report in 1883 by Captain St. John Mitchell on upland Assam was titled 'The North-East Frontier of India', and another influential report in 1884 by Alexander Mackenzie referred to 'the North-East frontier' of Bengal shown on an Indian Survey map to the scale of 1 inch to 32 miles.[53]

For much of the second half of the nineteenth century, explorers around the world had been mystified about what happened to the Tsangpo River after it disappeared from the map in southeastern Tibet. In a run of only 320 km, four of the major rivers of Asia descend from the Tibetan Plateau, confined in great gorges—the Yangtze, the Mekong, the Salween, and the Irrawaddy. River explorers were convinced the Tsangpo was a tributary of one of these rivers. On the plains of Assam, three more rivers unite to form the Brahmaputra—the Lohit, the Dibang, and the Dihang. A few suspected that the Tsangpo had bent sharply to the south and emerged as the Brahmaputra, but if that were the case, this would be an incredible natural phenomenon. There had to be a majestic waterfall bigger than the Niagara or Victoria, and may well be the new wonder of the world.

The exploration of the Tsangpo and Brahmaputra is a fascinating odyssey of explorers, writers, botanists, pilgrims and pilgrim-spies. But what this exploration really did was to introduce 'mensural recording', moving away from the earlier trigonometric surveys. In trying to solve the Tsangpo-Brahmaputra riddle[54] (an illiterate tailor from Darjeeling, Kinthup, eventually mapped the river in 1880, but the riddle was solved only in 1997 when Ian Baker finally reached the bottom of the falls, in a gorge within a gorge),

> the Indian Survey densely mapped the identity of a river that largely defined 'British Assam' and, by extension, the geo-body of Northeast India. Writing in the 1940s in his *Discovery of India*, Jawaharlal Nehru reassured himself about the Indian identity of the Tsangpo-Brahmaputra, which forces 'its way into India through deep chasms cut in the heart of the northeastern mountains', but his elite nationalist eyes saw it as 'rather cut off from the main current of history'.[55]

Although mapping this region was not the intended outcome of this exploration, once this uncharted terrain was mapped, a British census official was confronted with a bigger challenge: the 'gap between cartographic... and ethnographic Assam. The map of British Assam loosely included the whole of Northeast India—even Sylhet and the princely state of Manipur.'[56] They demarcated the borderland with internal and external boundaries. This was a colonial administrative policy in frontier regions to keep rebellious population at bay, preventing them from entering revenue earning areas and ensuring control. These areas were seen as mere geographical territory that had to be retained by force. Thus, the post-independence obsession with securitising the borders stems from a colonial idea of territoriality.

It is often forgotten in today's context, yet well-established, that the so-called Northeast 'is a result of overlapping territoriality and sovereignty, which characterizes the indigenous polity of this region and has been since a very long time'.[57]

If you 'reshuffle the geography' as Karlsson suggests, 'alternate starting points' could help us try and understand the 'making of a region' where the flow of human beings has been going on over centuries.[58] These borderlands have had multiple jurisdictions for centuries. Concepts of sovereignty and governance are found in various systems, for example, in monastic dual governance. Pre-colonial Northeast India was structured around networks of monasteries that extended over large territories. Wealthy women were patrons and dual governance was a feature of these networks. For example, as historian Indrani Chatterjee, who has studied this subject extensively, notes: 'In Bhutan between 17th to 19th centuries deb raja (druk desi) was the secular head and dharma raj (je khenpo) was the chief abbott'. In

Assam, the Bar Gosain was a minister in the Ahom courts and a king in Jaintia hills. The ascetics or gurus became ministers who ran the affairs of the state. With the coming of the East India Company, these networks were broken, and their lands seized for tea plantations. Chatterjee argued in a public lecture in 2017 that 'the borders of the North-East in modern terms began, I would argue, with the war in the Western Himalayas and because of the Gorkha expansion into Garhwal and Kumaon and the Anglo-Gorkha war'.[59]

Clearly, the various sub-national narratives prevalent in India's Northeast will be difficult to corroborate historically, but it is easier to read the assertions from the non-state space of James C. Scott's very popular *The Art of Not Being Governed*. However, I disagree with the use of Scott's conceptual framework for the study of the region. As Karlsson says, 'The Art of Not Being Governed transgresses the rigid boundary between South Asian and Southeast Asian studies. Northeast India has tended to fall in between these two academic specializations, being neither a proper part of South Asia nor of Southeast Asia.'[60]

The Anti-National as the Anti-hero

> The first right of a citizen is to secede.
>
> The people should gird themselves up and kill a cruel king who does not protect his subjects, who extracts taxes and simply robs them of their wealth, who gives no lead. Such a king is Kali (evil and strife) incarnate. The king who after declaring, 'I shall protect you', does not protect his subjects should be killed (by the people) after forming a confederacy, like a dog that is afflicted with madness.[61]

It is 15 January 2020. Posters have been circulated through social media for a large gathering of artists, students and civil society in New Delhi's Jamia Millia Islamia. In December 2019, this university witnessed an obscene example of state violence that was let loose on unarmed and unsuspecting students. This was the beginning of the 'nationwide' protests against the amended Citizenship Act and the NRC. The protests did not stop there, and spread across states after this day. The state, however, hardened its stand and unleashed every possible means to beat the citizenry into obedience.

I followed the protests during this time. There cannot be a more opportune moment in our history to write about the 'anti-national' than now. I recall what Dharampal had written about civil disobedience in 1810, when people in many states rose to non-violent protest against additional taxation at a time of economic duress. He was invoking the mass protests at Banaras, Patna, Saran, Murshedabad and Bhagalpur against the British imposition of taxes on houses and shops. Dharampal argues that the British had to beat people into a 'state of unquestioning obedience' because of their extreme insecurity:

> If the dates, (1810–12) were just advanced by some 110 to 120 years, the name of the tax altered and a few other verbal changes made, this narrative could be taken as a fair recital of most events in the still remembered civil disobedience campaigns of the 1920s and 1930s.[62]

He, however, clarifies that it is not the same, because people could at least express resistance then, whereas a century later, people could no longer move on their own till Gandhi's satyagraha created another phase of mass uprising. In his extraordinary collation of documents of Indian and British source materials pertaining to the right of the citizen to dissent and to hold the government of the day accountable, Dharampal's work appears to be extremely significant to a regime that harks back to ancient Indian traditions.

Dharampal draws from James Mill's observation that 'in the late seventeenth and eighteenth century…"in the ordinary state of things in India, the princes stood in awe of their subjects."'. Further, he quotes Gandhi: '[The idea that] we should obey laws whether good or bad is a new fangled notion. There was no such thing in former days. The people disregarded those laws they did not like.' The Gandhian notion of 'passive resistance' is connected to this practice; Dharampal cites Gandhi's explanation that '[t]he fact is that, in India, the nation at large has generally used passive resistance in all departments of life. We cease to cooperate with our rulers when they displease us. This is passive resistance.'[63]

Protest is a citizen's right, but it would be interesting to see how the citizens then protested in accordance with rules of the state and tradition of civil disobedience. According to Dharampal's records, in 1810, the Government of Bengal (Fort William) decided to levy a new house tax. The first protests broke out in Banaras on account of the reasons systematically cited by the citizens:

> (i) Former sooltauns never extended the rights of Government (commonly called malgoozaree) to the habitations of their subjects acquired by them by descent or transfer. It is on this account that in selling estates the habitations of the proprietors are excepted from the sales. Therefore the operation of this tax infringes upon the rights of the whole community, which is contrary to the first principles of justice.
> (ii) It is clear that the house tax was enacted only for the purpose of defraying the expenses of the police. In the provinces of Bengal and Behar, the police expenses are defrayed out of the stamp and other duties, and in Benares the police expenses are defrayed from the land revenue (malgoozaree). Then on what grounds is this tax instituted?
> (iii) If the Shastra be consulted it will be found that Benares to within five coss round is a place of worship and by Regulation XV 1810 places of worship are exempted from the tax.
> (iv) There are supposed to be in Benares about 50,000 houses, near three parts of which are composed of places of worship of Hindoos and Mussulman and other sects and houses given in charity by Mussulman and Hindoos. The tax on the rest of the houses will little more than cover the expenses of the Phatuckbundee. Then the institution of a tax which is calculated to vex and distress a number of people is not proper or consistent with the benevolence of Government.[64]

There were other such reasons; for example, the argument that people who did not even have enough to repair their houses would not be able to pay taxes. In the face of severe hardship and a steady price rise over ten years, how did the government expect the citizens to pay more?

On 25 December 1810, the acting magistrate wrote to the Governor-General-in-Council that 'a very serious situation has been excited among all ranks and descriptions of the inhabitants of the city by the promulgation of Regulation XV, 1810'. He went on to describe further how the 'clamorous' and 'tumultuous' mob revived the agitation after suspending it for a few hours as troops were mobilised:

> [T]he agitation was revived: an oath was administered throughout the city both among the Hindoos and the Mahommedans, enjoining all classes to neglect their respective occupations until

> I should consent to direct the collector to remove the assessors and give a positive assurance that the tax should be abolished. It was expected that the outcry and distress occasioned by this general conspiracy would extort from me the concession they required. The Lohars, the Mistrees, the Hujams, the Durzees, the Kahars, Bearers, every class of workmen engaged unanimously in this conspiracy and it was carried to such an extent, that during the 26th the dead bodies were actually cast neglected into the Ganges, because the proper people could not be prevailed upon to administer the customary rites. These several classes of people, attended by multitude of others of all ranks and descriptions, have collected together at a place in the vicinity of the city, from whence they declare nothing but force shall remove them unless I consent to yield the point for which they are contending.[65]

On 31 December 1810, the acting magistrate sent another report:

> Several thousands of people continue day and night collected at a particular spot in the vicinity of the city, where, divided according to their respective classes, they inflict penalties upon those who hesitate to join in the combination. Such appears to be the general repugnance to the operation of the Regulation, that the slightest disposition evinced by any individual to withdraw from the conspiracy, is marked not only by general opprobrium but even ejectment from his caste.[66]

As the protests continued, the acting magistrate kept sending missives till the Government in Bengal took note, and 'to warn the refractory part of the community of the serious evils, which under the foregoing orders, they are liable to bring upon themselves by a further perseverance in their present seditious conduct'.[67]

Mark the word 'seditious', initially used by the British and later appropriated by successive Indian governments to crush any dissent.

By 13 January 1811, following the Bengal Government's rejection of the public petition, people started to gather together again, and the magistrate saw no alteration in their mood despite official proclamations. In his concluding note, the magistrate cautioned that the collection of increased tax should not be attempted without larger military reinforcements since the people will not be 'reconciled easily'.

The protest in Banaras that spilled across the Presidency to Patna, Sarun, Moorshedabad and Bhagalpur continued, until people probably realised that such a mode of protest was futile against an 'alien' government that was not accustomed to their 'subjects' raising their voices. People still protest in much the same manner, but over 200 years later, the difference is that while in the past, people could mobilise on their own, such actions are now banned immediately and the protesters branded as 'anti-nationals'.

K. Santhanam, who wore many hats, from being the first editor of *The Indian Express* to setting up the Central Vigilance Commission (CVC), maintained that the quickest way to defend fundamental rights is civil disobedience. Dharampal, too, quotes Santhanam while discussing what constitutes a denial of rights. The argument clearly puts the onus on the state and its failings:

> What acts of state destroy a state? What constitutes denial of fundamental rights? Answers to these cannot be determined by recourse to mere legality. To take one glaring example: large scale hunger and insecurity are both fast corroding the foundations of the Indian state and its constitution, as well as constituting a denial of the most fundamental human right...the inability or insensitivity of the state in eliminating them...is fast leading India to a subversion of the constitution and state structure. The practice of non-cooperation and civil disobedience for eliminating hunger and insecurity... could have, and may yet if initiated in time, make such subversion much more difficult, if not impossible.[68]

The 'anti-national' is, in a sense, the typical anti-hero of literature and films. In reality, the anti-national/anti-hero emerges from the pages of history in times of social crisis to occupy public spaces like Shaheen Bagh in 2020, for example.

The anti-hero reappeared in the latter half of the twentieth century when once again, power and resistance took centrestage in postcolonial hegemony. This coincided with an almost unprecedented rise in armed political resistance against newly-formed states. India is a case in point, where armed and unarmed insurrections in the last seventy years are unparalleled anywhere in the world. While movements like Quit India, Civil Disobedience, and the Revolt of 1857 shaped India's freedom struggle, the post-Independence years were fraught with increasing resistance: the Anti-Hindi movement in the south of India, the Assam Agitation in the east, Navnirman Andolon that started in Ahmedabad before spreading to Bihar, the

Mandal Commission protests, Telengana statehood protest, Bodoland (Udayachal) demands that later turned into full-blown terrorist violence, protests against the Emergency (of 1977–79), Narmada Bachao Andolan, CAA protests or protests against Farm Laws. The most violent theatres, of course, were Punjab, Jammu and Kashmir, Nagaland, Mizoram, Manipur, Tripura, Assam, Arunachal Pradesh, Meghalaya and the LWE (Left Wing Extremism) corridor that cuts right through the 'mainland' of the country in Bengal, Jharkhand, Bihar, Chhattisgarh, Andhra Pradesh, Odisha and Maharashtra. Violence induces more violence from both the state and the non-state. Even non-violent protests are very often violent because the state monopolises legitimate force, which triggers violence. Even as early as 1960, a *Times of India* editorial on police firings read, 'Not the least depressing part of this dismal situation is that police firings are no longer regarded as something greatly out of ordinary. Familiarity has bred cynicism both among rulers and ruled.... There is new and frightening normalcy, with violence constantly in the air'.[69] After the First World War, Europe had witnessed an era of anti-heroes, where, as Yeats writes, 'the center cannot hold' and 'things fall apart'. It would be a mistake to consider an anti-hero the opposite of a hero. The same character could be seen as an anti-hero or a hero—it only depends on the time when this character emerges.

A word not in circulation outside literary usage is the picaro of the picaresque novels. Is Don Quixote a picaro? Cervantes, its creator, would agree. The picaresque is an untidy, chaotic, yet colourful world. It is characterised by a feudal social order, decaying towns and cities, where one survives through wit and trickery. The knights have evaporated into fantasy, faced with an unforgiving reality. On that stage was born Cervantes and the picaresque, and a confused but caring Quixote and Sancho Panza.

I began this book with a description of Don Quixote tilting at windmills. Quixote says his quest is to end injustice. He is neither a fool nor a madman. He sees what we see; yet, he sees something else, too. Together with Sancho, they know more than we do. 'Do we know exactly who we are?' Do we know what is the quest of the anti-hero and the anti-national? Not until we are ourselves Quixotic:

> His fantasy filled with everything he had read in his books, enchantments as well as combats, battles, challenges, wounds,

> courtings, loves, torments, and other impossible foolishness, and he became so convinced in his imagination of the truth of all the countless grandiloquent and false inventions he read that for him no history in the world was truer.[70]

The Beginning of an End[71]

The train has not moved in the past five hours. It is somewhere in Maharashtra, and with no stations nearby, there is no water or food. The nightmare has just become real. Jolly rests her head on the window bars and moves between sleep and wakefulness, hunger and thirst, hopelessness and fear. This is no regular train journey; everyone is trying to cover their faces and keep their distance from an invisible enemy. Her father has passed out from exhaustion. The entire compartment is a hellish pile of masked, hungry people. The fear in their eyes has now been replaced by sleep or blank stares.

A train passes by at high speed. She wakes up with a start and her whole life flashes before her. Jolly came to Mumbai when she was six years old. Her mother worked as a domestic help and her father worked in a factory. They occupied a small chawl in Dharavi. She lost her mother when she was ten and now, at thirteen, she manages to earn a little and looks after the house. Where is she headed? Her home has been Dharavi, so why are they going 'home' to Gosaigaon where she does not belong? How will life be any different there? Her father, who was asked to leave the factory where he worked, thinks that returning to the village may help them survive. Whatever they had saved has been spent in the past forty days. She had packed some rotis and *achaar* (pickles) for the journey, but it seems endless.

Jolly's father had changed three jobs in the past year and is now unemployed. The village back 'home' does not guarantee any livelihood either. They had an acre of land between three brothers, but since the last riots,[72] the land has been fallow. Jolly's idea of 'riots' is of people hitting each other, frustrated with living. She has no idea that back 'home', the riots are deeply racist and political. But she has always been curious about why she was born as Fatima but lives as Jolly. No one has clearly explained this to her.

Over the past few years, she has heard her father speak anxiously about some 'papers' and about their identities. The words 'Musalman' and 'Miya' were used repeatedly in those conversations. Jolly could not grasp why papers are important in determining who she is. She is a human being, and a girl who had to grow up faster then her friends. On 15 August, she dresses up and goes for the flag hoisting ceremony. She would have loved to go to school, but that did not happen. So how will 'papers' help her? Her father would explain what she should say if officers came and questioned them. Living in Dharavi, she had no idea of any other identity, until December, when there were protests and she joined them too. They sang songs and she joined the chorus. It had something to do with citizenship and 'papers'. It was totally incomprehensible to her.

The train started moving as Jolly was recalling her mother's burial. She just died suddenly, without warning, before they could even take her to hospital. The only thing she realised that day was that she had to fend for herself. Her father was usually away all day, and would return late at night, often drunk. Abdul would not let her be at peace, so she gave in. Surrendering to one is better than being abused by everyone. Thank goodness for NGOs like ACORN Foundation, who work to improve the lives of hawkers and street dwellers; now she has a community to spend time with. They recycle waste to create art and display it across the city, so as to awaken a sense of optimism and humanity in fellow people. The Dharavi project or Artefacting Mumbai is an immersive documentation of the world's biggest slum in its squalid environs. Jolly was part of that journey. She has rarely stepped out from this sea of humanity where every possible activity can be encountered. You grow up much faster in Dharavi than anywhere else. She was lucky not to end up in the brothel. With Abdul, it is just one man. In the real world a single girl like her would have to fight many Abduls. Like the electric poles breaking up the vision from a speeding train, her thoughts are violently interrupted, moving between her past and present. Speed often helps in moving on.

Abdul is a good-looking man with almond eyes. Through his stories about his village in Kashmir, she learnt about how young girls and boys take up guns and shoot the police and the army. But why do they do that? It sounds like a beautiful place where everything is pretty. Last year, Abdul's cousin was shot in the eyes and he is now blind. They have apple trees in their garden. She has never tasted an apple. How can apples grow in your house garden? They even see snow. She has only heard that snow is very white. They also have flowers, lots of flowers. There was a time when she used to sell flowers at road intersections.

The train arrives at a station where they speak in a language she finds familiar, although she cannot comprehend the words. It may take another two days to reach her father's village, where another life awaits her. No one wants to get off the train and there is nothing in the station to eat. Some are trying to fill water. Everyone has a mask or a dupatta or *gamcha* covering the mouth. Even the few stray dogs look hungry. Why are adults so scared of one invisible virus when there are so many others floating around? It is only us, human beings, trying to flee and getting caught.

When I began writing this book, the NRC exercise was underway in Assam, and almost as if in a sequence, the state of Jammu and Kashmir was bifurcated. In the same vein, the Citizenship Amendment Act was passed in late 2019 and hundreds of protests were brutally crushed in its aftermath, eventually leading to a riot in the capital city. Days after the manuscript was ready, the world went underground due to a pandemic, and after three months in total isolation, as I wrote the conclusion to the book, I was confronted with newer and unrecognisable realities.

If one pauses to search for the appropriate words to describe the years 2019–21, nothing seems adequate to capture their essence or make sense of them.

In August 2019, some 1.9 million people in the state of Assam failed to make it to the National Register of Citizens. Jolly's family was excluded from the list, but since they were in Mumbai, they escaped the summons. Apparently, there was a clerical error in the spelling of their names. How do they even ascertain who gets into the list and who stays out? When Jolly learnt there was to be a list, and that if her name is not on it she may end up in a big, newly constructed jail, she was really scared. She told Abdul, and they decided to run away to a place where no one would recognise them. She did not want to go to a jail, and that is why she was so reluctant to return to her father's village. Perhaps they would sell her to someone. She had met so many inside Dharavi who were sold by their families. By thirteen, she recognises that she is worth only her body. So why are the officers so interested in names? The body of the citizen is lucrative. Perhaps they should have a list of able-bodied citizens who can do more work, a list of bodies of women who can earn by selling themselves or working as slaves in people's homes. The diseased and infirm could be in one list, as those easily dispensable. Jolly would surely make it to some list. If she is useful, then they might not throw her into those big jails filled with Muslims like her father. She dislikes being referred to by a religion she does not even profess. Her mother was not a Muslim, and that is why her father left home, because his community excommunicated him. After she died, they asked him to remarry. But he is either drunk or in the brothel. Now, in the village, Jolly fears they may get him remarried. She will have to look around for employment and then escape. But she loves him too; he is all she has. And unlike other fathers, he has never raised his hand on her.

There is no denying that the process of delegitimisation has created desperate situations. The NRC is prone to the inevitable clerical errors, and has put millions through unmitigated misery and stigmatised people and communities based primarily on language and religion. Amid anxieties and the announcement of a nationwide registry, detention centres that appear more like concentration camps were being built to house the people whose names were missing from a list prepared by untrained government staff, egged on by chauvinistic groups. The chilling fact was that many who were employed to build the detention centres feared they would find themselves or their family members jailed there. A report published by *Al Jazeera* describes one detention centre: 'Spread around nearly 300,000 square feet…of land, the detention centre in Goalpara's Matia village, 126 km…from Guwahati, can house 3,000 people.'[73] The outer wall is 6 feet high and the inner one spans 20 feet. Six watch towers will monitor the inmates and a 100-metre-high beam will keep vigil. The government had been housing suspected foreigners in jails and other facilities. Since 2008, 100 people have died in these centres, and many have committed suicide. Karanataka, Goa, Punjab, Delhi and Maharashtra have reportedly opened their detention centres. It is feared that the majority of the inmates will be Muslims.[74]

August 2019 is a month to remember: after the Assam NRC, the government rolled out its 'Akhand Bharat' Kashmir policy and imposed President's rule in the state. By October, the special provisions accorded to the region had been abrogated, the state was bifurcated and the world's longest known lockdown was imposed on its civilian population. Leaders were arrested, hundreds of people detained, and some even killed. In 2019, the state had fifty-five internet shutdowns and the internet has not been fully restored in view of terrorist attacks. Since then, there have been several occasions when the communication network cut off the people from the outside world. There is fatigue and mistrust. Eight million people in Kashmir have been deprived of access to education, livelihood, entertainment and even communication.[75]

In December 2019, the government passed the contentious Citizenship (Amendment) Act (CAA), aggravating fears and leading to huge protests across the country.

Then emerged the phenomenon of Shaheen Bagh, which captured the imagination of young India. Across several Indian states, a spontaneous movement led primarily by students fuelled a kind of energy unfamiliar to urban India. Rural India, too, was part of the chorus of voices that demanded justice and equal rights for all, fighting against discrimination based on religion and ethnicity. The voice was by the Indian, not only for the Indian, but also for the human being in India. How can one dispense with a human being and just cast them away? It framed its demand not through compassion, but justice. The state, taken aback by this outpouring of emotions, decided to crack down. The more the state hardened its stance, the more the voices that joined the chorus. Amidst the din, many Indians found themselves cornered, intimidated and arrested.

Shaheen Bagh starts from Jamia Millia Islamia University's Gate No. 7, which leads to the university's central quadrangle where a poorly sculpted statue of Delhi's most famous poet, Mirza Ghalib, stands guard. This nondescript locality in a Muslim-majority area suddenly awakened the nation's conscience by sustaining a protest against the government's proposed Citizenship (Amendment) Act. It is significant to note that through the coldest nights of December and January in the chilliest winter Delhi had experienced in 109 years, Shaheen Bagh emerged as the meeting ground for a pluralistic society, where Sikhs joined hands with Muslims in a fight against fundamentalism, where every community was eager to take the stage in protest. This is significant for anyone who knows the history of these two religions. Minorities were looking out for one another against Hindu majoritarian politics. Ghalib looked stunned at the sheer number of women from his own community, who, with the tricolour pinned on their hijabs, defined the protest. This was a moment to reckon with.

The protests grew sharper and spread across campuses and town halls and streets. This was a new India where the youth sang Faiz anthems and marched through barricades. But the legislative, the judiciary and even some sections within civil society perceive protest as a disruption that should be muzzled. That is the paradox of democracies; the elected state becomes a self-styled despot, out to punish the citizenry when it raises its voice in protest. The movement was immediately de-legitimised, and any utterances against the government became seditious. The dissenting citizen had to be forced into being an obedient citizen.

In February, blood was spilled on the streets. The capital city was shaken by murders, looting, and arson, as the police stood by, mere bystanders. The state, just like it had in 1984 or 2002, waited and watched till Arshad Alam, Amaan Iqbal, Deepak Kumar, Mohammad Hamza and forty-nine others died.[76]

Before the mourning was over, just as people had begun picking up the pieces to start afresh, the world went underground and everything was locked and barred. Death stalked the streets and a different kind of fear and stigma engulfed us.

By 11 March 2020, the police had filed over 700 FIRs, mostly against Muslims. The Muslim victims found it hard to file complaints of their own. By June, the police had filed a chargesheet against twenty Hindus for the murders of Hashim Ali and Amir Ali, two brothers caught in the violence while returning home. They were thrashed, stabbed, stripped naked and their bodies were dumped in a drain. The Muslims have been accused of plotting the conspiracy of a riot, and the Hindus were charged with violence 'as an act of revenge and retaliation'.[77]

By the third week of March, India and the Indian media suddenly discovered a new subject, 'the migrant worker'. Given that our last national census was conducted in 2011, the population figure of 1.3 billion may no longer be accurate, and the estimate of 400 million internal migrants may also be grossly understated. But let us assume there were 400 million internal migrants who had to return home after the world's most severe lockdown was imposed and they found themselves without jobs or money. There were no other means of transport, so they started walking. Many lost their lives on the way. The 'Gulagisation' of India was nearly complete.

We are so familiar with the stories and pictures of our citizenry walking across hundreds and thousands of kilometres, we can now recount them in our sleep. We created a new race, a community, as if they had never existed before the lockdown. The migrations recorded in India between 2001–11 show that this country had witnessed an extraordinary movement of human beings. But no one really sat up and took notice of this shift in demography. Urban India started adding more people than rural India ever did, except when 20 million perished in the so-called Spanish Flu of 1918.[78] While data may suggest that India is recovering from job losses and that salaried and informal job holders are going back to their pre-pandemic occupations, the reality is somewhat different. Researchers have pointed out that the recovery is sharply gendered; while 90 per cent of men have come back to work, 60 per cent women failed to return. Most people who lost their occupations became self-employed and others had to agree to income cuts. Families who have borrowed to survive the pandemic are burdened with debt. Many families who have lost their bread-winners seek to avail social welfare schemes to sustain themselves. The economic shock is yet to be absorbed, while the brutality and indifference towards migrant labourers may have only deepened.[79]

Who is this migrant worker? Why is a bona fide Indian citizen labelled a migrant? How did urban India not notice that millions of their own citizens existed in their own backyards? Now, when they began returning home, suddenly the domestic worker, the canteen boy, the construction worker, the apartment guard, the dhabas on the highway have become sources of stories. In the preceding chapters of this book, we have referred to the invisible Indian, the migrant Indian, the tribal Indian and the anti-Indian. The migrant worker is the new Indian, cast away, pitied by urban India, offered token help, but largely rejected and dismissed, only to be eventually held hostage by the virus and by their employers.

The civilisational crisis, as many are referring to these times, is not limited to India; however, the crisis in this country is unique.

When millions of people were locked down under insecurity, hunger, unemployment and deprivation, the government arrested citizens under draconian laws, accusing them of disrupting public order, triggering riots or indulging in anti-national activities. Those arrested ranged from academics to activists and students. Even a pregnant activist was jailed for merely questioning what many consider an unconstitutional act, the CAA.[80]

Migrant workers Tarini and Ayesha and Rony had been waiting for over three months in makeshift shanties, scavenging for food, exhausted of fear, and still hoping to get on some vehicles moving towards the highway.[81] India is not a country you can visualise in your mind. That helps. Rony could never have mustered the courage to get off NH 44 and start walking towards a home that was roughly 1,500 kilometres away. He had never dreamt of such a thing, and nor had the girl who bought a bicycle for Rs 2,000, seated her ailing father on it, and cycled 1,200 kilometres back to their village.[82]

Special trains, named Shramik Specials ('Worker Specials'), were pressed into service to carry the migrant workers back home.[83] The Shramik Special started from Bhayander in Mumbai to Gorakhpur in Uttar Pradesh, but the driver of the train lost his way and reached Rourkela instead. Jolly's train was similarly diverted. She had never seen these places, but most of them look desolate. The standing crop looks beautiful; in Mumbai, she has only seen the sea and chawls. Three hundred such trains were suddenly on the rails of India, many losing their way.

As the world entered June 2020, American streets were hit by protests against George Floyd's murder by the Chicago police in a global campaign, #blacklivesmatter.[84] There are moments in history that trigger larger debates, and race has always been one of those issues that have not found any recourse beyond angry protests and victimhood. Have there been Floyds in India? Just recall the number of citizens lynched on suspicion of selling or consuming beef. Count the number of police and army encounter deaths. Or picture the police beating people for simply not wearing a mask during the lockdown.[85]

The larger picture is one of injustice, of comprehending that if the state wishes it, anyone can be made to suffer, because suffering is the supreme sacrifice that contributes to nation-building. That 'anyone' is increasingly the marginal voice, the minority who can be recognised by the clothes they wear, and those among the majority who dare to protest against this injustice.

This book straddles the notion of citizenship, the idea of nationality, and the sense of identity through oral literature, case studies, memoirs, genealogy, reportage and archival accounts, both personal and collective. What comes through from these heterogeneous experiences is the banality of everydayness, where voices speak up and often their experiences collide and where the 'nation' is no longer in our 'imagination'. It is indeed the heart of darkness!

> *He cried in a whisper at some image, at some vision—he cried out twice, a cry that was no more than a breath: 'The horror! The horror!'*
>
> Marlowe in Joseph Conrad's *Heart of Darkness*[86]

Endnotes

1. *Shorter Oxford English Dictionary on Historical Principles*, 6th ed., Vol. 2: s.v. 'nation'.
2. Ibid.: s.v. 'nationalism'.
3. Ibid.: s.v. 'dissent'.
4. See https://www.merriam-webster.com/dictionary/anti-national (accessed August 2022).
5. Partha, Mitter. 1994. 'Preface'. In *Art and Nationalism in Colonial India, 1850-1922: Occidental Orientations*, xxv. Cambridge: Cambridge University Press.
6. Brahmoism is a theistic movement, founded by Raja Rammohan Roy in nineteenth-century Bengal, which denounced idol worship and the caste system among the Hindus. The Brahmos campaigned for reforms like education for women and widow remarriage, and opposed child marriage. Two new groups were later formed from the original society, but reform was the basic tenet. See 'Brahmo Samaj', *Britannica.com*. Available at https://www.britannica.com/topic/Brahmo-Samaj (accessed August 2022).
7. Upendrakishore Raychaudhuri was the father of the writer-satirist Sukumar Ray and grandfather of filmmaker Satyajit Ray. He was known for his work in children's literature and his art—illustrations and landscape oil paintings, where he synthesised Western and Indian art styles and made them his own. He had an eclectic range of work, from half-tone block printing to composing songs, writing and painting. See Ray, Satyajit. 2021. 'Ray 100: Satyajit Ray on His Grandfather Upendrakishore Ray Chowdhury, Whom

He Never Saw.' *Scroll.in*, 2 May. Available at https://scroll.in/article/993815/ray-100-satyajit-ray-on-his-grandfather-upendrakishore-ray-chowdhury-whom-he-never-saw (accessed August 2022).

8. Pillai, Manu S. 2017. 'The Dark Shades of Raja Ravi Varma'. *Mint Lounge*, 6 April. Available at https://lifestyle.livemint.com/news/talking-point/the-dark-shades-of-raja-ravi-varma-111646837181442.html (accessed August 2022).

9. Nivedita. 1907. 'The Function of Art in Shaping Nationality'. *Modern Review*. Available at https://southasiacommons.net/artifacts/2343259/modern-review-january-1907/3159158/ (accessed August 2022).

10. See Thapar, Romila. 1996. 'The Theory of Aryan Race and India: History and Politics'. *Social Scientist* 24 (1/3): 3–29.

11. Sen, Ronojoy. 2022. 'Breaking the Stereotype'. *Outlook*, 4 February. Available at https://www.outlookindia.com/website/story/breaking-the-stereotype/296142 (accessed August 2022).

12. See Banerjea's lecture at the Anniversary Meeting of the Young Men's Union, Calcutta, 24 June 1876, titled 'Study of Indian History'. In Banerjea, Surendranath. 1918. *Speeches and Writings of Hon. Surendranth Banerjea, Selected by Himself*. Madras: G. A. Nateson and Co.

13. See Mitter, Partha. 1994. *Art and Nationalism in Colonial India, 1850-1922: Occidental Orientations*. Cambridge: Cambridge University Press.

14. For more details on this history, see Basak, Sanjay. 2021. 'In West Bengal, the Fight is for Hindu Votes'. *The Asian Age*, 18 March. Available at https://www.pressreader.com/india/the-asian-age/20210318/281599538262047 (accessed August 2022)

15. Das, Ranjana. 2012. 'The Nation and the Community: Hundus and Muslims in the Novels of Bankim Chandra Chatterjee'. *Proceedings of the Indian History Congress* 73: 578–87.

16. For more details, see Gupta, Amrita. 2020. '1905: Cartography, Nationalism and Iconography'. *Partition Studies Quarterly*, 11 July. Available at https://partitionstudiesquarterly.org/article/1905-cartography-nationalism-and-iconography/ (accessed August 2022).

17. Ibid.

18. See Nivedita's 'Abanindra Nath Tagore: Bharat Mata'. 2018. In *The Complete Works of Sister Nivedita* 3, p. 57. Kolkata: Advaita Ashrama. The article originally appeared in *Prabasi*, 1906.

19. Ibid.

20. Mitra, Subrata K. and Lion Konig. 2013. 'Icon-ising National Identity: France and India in Comparative Perspective.' *National Identities* 15 (4): 357–77, especially p. 357 for this quote. Available at http://dx.doi.org/10.1080/14608944.2013.829430 (accessed August 2022).

21. Ibid.

22. Ibid., 358.

23. Ibid., 363.

24. Ibid., 364.

25. Ibid., 373.

26. Laxman, R. K. 2000. 'The Tunnel of Time'. In *Collected Writings*, 144. New Delhi: Penguin.

27. Laxman, R. K. 2012. *The Very Best of the Common Man*. New Delhi: Penguin.

28. Milosz, Czeslaw. 1985. *The Captive Mind*, trans. Jane Zielonko, vii. London: Penguin.

29. Ibid., xi.

30. Zareena's grandniece, Lalsawmliani Tochhawng, speaking to the author, New Delhi, 2020.

31. Satyabrata Pal in an interview with the author, New Delhi, 2010.

32. See Buhril, David. 2016. '50 Years Ago Today, Indira Gandhi got the Indian Air Force to Bomb its Own People'. *Scroll.in*, 5 March. Available at https://scroll.in/article/804555/50-years-ago-today-indira-gandhi-got-the-indian-air-force-to-bomb-its-own-people (accessed August 2022).

33. What Mr Pal is referring to is the use of vigilante forces by the state. For example, in Assam the surrendered United Liberation Front of Assam (ULFA) terrorists—known as SULFA—were used by the state government to target their former cadres in the ULFA, who often settled personal scores. In Jammu and Kashmir, the Rashtriya Rifles employs surrendered terrorists or *ikhwans* and legitimises them to fight alongside the Indian army. In the Left-wing Extremist (LWE) areas, the then Chhattisgarh government raised tribal youths as special police officers to fight the Maoist guerrillas. But it turned into a vendetta, displacing their own tribal people, and was eventually struck down by the Supreme Court as illegal. For more details, see Pal, Satyabrata. 2011. 'Security and Human Rights'. Internal Security Lecture Series, Institute for Defence Studies and Analyses, December, New Delhi. Available at https://www.youtube.com/watch?v=0tDuGran1qo (accessed August 2022).

34. A curved metal machete with a broad blade, used especially by the Gorkhas.

35. Pal, 'Security and Human Rights.'

36. Nehru, Jawaharlal. 1948. 'In the Valley of the Brahmaputra'. 9 December 1937, in *The Unity of India, Collected Writings, 1937–40*. London.

37. Ibid.

38. Aram, M. 1974. *Peace in Nagaland*, 117. New Delhi: Arnold Heinemann.

39. Nag, Sajal. 2009. 'Nehru and the Nagas: Minority Nationalism and the Post-Colonial State.' *Economic and Political Weekly* 44 (49), 5 December. Available at https://epw.in/journal/2009/49/special-articles/nehru-and-nagas-minority-nationalism-and-post-colonial-state.html (accessed August 2022).

40. See the Lok Sabha Debates, Series 1, Vol. 6, No. 27, columns 4229–30. Cited in Nag, 2009. 'Nehru and the Nagas'.

41. Berry, Ellen. 2016. 'An Epidemic of Dead Eyes in Kashmir as India Uses Pellet Guns on Protestors'. *The New York Times*, 28 August. Available at https://www.nytimes.com/2016/08/29/world/asia/pellet-guns-used-in-kashmir-protests-cause-dead-eyes-epidemic.html (accessed August 2022).

42. Waheed Mirza. 2016. 'India's Crackdown in Kashmir: Is this the World's First Mass Blinding?' *The Guardian*, 8 November. Available at https://www.theguardian.com/world/2016/nov/08/india-crackdown-in-kashmir-is-this-worlds-first-mass-blinding (accessed August 2022).

43. Rania, Abouzeid. 'Conflict in Kashmir Takes a Grim Toll on Unwitting Victims'. *National Geographic*, June. Available at https://www.nationalgeographic.com/magazine/2018/06/kashmir-conflict-anger-indian-police/ (accessed August 2022).

44. The Camp David Accords of 1978 are agreements between Israel and Egypt, with the mediation of the United States, which did not include Palestinians, though the framework of peace envisioned full autonomy for Palestine in West Bank and Gaza. The Delhi Agreement of 1952 was an agreement between the Kashmir Government and the Government of India to endorse the decisions of the Constituent Assembly of J&K.

45. This account is based on an interview and is reproduced here with the respondent's consent, as narrated to the author.

46. See *The Telegraph's* news report on Sajik Tampak, 2004. 'Army Brigade Set Up in Sajik Tampak Valley', 7 May. Available at https://www.telegraphindia.com/north-east/army-brigade-set-up-in-sajik-tampak-valley/cid/750831 (accessed August 2022). For further insight into the political dynamic of this region, see Bhattacharjee, Kishalay. 2010. 'After 69 Days'. *Himal Southasian*, 1 July. Available at https://www.himalmag.com/after-69-days/ (accessed August 2022).

47. A decisive battle was fought between 8 March and 18 July 1944 on the Red Hill, on the outskirts of Imphal. This became a turning point for one of the most memorable battles of the Second World War (1939–45). The Japanese defeat at the Red Hill and then in Kohima became the springboard for the Fourteenth Army's subsequent re-conquest of Burma. See Bhattacharjee, Kishalay. 2015. 'On This Day 71 Years Ago: Memories of the Battle of Red Hill, Imphal'. *Scroll.in*, 29 May. Available at https://scroll.in/article/730790/on-this-day-71-years-ago-memories-of-the-battle-of-red-hill-imphal (accessed August 2022).

48. Manipur, a sovereign princely state, signed the Instrument of Accession on 11 August 1947. On 21 September 1949, the Manipur king was made to sign a Merger Agreement under house arrest at his Shillong residence. In less than a month, Manipur was made part of India. From a sovereign state

with an elected government and a constitution, Manipur became a mere administrative territory under a single bureaucrat (*dewan*) and his appointed council. Manipuris say that they never got over the shock of this loss of pride and sovereignty. It was only in 1956 that Manipur became a union territory, and statehood came as late as 1972. Many in the state feel that the violent rebellions that occurred over the decades could have been averted if there was dignity in the merger and if statehood had been declared earlier. See Pilai, G. K. 2011. 'Manipur: The Way Out'. Internal Security Lecture Series, organised by Institue of Defence Studies and Analyses (IDSA), 26 September. Available at https://www.youtube.com/watch?v=KCt87g_AFX4 (accessed August 2022).

49. See Daniyal, Shoaib. 2015. 'India-Bangla Land Swap: Was the World's Strangest Border Created by a Game of Chess?' *Scroll.in*, 8 May. Available at https://scroll.in/article/725804/india-bangla-land-swap-was-the-worlds-strangest-border-created-by-a-game-of-chess (accessed August 2022).

50. Mukhia Sudeep. 2015. 'Fake Fathers of Mashaldanga'. *Ourstories.org.in*.

51. Pugh, B. M. 1976. *The Story of a Tribal: An Autobiography*. Kolkata: Orient Longman. Quoted in Karlsson, Bengt G. 2013. 'Evading the State: Ethnicity in Northeast India through the Lens of James Scott'. *Asian Ethnology* 72 (1): 321–31, especially p. 327.

52. Ibid., 329.

53. Zou, David Vumlallian and M. Satish Kumar. 2011. 'Mapping a Colonial Borderland: Objectifying the "Geo-Body" of India's Northeast.' *The Journal of Asian Studies* 70 (1): 141–70.

54. See Ward, Frank Kingdon. 2008. *Riddle of the Tsangpo Gorges*, ed. Kenneth Cox. Woodbridge: Garden Art Press. See also Baker, Ian. 2004. *The Heart of the World: A Journey to Tibet's Lost Paradise*. New York: Penguin Press.

55. Zou and Kumar, 'Mapping a Colonial Borderland', 155.

56. Mullan, quoted in ibid., 157.

57. Ibid., 144.

58. Karlsson, quoted in ibid., 323.

59. Chatterjee, Indrani. 2017. 'The Impossible Dream? Decolonising the History of Borders.' *Beyond Borders* series of lectures, New Delhi, 20 December.

60. Karlsson, 'Evading the State'.

61. *Mahabharata*. 1946. Quoted in Kane, P. V. 1946. *History of Dharmasastra* 3: 26.

62. Dharampal. 2000. *Civil Disobedience in Indian Tradition*, 42. Sarva Seva Sangh Prakashan, republished by Other India Press, Mapusa.

63. Ibid.

64. Dharampal. 2000. *Collected Writings, Vol. II*, 19–20. Mapusa, Goa: Other India Press.

65. Ibid., 21.

66. Ibid., 22.

67. Ibid., 26.

68. Santhanam, K. 1960. *Satyagraha and the State*, 62. Bombay: Asia Publishing House.

69. Bayley, David H. 1963. 'Violent Public Protest in India: 1900–1960'. *The Indian Journal of Political Science* 24 (4): 309–25.

70. Cervantes. 2009. *Don Quixote*, translated by Edith Grossman, 21. Penguin Random House.

71. The personal accounts here are fictionalised narratives based on real stories I collected from Dharavi during the protests, tracing them to Assam.

72. The Bodo-Muslim riots in Lower Assam, in 2012, 2015 and 2016.

73. Hussain, Tawqeer. 2020. '"How is it Human?": India's Largest Detention Centre is Almost Ready'. *Al Jazeera*, 2 January. Available at https://www.aljazeera.com/news/2020/1/2/how-is-it-human-indias-largest-detention-centre-almost-ready (accessed August 2022).

74. See *The Hindu*. 2019. '89% of People Excluded from Assam NRC Suffering from Mental Torture, Finds Survey', 24 August. Available at https://www.thehindu.com/news/national/89-of-people-excluded-from-assam-nrc-suffering-from-mental-torture-finds-survey/article29238522.ece (accessed August 2022). See also Siddique, Nazimuddin. 2020. 'Inside Assam's Detention Camps: How the Current Citizenship Crisis Disenfranchises Indians'. *Economic and Political Weekly* 55 (7). Available at https://www.epw.in/engage/article/inside-assams-detention-camps-how-current (accessed August 2022).

75. See internetshutdowns.in. See also Perrigo, Billy. 2020. 'India's Supreme Court Orders a Review of Internet Shutdown in Kashmir. But For Now, It Continues'. *Time*, 10 January. Available at https://time.com/5762751/internet-kashmir-supreme-court/ (accessed August 2022).

76. *The Wire*. 2020. 'Delhi Riots Death Toll at 53, Here Are the Names of the Victims', 6 March. Available at https://thewire.in/communalism/delhi-riots-identities-deceased-confirmed (accessed August 2022).

77. See *The Hindu*. 2020. 'Parliament Proceedings live | 700 FIRs Registered; 2647 People Detained/Arrested in Connection with Delhi Violence: Home Minister', 11 March. Available at https://www.thehindu.com/news/national/parliament-live-march-11-2020/article31037560.ece (accessed August 2022). See also Pandey, Amit and Shahid Tantray. 2020. 'Hate Speech—A Hindu Rioter Speaks: Delhi Violence was "Revenge" against Muslims, Police Gave Free Reign'. *Caravan*, 31 July. Available at https://caravanmagazine.in/crime/delhi-rioter-testimony-hindu-revenge-muslims-police-free-reign (accessed August 2022). For international reportage on the riot, see Bal, Hartosh Singh.

2020. 'Why Delhi Police Did Nothing to Stop Attacks on Muslims'. *The New York Times*, 3 March. Available at https://www.nytimes.com/2020/03/03/opinion/delhi-pogrom.html (accessed August 2022).

78. Sainath, P. 2020. 'The Migrant and the Moral Economy of the Elite'. *People's Archive of Rural India*, 8 June. Available at https://ruralindiaonline.org/en/articles/the-migrant-and-the-moral-economy-of-the-elite/ (accessed August 2022).

79. For a detailed analysis, see Nath, Paaritosh, Nelson Mandela S. and Aishwarya Gawali. 2022. 'Loss, Recovery and the Long Road Ahead: Tracking India's Informal Workers Through the Pandemic'. Centre for Sustainable Employment Working Paper No. 47. Bengaluru: Azim Premji University. Available at https://cse.azimpremjiuniversity.edu.in/publications/loss-recovery-and-the-long-road-ahead-tracking-indias-informal-workers-through-the-pandemic/ (accessed August 2022). See also Nandi, Shreya. 2020. 'Experts Call for a Spending Boost'. *Livemint.com*, 30 December. Available at https://www.livemint.com/budget/news/experts-call-for-a-spending-boost-11609293876285.html (accessed August 2022). See also the detailed report by Abraham, Rosa, Amit Basole and Surbhi Kesar. 2021. 'Pandemic Effect: 9 Months On, More Younger Workers Remain Jobless'. *IndiaSpend*, 20 January. Available at https://www.indiaspend.com/economy/pandemic-effect-9-months-on-more-younger-workers-remain-jobless-716310 (accessed August 2022).

80. See Haider, Suhasini. 2021. 'UN Rights Panel Slams Detention of Safoora Zargar'. *The Hindu*, 13 March. Available at https://www.thehindu.com/news/national/un-rights-panel-slams-detention-of-safoora-zargar/article34061744.ece (accessed August 2022).

81. Fictionalised account based on real-life reportage.

82. *Deccan Herald*. 2020. '"I was Determined", Says the Girl Who Cycled Injured Dad Across India', 27 May. Available at https://www.deccanherald.com/national/i-was-determined-says-girl-who-cycled-injured-dad-across-india-842490.html (accessed August 2022).

83. See Bhargava, Yuthika. 2020. 'Coronavirus Lockdown | Railways to Run 'Shramik Special' Trains to Move Migrant Workers, Other Stranded Persons.' *The Hindu*, 1 May. Available at https://www.thehindu.com/news/national/railways-to-run-shramik-special-trains-to-move-migrant-workers-other-stranded-persons/article31481996.ece (accessed December 2022).

84. Aratani, Lauren. 2020. 'George Floyd Killing: What Sparked the Protests—and what has been the Response?' *The Guardian*, 29 May. Available at https://www.theguardian.com/us-news/2020/may/29/george-floyd-killing-protests-police-brutality (accessed August 2022). For instance, see *The Indian Express*. 2020. 'Man Beaten in Delhi on Suspicion of Conspiracy

to Spread COVID-19', 9 April. Available at https://indianexpress.com/article/cities/delhi/man-beaten-in-delhi-on-suspicion-of-conspiracy-to-spread-covid-19-6354586/ (accessed December 2022). For more information on the issue of enounters, see Jain, Bharti. 2022. '655 Cases of Death in Police Encounter across India; 191 in Chhattisgarh and 117 in UP'. *The Times of India*, 8 February. Available at https://timesofindia.indiatimes.com/india/655-cases-of-death-in-police-encounter-across-india-191-in-chhattisgarh-and-117-in-up/articleshow/89437291.cms (accessed December 2022). See also Karthikeyan, Suchitra. 2022. 'Explained | Police Encounters in India: Cases, Convictions and Court Orders'. *The Hindu*, 3 June. Available at https://www.thehindu.com/news/national/explained-police-encounters-in-india-cases-conviction-court-orders/article65463140.ece (accessed December 2022).

85. Numerous such incidents were reported in the press, and some of them have been mentioned in the Appendix at the end of the book.

86. Conrad, Joseph. 1974. *Heart of Darkness*, 100. UK: Penguin.

Appendix

Timeline of Events, January 2020–December 2021

It is now a cliché to say that the last few years have been extraordinary, given the magnitude of collective grief experienced, and the utter irresponsibility of lawmakers across the world in addressing global issues that have brought the planet to the brink of disaster. It is no coincidence that individual liberty and rights, including the idea of citizenship—one of the most important political ideas of our times—were challenged as the world battled a global pandemic.

This book was written during those dark hours. While it was conceived as a study of identity, citizenship and nationality in India, it is critical to take note of the timeline of events that accompanied the research. It should serve as a reminder of the questions that the participants in this research have raised. It could also serve as a testimony of how India lived through these two years. The chronology from January 2020 to December 2021 is not an arbitrary timeline, but rather one that encapsulates momentous events, starting from nationwide protests against the new citizenship law and a national register of citizens; to the paralysis in Jammu and Kashmir following the abrogation of Article 370 and largescale human rights violations and preventive arrests; a formidable farmers' agitation on the borders of the Indian capital; and the incarceration of several citizens, allegedly as a result of political vendetta. This period was also the most difficult in terms of dealing with the pandemic.

2020

January

5 January: A masked mob, armed with rods and sticks, attacked the campus of Jawaharlal Nehru University (JNU), New Delhi, injuring more than forty students and teachers. The violence was allegedly an attack by the Akhil Bharatiya Vidyarthi Parishad (ABVP), the student wing of the RSS, on the Left-dominated students' union in JNU, weeks after the Delhi Police beat up students inside Jamia Millia Islamia University in Delhi. Students there were protesting the controversial Citizenship (Amendment) Act. This triggered protests at over sixty universities and colleges across India.

10 January: The Citizenship (Amendment) Act came into force. The Delhi High Court dismissed a plea to remove the protesters occupying Shaheen Bagh.

17 January: Inspired by the protest at Shaheen Bagh, around 10,000 women gathered at the YMCA ground in Mumbai to protest in the evening.

19 January: In Delhi, hundreds of protesters participated in a candle-light march from Jamia Millia Islamia to Shaheen Bagh.

30 January: The COVID-19 virus confirmed to have spread to India. The first case of COVID-19 detected in Kerala.

February

1 February: A person fired shots in the air at Shaheen Bagh, the epicentre of protests against the Citizenship (Amendment) Act, chanting 'Jai Shri Ram', saying that in India only the Hindus deserve rights. Two days earlier, another person had shot at non-violent protesters near Jamia University. Thousands of LGBTQI rights activists protested against the CAA in Mumbai.

11 February: Jamia Millia Islamia students staged a march to the Parliament.

23–29 February: Communally-charged clashes between pro-CAA and anti-CAA protesters escalated and violence erupted in north-east Delhi. Fifty-three people, mostly Muslims, were killed, and hundreds wounded. Reports emerged that the police had stood by and done nothing. In some cases, they had participated in the violence.[1]

March

20 March: The BJP formed a government in Madhya Pradesh after Chief Minister Kamal Nath of the Congress lost his majority and was compelled to resign before a floor test.

22 March: India observed a 14-hour lockdown in a 'Janata Curfew' to prevent the spread of the COVID-19 virus.
23 March: Maoists attacked paramilitary personnel in Chhattisgarh, killing seventeen in a well-planned ambush. Around 300–350 Maoist rebels are believed to have carried out the attack. This was seen as a sign of deepening conflict between Naxalites and the Indian government.
24 March: Prime Minister Modi announced a 21-day lockdown throughout India, starting from midnight of 25 March until 14 April, to prevent the spread of COVID-19. This triggered a crisis among the migrant workers across cities, as, stranded with no jobs, little money, and no means of transport, they had to walk their way back home.

April

India reeled under an extended lockdown throughout the month of April, hoping to check the spread of the COVID-19 pandemic in the country.

1 April: Reports started trickling in from major media outlets that the Tablighi Jamaat, a puritanical Islamic group, had held a gathering in March at Nizamuddin Markaz in Delhi, and was responsible for the spread of COVID-19. Of the 14,378 coronavirus cases in the country at the time, 4,291 cases were linked to the event by the government and many organisers of the event were arrested.[2] This has since been revealed to be misinformation and empirical data did not fully support the claim.
6 April: Death toll due to COVID-19 reached 100.
14 April: Thousands of migrants gathered at Bandra station, hoping to get home by train, since most forms of public transport had been halted due to the lockdown. The police dispersed the crowds with batons.
29 April: India recorded 1,000 deaths due to COVID-19.

May

1 May: The lockdown was extended for two weeks, starting 4 May.
5 May: Skirmishes began between about 150 Indian and Chinese soldiers at the Nathu La crossing. Several were injured following fistfights and stone-throwing.

8 May: Train runs over migrant workers in Aurangabad, killing sixteen. The nationwide COVID-19 lockdown that started on 25 March exposed us to the distress of millions of ordinary Indians, from migrant workers to pastoral nomads. But it is easy to be inured with 24x7 information and visuals of the same. However, the incident of the freight train running over exhausted migrants who were sleeping on the railway tracks shocked the citizenry and forced us to confront how people have been pushed beyond the limits of desperation.[3]
17 May: The Ministry of Home Affairs extended the lockdown again till 31 May.
19 May: India recorded more than 1 lakh total COVID-19 cases.

June

5 June: The President of India promulgated three ordinances related to agriculture, which would be later proposed as a bill and consequently passed as an act.
12 June: India became the fourth-worst coronavirus hit country with more than 3 lakh cases.
15-16 June: Twenty soldiers of the Indian Army, including a colonel, were killed in a violent skirmish linked to tensions between India and China at Line of Actual Control (LAC) in the Galwan Valley of Ladakh. The violent face-off came amid a 'de-escalation process' in the Galwan valley, following a standoff between both countries' troops along the LAC during the previous month.[4]
17 June: Twenty Indian officers killed in action over the Galwan valley border dispute.

July

6 July: India becomes third-worst hit country in terms of coronavirus infections, with 6.97 lakh cases.[5]
19 July: Activist Sharjeel Imam was charged with sedition on allegations that he incited people to participate in anti-CAA protests, which were perceived as detrimental to the sovereignty of India.[6]

August

5 August: Prime Minister Narendra Modi attended a ceremony for the founding of a Ram Mandir in Ayodhya. An article in *The Guardian* observed: 'The issue has divided Indians, alienated Muslims, helped propel the BJP to power and thrown its rivals into disarray.... The BJP has succeeded in turning the controversial issue of whether the temple should be built into a touchstone of Hindu identity, a marker of the Hindu nationalism that forms part of its core ideology known as Hindutva.'[7]

11 August: A communally charged Facebook post by Naveen, a nephew of a Congress member in Bengaluru, triggered a violent clash. Places and vehicles were vandalised overnight as hundreds rioted. Three Muslims were reported to have died, several people injured and 110 rioters arrested. Armed police fought to maintain peace on the streets and Section 144 of the Indian Penal Code (IPC) was put into effect to impose a curfew on the whole city of Bengaluru.

24 August: The Supreme Court quashed three FIRs against thirty-five petitioners—twenty-nine of whom were foreign nationals—who attended the Tablighi Jamaat event in Delhi and then travelled to different parts of the country. The court observed, 'A political government tries to find the scapegoat when there is pandemic or calamity, and the circumstances show that there is probability that these foreigners were chosen to make them scapegoats.'[8]

September

7 September: India recorded the second highest number of COVID-19 cases in the world, with a total of 41.13 lakh cases.

14 September:

1. Three Bills related to agriculture, which propose wide-ranging agricultural reforms, were introduced in the Parliament.
2. A Dalit woman was gangraped in Hathras, Uttar Pradesh, allegedly by four upper-caste men. She died of her injuries two weeks later. Her death sparked protests all over the country.

30 September: A special court acquitted all thirty-two accused in the demolition of the Babri Masjid in 1992. This included leaders from the ruling party, the BJP, like former deputy Prime Minister L. K. Advani, Murli Manohar Joshi, Uma Bharti, Vinay Katiyar and several others. The special court judge said that '[t]he demolition was not pre-planned'.

October

31 October: Uttar Pradesh Chief Minister Yogi Adityanath announced that a law to curb 'Love Jihad' was being prepared by his government. This came after an Allahabad High Court stated that conversion 'just for the purpose of marriage' is not valid.[9]

November

5 November: More than 200 farm unions from twenty-two states organised a nationwide road blockade against the new laws introduced by the Union government. These laws relaxed restrictions governing the purchase and sale of farm produce, eased constraints on stocking, and enabled contract farming.

24 November:

1. The 'Love Jihad' ordinance was cleared by the Uttar Pradesh state cabinet. The law proposed jail time of one to five years for those found guilty of forced conversions for marriages.
2. The same day, the Allahabad High Court went back on its earlier remark that conversion only for marriage is not acceptable. Hearing a plea by petitioners Salamat Ansari and Priyanka Kharwar a.k.a. Alia, both residents of Kushinagar district, the court stated: 'To disregard the choice of a person who is of the age of majority would not only be antithetic to the freedom of choice of a grown-up individual but would also be a threat to the concept of unity in diversity.'[10]

25 November: After a series of local protests, farmers from Punjab and Haryana decided to move their protests to the capital city. They made a 'Delhi Chalo' ('Let's go to Delhi') march call.

26 November: The police at Haryana's Ambala district used water cannons and tear gas to stop farmers from reaching Delhi. Reports say the Haryana government had dug trenches on the roads leading to Delhi as part of their efforts to stop farmers from travelling to the capital.

27 November: Farmers set up camps on the highways at the city's border, in defiance of police permission for the protest only at a site in Delhi's Burari.

28 November:

1. Uttar Pradesh Governor Anandiben Patel approved The Uttar Pradesh Prohibition of Unlawful Conversion of Religion Ordinance, 2020 which is based on the right-wing's claims of 'Love Jihad'.
2. Home Minister Amit Shah offered to hold talks with the farmers if they agreed to vacate Delhi's borders and move to the designated protest site in Burari. Rejecting his offer, the protesting farmers demanded permission to hold their protest at Delhi's Jantar Mantar.

December

1 December: The NDA-II government held the first round of talks with leaders of thirty-five farm unions. The meeting remained inconclusive.
3 December: A marathon eight-hour meeting between the government and farmer union heads ended in a deadlock.
4 December: The protests grabbed attention for their efficiency and preparedness for the long haul. Farmers claimed they had enough arrangements to sit at Delhi's borders indefinitely. Many protesters had tractors installed with air conditioners and heaters to brave the weather.
8 December: Protesting farmers called for a nationwide shutdown and demanded a complete rollback of the new farm laws. The shutdown gathered support from many opposition parties and trade unions, especially in Punjab and Haryana. A meeting between Home Minister Shah and a selected group of farmers' representatives failed to achieve a breakthrough.
11 December: The Bharatiya Kisan Union, one of the farmer bodies, moved the Supreme Court against the three farm laws.
16 December: The apex court suggested that the Centre put the new farm laws on hold while putting forward the idea of constituting an impartial and independent committee to end the impasse between protesters and the state.
19 December: India's coronavirus cases crossed 1 crore.
21 December: Farmers held a one-day hunger strike at protest sites near the borders of Delhi.

22 December: More than thirty-five social and political organisations, farmers' groups, and trade and labour unions held a peaceful protest in Mumbai to show their support. Farm unions in Mumbai held a protest in solidarity with protesting farmers at Delhi's borders.
25 December: Seventy-five Kashmiri political leaders were arrested to 'prevent unrest' after local elections. 'The detentions undermine the verdict of the people,' says Imran Nabi Dar, spokesman for the National Conference, a regional party and a key member of the People's Alliance for Gupkar Declaration (PAGD).[11]
26 December: The Madhya Pradesh government approved an anti-conversion bill similar to the law passed in Uttar Pradesh. 'Under [the] new Bill, forcing religious conversion on someone will attract 1-5 years of imprisonment and a minimum Rs 25,000 fine,' said Narottam Mishra, State Minister.[12]
30 December: Some headway was made in a fresh round of talks between the government and union leaders—the former agreed to drop the penal provisions against farmers in an ordinance relating to stubble burning and to put on hold a proposed electricity amendment law.

2021

January

4 January: Reliance Industries, owned by one of India's wealthiest persons, Mukesh Ambani, stated that it would never enter contract farming. A fresh meeting between the farmers and the government ended without a solution as the union leaders continued to press for the withdrawal of the three farm laws.
12 January: The Supreme Court put on hold the implementation of the three farm laws and set up a committee to evaluate any changes to the laws. The committee was given a two-month deadline.
15 January: Another round of talks between the farmers and the government failed to end the deadlock.
16 January: India began its COVID-19 vaccination programme.
20 January: In a fresh round of talks, the government proposed to suspend the three farm laws for one-and-half years and set up a joint committee to discuss the legislation. The farmers, however, rejected

the proposal and continued their demand for a complete rollback of the laws.

22 January: The government hardened its stand and said that the next round of talks would be held only when the farmers agreed to discuss the proposal to suspend the laws rather than withdraw them.

24 January: The Delhi police allowed farmers to hold a tractor rally on 26 January in the national capital to mark the completion of two months of their protest. The permission was limited to a fixed route through the city.

26 January: Chaos unfolded when a group of farmers deviated from the permitted route for the tractor rally on Republic Day. In an attempt to stop the farmers, the police used tear gas, but the situation turned violent after some farmers allegedly pelted stones at them. Protesting farmers vandalised bus and police vehicles and broke the barricades at Delhi's ITO. One farmer died in the violence. The farmers alleged that he was shot at by the Delhi police. However, the police denied the allegation and claimed that the man died after his tractor was toppled when he tried to break through the barricades.[13]

Violence intensified after a group of protesters reached the Red Fort and breached the monument's security. While some waved their farmers' union flags, others hoisted the Nishan Sahib flag, which is sacred to the Sikh community. Through its leaders' statements, the Samyukt Kisan Morcha (SKM), an amalgam of the protesting farm unions, dissociated itself from the violence and claimed 'anti-social elements' had infiltrated the rally. Following the clashes between the protesting farmers and the police, Amarinder Singh, chief minister of Punjab, urged farmers to leave Delhi and return. He emphasised that 'genuine farmers' were not involved in the violence.[14]

27 January: Delhi Police filed twenty-two FIRs against farmer leader Rakesh Tikait and others in connection to the violence on Republic Day.

28 January: The leaders of the protesting unions called off their plan to march to the Parliament on 1 February. A few farm unions from Uttar Pradesh—Bharatiya Kisan Union (Bhanu) and Rashtriya Kisan Mazdoor Sangathan—ended their protest and dissociated themselves from the agitation. At night, the Uttar Pradesh police forcefully removed the protesting farmers sitting on the Delhi-Saharanpur highway.[15]

February

1 February: The Ministry of Home Affairs extended the internet ban imposed on the Delhi border areas of Ghazipur, Singhu and Tikri, the main sites where farmers had gathered in protest.

5 February: 4G internet services restored in the entirety of Jammu and Kashmir after eighteen months.

6 February: Highways in India were blocked by tens of thousands of farmers protesting in a three-hour 'chakka jam'.

13 February: Climate activist Disha Ravi was arrested on charges of sedition in the 'Toolkit' conspiracy case related to the farmers' agitation. According to the police, a document by Ravi was inadvertently posted on Twitter by Swedish climate crusader Greta Thunberg and received international attention. Thus, the term 'toolkit' was coined. Ravi was accused of collaborating with a pro-Khalistani group to create a toolkit to defame India. She was named as one of the 'key conspirators' in the case. She was arrested at her home in Bengaluru, flown to Delhi, placed in the custody of Delhi police without access to a lawyer, and charged with sedition and criminal conspiracy.[16]

18 February: 'Rail Roko' protest organised by famers across India from 12 PM to 4 PM.

19 February: India crossed one crore vaccinations against COVID-19 in thirty-four days and is second fastest after the USA.

23 February: Activist Disha Ravi was granted bail by a sessions court in Delhi.

March

1 March: The second phase of vaccination began in India and all above 60 years were made eligible for the vaccine.

3 March: Freedom House's annual 'Freedom in the World' report downgraded India from 'free' to a 'partly free' status. The report scored India a 67/100, four points below the previous year. The reason for the drop was 'a crackdown on expressions of dissent by the media, academics, civil society groups, and protesters' and that political rights had been particularly infringed upon after 'Modi's reelection in 2019'. It cited the 'love jihad' law that prohibited conversion, the COVID-19 lockdown that left millions of migrants stranded, the Tablighi Jamaat members who were blamed for the spread of the virus, and many more incidents that had factored into India's freedom score.[17]

4 March: Ministry of Home Affairs issued a notification under Section 7B of the Citizenship Act, 1955. Overseas Citizens of India (OCIs) are termed 'foreign nationals' and several rights and liberties are curtailed and restricted under the notification. OCIs now require a Special Permit to 'undertake Research' or 'any Missionary or Tabligh or Mountaineering or Journalistic activities'.[18]

5 March:

1. India's Department of Economic Affairs stated that the Indian economy would do better than the projected 8 per cent shrinkage estimated. 'Positive GDP growth in Q3 of FY21 for the first time since the onset of the pandemic adds to the positive sentiment as the economy is set to close the year with activity levels higher than measured in the second advance estimates of GDP,' the report said.[19]
2. The Punjab Assembly passed a resolution for the unconditional withdrawal of farm laws for Punjab's farmers.

6 March: The farmers' protest completed 100 days at the Delhi borders.

10 March:

1. Sweden's V-Dem Institute released their fifth annual democracy report, 'Autocratisation goes viral'. India is termed an 'electoral autocracy', a concerning change from the previous year's 'world's largest democracy' tag. The report stated that 'most of the decline occurred following BJP's victory in 2014 and their Hindu nationalist agenda' along with the increased media 'muzzling'.[20]
2. State Bank of India's report stated that India's budget gap in the fiscal year would reach 12.7 per cent. The pandemic forced states to borrow more, which led to an increase in debt.

11 March: Jamia Millia Islamia student activist Safoora Zargar's arrest was slammed by the UN Human Rights Council's (HRC) Working Group against Arbitrary Detentions (WGAD). The opinion on the detention highlighted a 'deprivation of liberty', breaching several human rights. It also stated that Zargar's stand against the Citizenship (Amendment) Act and participation in protests are why 'her current detention can clearly be interpreted as another move to curb her dissent by intimidating her and others associated with the Jamia

Coordination Committee'. The case was referred to three Special Rapporteurs for further action.[21]

12 March:

1. In a letter dated 10 March, the Ministry of Home Affairs (MHA) wrote to the chief secretaries of Nagaland, Manipur, Mizoram and Arunachal Pradesh, telling them to 'take appropriate action as per law to check illegal influx from Myanmar into India'. It expressed that state governments cannot issue a 'refugee status to any foreigner' and told them to prevent an influx of illegal migrants. This came in the context of the Myanmar coup, after which many in Myanmar were forced to flee for their lives and seek refuge.
2. According to data from the Petroleum Planning and Analysis Cell (PPAC) of the Ministry of Petroleum & Natural Gas, India's oil demand fell 5 per cent in February.

15 March: India achieved 3.15 crore vaccinations.

19 March: Reuters reported that over 1,000 people had fled from Myanmar to Mizoram since late February.

18 March:

1. A Pew Research Center analysis reveals that the middle class in India is disappearing as it had shrunk by 32 million by 2020. The number of people living in poverty is estimated to have increased by 75 million due to the COVID-19 pandemic.[22]
2. Amnesty International's report, 'Forgotten Behind Bars: COVID-19 and Prisons', revealed that India's measures to curb COVID-19 in prisons had been inadequate and several human rights had been violated. The state of prisoners during the pandemic was precarious and deplorable.

29 March: India recorded 68,020 cases, the highest daily case count since November, and total cases crossed 12 million.

30 March:

1. A report by the United Nations Economic and Social Commission for Asia and the Pacific (UNESCAP) called 'Economic and Social Survey of Asia and the Pacific 2021: Towards post-COVID-19 resilient economies' estimated an economic growth of 7 per cent in 2021–22 for India over a contraction of 7.7 per cent in the previous fiscal year. It stated, 'Despite a robust reduction in new COVID-19 cases and

the start of vaccine roll-out, India's 2021 economic output is expected to remain below the 2019 level.'[23]

2. Moody's Analytics, a financial intelligence company, stated that India's inflation was 'uncomfortably high' and 'worrisome'.[24]

31 March: World Bank's South Asia Economic Focus Report was released and predicted that India's real GDP growth for fiscal year (FY21–22) could range from 7.5 to 12.5 per cent. It commended India on bouncing back and said that it was 'amazing how far India has come compared to last year.'

April

1 April:

1. The National Investigative Agency (NIA) was revealed to have raided more than thirty-one places on 31 March in Andhra Pradesh and Telangana. The houses raided belonged to human rights, civil rights and labour rights activists, advocates and members of cultural troupes. The agency claimed that the raid went on for nine hours. They believed the thirty people raided were allegedly 'furthering the activities of the proscribed organisation, CPI (Maoist) in Andhra Pradesh in the guise of frontal organisations' and lodged charges of UAPA (Unlawful Activities [Prevention] Amendment Act, 2008), sedition, criminal conspiracy, and the Arms Act against them. Six of the accused were arrested.[25]
2. Crowds began arriving in Haridwar for the Kumbh Mela. The ceremonies and holy baths in the Ganges began.

3 April: The Uttar Pradesh Police filed a 5,000-page chargesheet against journalist Siddique Kappan. Kappan was arrested in October 2020 for reporting on the Hathras gangrape case. He stands accused of attempting to create communal tension under the Unlawful Activities (Prevention) Act, sedition and parts of the IT Act. His lawyer commented that Kappan was just doing his job as a journalist.

6 April:

1. Assam writer Sikha Sarma was arrested under the charge of sedition for an alleged Facebook post. The post came in the wake of a Maoist attack in Chhattisgarh. The post read: 'Salaried professionals who die in the line of duty cannot be

termed martyrs. Going by that logic, electricity department workers who die of electrocution should also be labelled martyrs. Do not make people sentimental, media.'

2. Concerns grew over the Kumbh Mela as government officials worried it might turn into a super spreader. This was reported by *India Today* and the same day, the Ministry of Health and Family Welfare tweeted that this report was 'fake news'.

7 April: Reserve Bank of India (RBI) forecast GDP growth for FY22 at 10.5 per cent.

8 April: Fearing another lockdown, hundreds of migrant workers in Delhi and Mumbai boarded trains and buses to return to their villages. The Ministry of Railways and Northern Railway denied these reports and claims of a mass exodus.

10 April: Patna Police lodged a case against two voluntary city groups under the sedition act, accusing them of teaching 'provocative and anti-national' lessons on the CAA and the NRC to street children at a Danapur residential school. They were charged because of a recommendation by the National Commission for Protection of Child Rights (NCPCR), who took suo moto cognisance of the matter.

12 April: Reports of crowds at Kumbh Mela triggered concerns over a 'super spreader' event leading to a rise in coronavirus cases. Hundreds of thousands gathered at the Ganga to take a holy dip.

13 April: Eighty OCIs moved the Supreme Court of India to direct the Centre to stop treating them like 'second class citizens' and restricting their free speech and anti-government views.

14 April:

1. The Foreign Affairs Committee of the European Parliament adopted a report expressing concerns over the 'deteriorating human rights situation in India'. The report highlighted the unsafe working conditions for human rights activists and journalists, along with raising an alarm about CAA.[26]
2. The Guwahati High Court dismissed the petition against granting bail to Akhil Gogoi, an Assam peasants' rights activist. Gogoi was arrested and granted bail in a case related to anti-CAA protests in Assam in 2019. The judges stated that a person can be charged under the UAPA if there is a threat of terrorism or hurting India's sovereignty, integrity and unity. 'Unlawful act of any other nature, including acts [of] arson

and violence aimed at creating civil disturbance and law and order problems, which may be punishable under the ordinary law, would not come within the purview of Section 15 (1) of the Act of 1976 unless it is committed with the requisite intention,' the court said.[27]

3. An estimated 9,43,452 people took a dip in the Ganges during the Kumbh Mela. Over the five days of the Kumbh Mela, 10–14 April, 1,700 people tested positive for COVID-19.[28]

17 April: At least 5,037 people from the Kumbh Mela tested positive for COVID-19.[29]

19 April: The government announced Phase 3 of vaccinations from 1 May. Everyone above the age of 18 would be eligible to take the vaccine.

20 April:

1. The Kerala Union of Working Journalists moved a plea in the Supreme Court to shift Kerala journalist Siddique Kappan to AIIMS as he had tested positive for COVID-19 and collapsed with serious injuries.[30]
2. Media watchdog Reporters Sans Frontières released the World Press Freedom Index 2021. India was at 142 out of 180 countries and the report stated that it was still 'bad' for journalism, with journalists in grave danger. RSF said that journalists are 'exposed to every kind of attack, including police violence against reporters, ambushes by political activists, and reprisals instigated by criminal groups or corrupt local officials'.[31]
3. Hospitals in Delhi pleaded for more oxygen as they revealed that they had oxygen for merely another eight to twenty-four hours. Meanwhile, some private hospitals only had enough for four to five hours.

21 April: Twenty-two patients died in Nashik, Maharashtra because of a leak in the tank supplying oxygen to the patients.

22 April:

1. The annual report on religious freedom by the United States Commission on International Religious Freedom (USCIRF) was released, which designated India as a 'country of particular concern'. It stated that India has been 'engaging in and tolerating systematic, ongoing, and egregious religious freedom violations, as defined by the International Religious Freedom Act (IRFA)'.

2. India hit a record single-day rise in coronavirus cases with 3,14,835 cases, which was, at the time, the highest single-day spike in infections recorded in any country since the beginning of the pandemic.[32]

23 April: State Bank of India revised India's GDP growth forecast downwards to 10.4 per cent for the Fiscal Year 2022.

24 April: Twenty-five COVID-19 patients died in Jaipur Golden Hospital in Delhi as the oxygen supply ran out.

25 April: Siddique Kappan's lawyer wrote to the Chief Justice of India (CJI) requesting a shift to Mathura Jail for Kappan from Mathura Medical College. According to his wife, Kappan was 'chained like an animal in a cot of Medical College Hospital, Mathura, without mobility, and he neither could take food, nor could go to the toilet for the last more than four days, and is very critical'. Eleven members of the Parliament also wrote to CJI Ramana to shift Kappan to AIIMS. Additionally, Kerala Chief Minister Pinarayi Vijayan wrote to Uttar Pradesh Chief Minister Yogi Adityanath for aid in moving the journalist to a hospital.

27 April: Last 'shahi snan' or holy bath at the Kumbh Mela. Seers kept the ritual symbolic because of the pandemic and the backlash over organising a huge festival that had caused many infections.[33]

28 April:

1. The Asian Development Bank (ADB) released its publication, 'Asian Development Outlook 2021', with a forecast that India's GDP would grow by 11 per cent in 2020–21. The report indicated that with vaccinations, the pandemic would be contained and India will be on the road to recovery.
2. The Supreme Court ordered the Uttarakhand Government to admit journalist Siddique Kappan to a hospital. The Solicitor General, Tushar Mehta, claimed that Kappan had tested negative and advised against moving Kappan as he would take away a bed from a Covid-positive patient. The bench told him to work out the details, but to get Kappan the medical attention he needed.

29 April: The Uttarakhand government announced that the Char Dham Yatra, a festival in May, was suspended as they feared a repeat of the Kumbh Mela. Only priests would be allowed inside to conduct rituals and no one else would be allowed to enter the portals.

May

1 May: India records 4,01,993 new coronavirus cases, setting another daily record. A fire in an Ahmedabad COVID-19 hospital ward killed eighteen patients.

3 May: The Manipur High Court allowed seven Myanmar refugees (who had fled to India following the Myanmar military coup) to travel to New Delhi so that they could get sanctuary from the United Nations High Commissioner for Refugees (UNHCR).

4 May: With a devastating Covid-19 crisis affecting the country, a Human Rights Watch report stated that Europe should press the Indian government to reverse its abusive and discriminatory policies to censor free speech and criminalise dissent, and release all human rights defenders.

7 May: Former Jammu and Kashmir chief minister and PDP president, Mehbooba Mufti, appealed for the release of political prisoners, who were at great risk in jails inside and outside Jammu and Kashmir. 'Throughout the world, most countries have released prisoners on parole in view of the alarming COVID crisis. A democratic and civilised country like India shouldn't drag its feet and must release these detainees immediately so that they can return home at a time when life feels so threatened,' she said, in a letter to the prime minister.[34]

11 May: Ratings agency Moody's revised India's GDP forecast for FY2022 downwards to 9.3 per cent.

13 May: Journalist Kishorechandra Wangkhem and activist Erendro Leichombam were booked under sedition and arrested for a social media post made in the wake of the death of Manipur BJP chief, Tikendra Singh.

17 May:

1. A mosque in Uttar Pradesh was razed to the ground by the local state administration despite a state high court order against such action. The Masjid Gareeb Nawaz Al Maroof mosque had stood there since colonial times. They have been paying its electricity bills for the last six decades. The administration claimed that it was an illegal structure and steadily refused to classify it as a mosque. The mosque committee had earlier sent all the official documentation to verify that the mosque was legal after they were issued a notice on 15 March. They

received no response and the BJP-ruled state government blocked access to the mosque before ultimately destroying it.

2. Nearly a dozen people were arrested and seventeen FIRs lodged against people accused of putting up posters that were critical of the government's handling of the pandemic.

19 May: Spokesperson for UN Secretary-General Antonio Guterres, Stephane Dujarric, said that an estimated 4,000–6,000 refugees from Myanmar had sought refuge in India.

22 May: Karnataka government announced a new vaccination policy where slum dwellers, auto and cab drivers, e-commerce delivery agents and construction workers would be given preference as stocks of vaccines were low. The drive was set to begin in the first week of June.

24 May: Police served a notice at Twitter's office after a tweet by the BJP spokesperson, Sambit Patra, was flagged as 'manipulated media'. He had shared documents that allegedly proved that the Congress was working against BJP's efforts to manage COVID-19.

27 May:

1. Twitter said it planned to ask for changes in India's new IT laws, which has more stringent provisions and may hinder free speech, and expressed worry over 'intimidation tactics' used by the Delhi Police. 'We, alongside many in civil society in India and around the world, have concerns with regards to the use of intimidation tactics by the police in response to enforcement of our global Terms of Service, as well as with core elements of the new IT Rules,' the company spokesperson added. The Ministry of Electronics and IT (MeitY) denied the allegation of intimidation tactics, calling it 'completely baseless' and claimed that India has always protected free speech.[35]
2. The farmers observed a 'black day' and burnt effigies of the government to commemorate six months of the farmers' protest.

28 May: The Ministry of Home Affairs issued a notification under the 2009 rules of the Citizenship Act, 1955 inviting non-Muslim refugees from Afghanistan, Bangladesh and Pakistan living in thirteen districts of Gujarat, Rajasthan, Chhattisgarh, Haryana and Punjab to apply for Indian citizenship.

The fresh notification stated:

> In exercise of powers conferred under Section 16 of the Citizenship Act, 1955 (57 of 1955), the central government

> hereby directs that powers exercisable by it for registration as citizen of India under Section 5, or for grant of certificate of naturalisation under section 6 of the Citizenship Act 1955 in respect of any person belonging to a minority community in Afghanistan, Bangladesh and Pakistan namely, Hindus, Sikhs, Buddhists, Jains, Parsis and Christians, residing in the districts mentioned and the states mentioned below.

This notification was not related to the Citizenship (Amendment) Act, for which rules were yet to be framed.
31 May:
1. The Supreme Court stated that 'it is time to define the limits of sedition' as it granted protection to two Telugu channels from being charged with sedition by the Andhra government because of their reporting on COVID-19.[36] The three-judge bench said that the sedition law was used indiscriminately against activists, journalists, and even the general public for non-controversial matters like trying to source an oxygen tank on social media during the coronavirus crisis.
2. The National Statistical Office (NSO) released GDP data that showed India's economy contracting by 7.3 per cent in 2020-21.

June

1 June: The Indian Union Muslim League (IUML) challenged the government order of 28 May that had invited non-Muslim refugees from Afghanistan, Bangladesh and Pakistan, residing in thirteen districts of India, to apply for citizenship. The application stated that the order was a way to execute the 'malafide designs' of the CAA and discriminate on the basis of religion while granting citizenship.
2 June: The Supreme Court said courts cannot be 'silent spectators when constitutional rights of citizens are infringed by executive policies' and disagreed with the Centre's stance that the judiciary should not be involved in COVID-19 and vaccination policies.
3 June: The Supreme Court dismissed a sedition case against journalist Vinod Dua and stated that citizens had the right to criticise the government as long as the intention is not to create violence.

15 June: A court in Mathura dropped the charges against journalist Siddique Kappan after the police failed to complete the inquiry against him.

16 June: The Institute on Statelessness and Inclusion, based in Europe, stated in a report titled, 'Together We Can: The COVID–19 Impact on Stateless People and a Roadmap for Change', that the 2,00,000 refugees in India were the worst affected by the COVID-19 pandemic in the country. 'The stateless in India have not received economic relief packages provided by the government…they don't have a bank account or proof of citizenship,' it said.[37]

26 June: To mark seven months of their agitation, farmers marched to Delhi.

29 June: The Pew Research Center released data from a survey of religions across India. The survey revealed that a majority of Indians believe in respecting other religions and say that 'they are very free to practice their faiths'. At the same time, however, the major religious groups saw themselves as different from others and wanted to remain separate from each other.

July

5 July: Father Stan Swamy died of COVID-19 complications. He was an activist who had spent his last year in jail and was not granted pre-trial bail even though his condition had been worsening. Swamy had impaired hearing in both ears, had undergone surgery for hernia, and had lumbar spondylosis. He suffered from Parkinson's disease, his memory was fading, and he had even tested positive for COVID-19 on 30 May. Later, when moved to a hospital, he succumbed to a cardiac arrest. After his death, the Office of the United Nations High Commissioner for Human Rights expressed that it was 'disturbed' and hoped that the Indian government was making sure no one is 'detained for exercising their fundamental rights to freedom of expression, of peaceful assembly and of association'.[38]

15 July:

1. The Supreme Court examined the pleas filed by the Editors Guild of India that challenged how often Section 124A (sedition) was being used. The Court stated that it was being misused and questioned the Centre on why this provision

had not been repealed yet. According to Home Ministry data, out of a total of 326 cases registered under the sedition law between 2014 and 2016, only six had resulted in convictions.

2. Farmers protesting the farm laws were charged with sedition. Five were arrested after a protest broke out at Sirsa against Haryana's Deputy Assembly Speaker Ranbir Singh Gangwa on 11 July, which then turned violent.

18 July: An investigation was carried out by seventeen media partners, including *The Wire* (India), into a leaked database of thousands of phone numbers, which were revealed to have been listed by government clients of Israeli surveillance firm, the NSO Group. The Pegasus spyware was accessed by Forbidden Stories, a Paris-based non-profit, and Amnesty International. Ten of the phones that were targeted by this spyware were Indian. Over 300 telephone numbers listed were of Indian ministers, opposition leaders, journalists, the legal community, businessmen, government officials, scientists, rights activists, and others. The NSO group limits its clients to only 'vetted governments', so no private entity was privy to this data. In its response, the Ministry of Electronics and Information Technology denied any government surveillance and called the accusations baseless.

20 July: The Asian Development Bank (ADB) slashed India's growth estimate for 2021-22 to 10 per cent from 11 per cent.

27 July: The International Monetary Fund (IMF) revised its estimates for India's GDP growth from 12.5 per cent to 9.5 per cent for the Fiscal Year 2022. The IMF listed the second wave of the pandemic as the major reason for this, since it had led to fewer growth opportunities.

August

5 August: *The Indian Express* reviewed official police data and revealed that the Jammu and Kashmir administration had booked over 2,300 people under the Unlawful Activities (Prevention) Act and 954 people under the Public Safety Act (PSA) since 2019. Forty-six per cent of those booked under UAPA and almost 30 per cent of those under PSA were still in jail when the report was published. During the first thirty days after J&K's special status was removed in 2019, 290 people were booked under PSA.[39]

9 August: The Centre revealed that over 8,400 Myanmar refugees had crossed into India after the Myanmar coup, of which 5,796 were pushed back. This came after several organisations and state governments had called upon the Centre to provide refuge to the people fleeing Myanmar.

17 August: The Karnataka High Court found policemen who interrogated children while armed to be in violation of the Juvenile Justice Act and child rights. The children were questioned because of a sedition case connected to an anti-CAA play staged by them at their school the previous year. 'Why children are subjected to all this? This has to be corrected, this can't go on like this,' the court stated.[40]

20 August: Nineteen opposition party leaders held an online meeting to discuss the NDA-II government's mismanagement during the pandemic and refusal to talk about the Pegasus spyware scandal. They issued a joint statement and announced their intention to organise protests across India from 20–30 September.

24 August: The State Bank of India estimated that India's GDP would grow by 18.5 per cent in the June quarter.

28 August: Haryana police turned violent when farmers in Karnal protested against a BJP meeting.

September

1 September: Activist Sharjeel Imam's bail petition hearing began. The Delhi Police claimed that his speech during the anti-CAA protests was 'divisive'. Special Public Prosecutor Amit Prasad claimed that Imam wanted to 'create complete anarchy' and had done a 'thesis on rioting'.

5 September:

1. Farmer leaders against the Centre's agricultural laws gathered in Muzaffarnagar in a show of strength. They announced a campaign against the ruling party in Uttar Pradesh.
2. Former UP Governor Aziz Qureshi was booked for sedition over his alleged comments against the Yogi Adityanath government. The complainant alleged that he had compared the government to a 'demon'.

6 September: Haryana suspended internet services in five districts to maintain law and order, in view of the farmers' protest. The Karnal district administration banned large gatherings and imposed Section 144.

7 September:

1. The farmers' protest continued in Karnal, where a huge group surrounded the mini secretariat. They put forward demands related to the lathi charge by police on 28 August.
2. The Tamil Nadu assembly passed an anti-CAA resolution, triggering a walkout by the opposition party, BJP.

11 September: The protest came to an end as the Haryana government initiated a probe into the event.

15 September:

1. Data released by National Crime Records Bureau (NCRB) shows that Manipur, Assam and Uttar Pradesh had the highest number of cases recorded under 'Offences against State'. These include sedition, UAPA, Official Secrets Act, damage to public property, imputation, and assertions prejudicial to national integration.
2. The UNCTAD Trade and Development Report 2021 revealed that India's economy contracted by 7 per cent in 2020, but was expected to grow by 7.2 per cent in 2021. It also said that economic growth could decelerate in 2022 due to COVID-19 and rising food price inflation.
3. The UNHRC revealed that 11,736 Afghans in India were recorded for new registration from 1 August to 11 September.

17 September: India created history by administering the highest number of COVID-19 vaccinations in one day, crossing more than 2.5 crore.

20 September: The Assam state government organised a drive against 'illegal encroachments' and evicted 800 families from 4,500 bighas of land in Darrang district. It drew criticism from Opposition party members and human rights activists. *The Indian Express* reported that the rehabilitated families received no help. During the eviction, a photographer and policemen beat an illegal settler to death.[41]

27 September: The farmers carried out a successful Bharat Bandh from 6 AM to 4 PM.

October

3 October:

1. PM Narendra Modi was mentioned in *Time* magazine's 100 Most Influential People list for 2021. In his profile, he was

described as having 'imprisoned and intimidated journalists who shine a light on its abuses and has passed laws crippling India's thousands of NGOs and advocacy groups'.

2. Leaked offshore data, containing millions of documents about the financial secrets of the richest and most influential people in the world, was published. Called 'The Pandora Papers', the investigation involved media outlets around the world, who found offshore dealings of powerful politicians, world leaders, and public officials.
3. Violence broke out in Lakhimpur Kheri, Uttar Pradesh, as protesting farmers blocked UP Deputy Chief Minister Keshav Prasad Maurya's visit to Banbirpur village. A jeep allegedly ran over farmers and people in a convoy opened fire on the protesters. Eight died and four were injured.

8 October: The World Bank released a report projecting that India's economy would grow by 8.3 per cent in the Fiscal Year 2021–22, lower than its previous forecast.

15 October: A Sikh Dalit man was lynched to death at Delhi's Singhu border by a Nihang Sikh group, who said he had committed sacrilege by picking up a copy of the Sarbloh Granth, a Sikh religious scripture.

21 October: India reached the landmark of administering 1 billion COVID-19 vaccine doses.

22 October: The Central government opposed a petition for granting electricity and water to 200 Pakistani Hindu migrant families in north Delhi. It claimed that they were illegally encroaching on defence land.

26 October: A Vishwa Hindu Parishad (VHP) protest rally in Tripura of 3,500 people destroyed a mosque and set fire to two shops belonging to people from the minority community. Section 144 was imposed. The protest was in response to an attack on Durga Puja pandals in Bangladesh.[42]

27 October: The Supreme Court appointed an expert committee to enquire into the Pegasus snooping row and whether the technology had been used to spy on Indian citizens.

28 October: After Pakistan's win against India in the T20 World Cup cricket match, three Agra teens were arrested and booked for sedition for supporting the Pakistan team on social media.

November

19 November: The Union government repealed the farm laws; the Prime Minister announced this in an address to the nation and apologised to the country.

> '*Main aaj deshvaasiyon se kshama maangte hue, sachche man se aur pavitr hraday se kahana chaahata hoon ki shaayad humaari tapasya mein hi koi kami rahi hogi, jiske kaaran diye ke prakaash jaisa satya kuchh kisaan bhaiyon ko hum samjha nahin pae. Aaj Guru Nanak Dev ji ka pavitra Prakash Parv hai. yah samay kisi ko bhi dosh dene ka nahin hai.*'
>
> ('Today, while apologising to the countrymen, I want to say with a sincere and pure heart that perhaps there must have been some deficiency in our efforts, due to which we could not explain the truth, like the light of a lamp, to some farmers. Today is the sacred birth anniversary of Guru Nanak Dev ji, so it is not a time to assign blame to anyone.')[43]

25 November: A survey of slums in East Delhi found that 27 per cent of respondents were unemployed and 48 per cent households were living in 'very deprived conditions'.
29 November: The two houses of Parliament cleared the Farm Laws Repeal Bill 2021.
30 November: The government informed the Parliament that over 6 lakh Indians had given up Indian citizenship between 2017 and 30 September 2021. A total of 4,177 people were granted Indian citizenship between 2016 and 2020.

December

4 December: A 21 Para Special Forces unit killed civilians returning to a coal mine in Tiru after mistaking them for Naga insurgents. Six died and two were injured. An hour later, concerned villagers, hearing the gunshots, clashed with the troops, resulting in serious injuries.
5 December: A mob in Nagaland attacked a camp of the paramilitary Assam Rifles in district headquarters Mon in protest against the incident.
6 December: 500 Hindu extremists attack a Catholic school in Madhya Pradesh. The mob, armed with iron rods and stones, chanted 'Jai Shri Ram'. The violence was triggered by misinformation that the

school was converting children. The school had requested protection before the attack, which was denied.[44]

8 December: The government sent a draft proposal to the farm unions and agreed to a concession, asking for the farmers' protest to end.

9 December: The farmers' protest was called off after the government met its demands. The Samyukt Kisan Morcha leaders meet at the Delhi borders.

11 December: The farmers dispersed.

17–19 December: A Dharma Sansad or Religious Parliament in Haridwar, Uttarakhand saw an outpouring of hate speech, incitement to violence, and anti-Muslim propaganda. Major religious leaders, right-wing activists, hardline fundamentalist militants and Hindutva organisations attended the event. The speeches spoke of Hindus needing to take back the country and calls for ethnic cleansing.[45]

21 December: The Karnataka state cabinet approved the anti-conversion 'love jihad' bill. The Karnataka Right to Freedom of Religion Bill 2021 was introduced in the state legislative assembly.

Endnotes

1. Gettleman, Jeffrey et al. 2020. 'How Delhi's Police Turned Against Muslims.' *The New York Times*, 12 March. Available at https://www.nytimes.com/2020/03/12/world/asia/india-police-muslims.html (accessed August 2022).

2. See *The Indian Express*. 2020. 'Of 14,378 positive Covid-19 cases, 4,291 linked to Tablighi Jamaat Meet: Health Ministry', 18 April. Available at https://indianexpress.com/article/coronavirus/of-14378-positive-covid-19-cases-4291-linked-to-tablighi-jamaat-meet-health-ministry-6368269/ (accessed August 2022).

3. See Abi-Habib, Maria and Sameer Yasib. 2020. 'India's Coronavirus Lockdown Leaves Vast Numbers Stranded and Hungry.' *The New York Times*, 29 March. Available at https://www.nytimes.com/2020/03/29/world/asia/coronavirus-india-migrants.html (accessed August 2022). See also Mody, Anjali. 2020. 'Coronavirus Lockdown: Narendra Modi has Cut India's Poor Adrift.' *Scroll.in*, 25 March. Available at https://scroll.in/article/957166/coronavirus-lockdown-narendra-modi-has-cut-indias-poor-adrift (accessed August 2022). Another report on the issue is Hebbar, Nistula. 2020. 'Migrant Labourers are the Most Disenfranchised Invisible Citizens: Political Scientist Ashwani Kumar.' *The Hindu*, 31 May. Available at https://www.thehindu.com/news/national/migrant-labourers-are-the-most-disenfranchised-invisible-citizens/article31717502.ece (accessed August 2022).

4. Myers, Steven Lee et al. 2020. 'In China-India Clash, Two Nationalist Leaders with Little Room to Give.' *The New York Times*, 17 June. Available at https://www.nytimes.com/2020/06/17/world/asia/china-india-border.html (accessed August 2022).

5. See De, Abhishek. 2020. 'Coronavirus India Timeline: Tracking Crucial Moments of Covid-19 Pandemic in the Country'. *The Indian Express*, 1 October. Available at https://indianexpress.com/article/india/coronavirus-covid-19-pandemic-india-timeline-6596832/ (accessed August 2022).

6. See *The Print*. 2020. 'Sharjeel Imam Charged with Sedition in anti-CAA Riots Case', 25 July. Available at https://theprint.in/india/sharjeel-imam-charged-with-sedition-in-anti-caa-riots-case/468342/ (accessed December 2022).

7. Dhillon, Amrit. 2020. 'Ayodhya: Modi Hails "Dawn of New Era" as Work on Controversial Temple Begins.' *The Guardian*, 5 August. Available at https://www.theguardian.com/world/2020/aug/05/ayodhya-narendra-modi-temple-foundation-stone-ceremony (accessed August 2022).

8. Mandhani, Apoorva. 2020. '"No Proof Tablighi Foreigners Spread Covid, Were Made Scapegoats"—Bombay HC Quashes FIRs'. *The Print*, 22 August. Available at https://theprint.in/judiciary/no-proof-tablighi-foreigners-spread-covid-were-made-scapegoats-bombay-hc-quashes-firs/487277/ (accessed August 2022).

9. 'Love Jihad' is a term used by Hindutva groups to refer to Hindu-Muslim marriages, where the girl is allegedly made to undergo religious conversion to marry a Muslim man. Though the Hindutva government was categorical that no such activity is legal, Adityanath, the chief minister of Uttar Pradesh, India's most populous state, directed his officers to explore whether a law against such 'jihad', apparently for women's safety, should be enacted. The Allahabad High Court's observation that 'conversion just for the purpose of marriage is unacceptable' while dismissing a petition filed by a couple came as a shot in the arm for Adityanath's war against Love Jihad. See *The Indian Express*. 2020. 'Yogi's Love Jihad Warning: "Your Ram Naam Satya Journey will Begin if You Don't Mend Ways"'. Available at https://indianexpress.com/article/cities/lucknow/yogi-adityanath-love-jihad-law-uttar-pradesh-6911537/ (accessed August 2022).

10. *Outlook*. 2020. 'Right To Choose A Partner Is A Fundamental Right: Allahabad HC', 24 November. Available at https://www.outlookindia.com/website/story/india-news-right-to-choose-a-partner-is-a-fundamental-right-allahabad-hc/365250 (accessed August 2022).

11. *Reuters*. 2020. 'India Detains 75 in Kashmir after Local Election', 26 December. Available at https://www.reuters.com/world/asia-pacific/india-detains-75-kashmir-after-local-election-2020-12-26/ (accessed August 2022).

12. *The Free Press Journal*. 2020. '"Another Great Step by Govt…": Twitter Reacts as MP Cabinet Approves Anti-Conversion Bill', 26 December. Available at https://www.freepressjournal.in/viral/another-great-step-by-govt-twitter-reacts-as-mp-cabinet-approves-anti-conversion-bill-2 (accessed August 2022).

13. See *The Indian Express*. 2022. 'Man's Death During 2021 Republic Day Farmers' Protest: Delhi HC Seeks UP Govt Response on Family Allegations', 29 January. Available at https://indianexpress.com/article/cities/delhi/mans-death-during-2021-republic-day-farmers-protest-delhi-hc-seeks-up-govt-response-on-family-allegations-7746641/ (accessed August 2022).

14. For reportage on the day's events, see *The Hindu*. 2021. 'Top News of the Day: Sikh Nishan Sahib Flag Hoisted as Farmers Enter Red Fort; India Urges Inclusivity at UNSC to Address Complex Issues, and More', 26 January. Available at https://www.thehindu.com/news/top-news-of-the-day-january-26-2021-sikh-nishan-sahib-flag-hoisted-as-farmers-enter-red-fort-india-urges-inclusivity-at-unsc-to-address-complex-issues-and-more/article33668458.ece (accessed August 2022). See also Arvin, Jariel. 2021. 'India's Farmers are Still Protesting—And Things are Turning Violent'. *Vox*, 26 January. Available at https://www.vox.com/2021/1/26/22242395/india-farmer-protest-republic-day-delhi (accessed August 2022).

15. See Rai, Sandeep. 2021. 'UP Police Clears Protest Site in Baghpat, Farmers Allege Brutality, Cops Deny Use of Force'. *The Times of India*, 29 January. Available at https://timesofindia.indiatimes.com/city/meerut/up-police-clears-protest-site-in-baghpat-farmers-allege-brutality-cops-deny-use-of-force/articleshow/80515056.cms (accessed August 2022).

16. *The Washington Post*. 2021. 'Opinion: The Arrest of this Activist Should Put India's "Democracy" Title in Question', 24 February. Available at https://www.washingtonpost.com/opinions/global-opinions/the-arrest-of-this-activist-should-put-indias-democracy-title-in-question/2021/02/24/a18b6ae4-7602-11eb-8115-9ad5e9c02117_story.html (accessed August 2022).

17. See the statement by Freedom House. 2022. 'India: Media Freedom Under Threat', 2 May. Available at https://freedomhouse.org/article/india-media-freedom-under-threat (accessed August 2022).

18. Sinha, Bhadra. 2021. 'What are the Changes OCIs will Face under Modi Govt's New Work Permit Rules'. *The Print*, 8 March. Available at https://theprint.in/india/governance/what-are-the-changes-ocis-will-face-under-modi-govts-new-work-permit-rules/617557/ (accessed August 2022).

19. *Business Standard*. 2021. 'Indian Economy to do Better than -8% Prediction: Finance Ministry', 5 March. Available at https://www.business-standard.com/article/economy-policy/indian-economy-to-do-better-than-8-prediction-finance-ministry-121030501070_1.html (accessed August 2022).

20. *Outlook.* 2021. 'Swedish Organization Declares India "Electoral Autocracy", Rahul Gandhi Amplifies', 12 March. Available at https://www.outlookindia.com/website/story/india-news-swedish-organization-declares-india-electoral-autocracy-rahul-gandhi-amplifies/376907 (accessed August 2022).

21. *The Wire.* 2021. 'UN Body Opines That Safoora Zargar's Arrest Violated International Treaties Signed by India', 13 March. Available at https://thewire.in/diplomacy/united-nations-safoora-zargar-arrest-india-international-law (accessed August 2022).

22. Kochhar, Rakesh. 2021. 'In the Pandemic, India's Middle Class Shrinks and Poverty Spreads While China Sees Smaller Changes'. Pew Research Centre, 18 March. Available at https://www.pewresearch.org/fact-tank/2021/03/18/in-the-pandemic-indias-middle-class-shrinks-and-poverty-spreads-while-china-sees-smaller-changes/ (accessed August 2022).

23. See UNESCAP. 2021. 'Economic and Social Survey of Asia and the Pacific 2021: Towards Post-COVID-19 Resilient Economies', 30 March. Available at https://www.unescap.org/kp/2021/economic-and-social-survey-asia-and-pacific-2021-towards-post-covid-19-resilient-economies (accessed August 2022).

24. See Noronha, Gaurav. 2021. 'India'a Inflation "Uncomfortably High": Moody's Analytics'. *The Economic Times*, 30 March. Available at https://economictimes.indiatimes.com/news/economy/indicators/indias-inflation-uncomfortably-high-moodys-analytics/articleshow/81760520.cms (accessed August 2022).

25. *The Hindu.* 2021. 'CPI (Maoist) case | NIA searches 31 locations in Andhra Pradesh, Telangana', 1 April. Available at https://www.thehindu.com/news/national/cpi-maoist-case-nia-searches-31-locations-in-andhra-pradesh-telangana/article34217695.ece (accessed August 2022).

26. *The Wire.* 2021. 'EU Parliamentary Committee Expresses Concern Over Human Rights Situation in India', 17 April. Available at https://thewire.in/rights/eu-parliamentary-committee-expresses-concern-over-human-rights-situation-in-india (accessed August 2022).

27. See *The Hindu.* 2021. 'Gauhati High Court Rejects Activist Akhil Gogoi's Bail Plea', 7 January. See https://www.thehindu.com/news/national/other-states/gauhati-high-court-rejects-activist-akhil-gogois-bail-plea/article33518131.ece (accessed August 2022).

28. See *The Indian Express.* 2021. 'Over 1,700 test positive for Covid-19 in Kumbh Mela over five-day period', 15 April. Available at https://indianexpress.com/article/india/over-1700-test-positive-for-covid-19-in-kumbh-mela-over-five-day-period-7275124/ (accessed August 2022). See also *BBC.* 2021. 'Haridwar: Hundreds Test Positive for Covid at Kumbh Mela',

14 April. Available at https://www.bbc.com/news/world-asia-india-56742231 (accessed August 2022).

29. See Mirror Now's Twitter thread on the numbers, available at https://twitter.com/MirrorNow/status/1383312582098837507 (accessed August 2022).

30. *The Wire*. 2021. 'SC Directs UP Govt to Shift Siddique Kappan to Delhi Govt Hospital; SG Opposes', 28 April. Available at https://thewire.in/law/siddique-kappan-supreme-court-delhi-hospital-aiims-rml-tushar-mehta (accessed August 2022).

31. Nair, Sobhana K. 2021. 'India Again Placed at 142nd Rank in Press Freedom'. *The Hindu*, 21 April. Available at https://www.thehindu.com/news/national/india-again-placed-at-142nd-rank-in-press-freedom/article34377079.ece?homepage=true (accessed August 2022).

32. *Reuters*. 2021. 'India Records World's Biggest Single-Day Rise in Coronavirus Cases', 22 April. Available at https://www.reuters.com/world/india/india-records-worlds-biggest-single-day-rise-coronavirus-cases-2021-04-22/ (accessed August 2022).

33. Venkataramakrishnan, Rohan. 2021. 'Imagine the Headlines if Any Other Religion Had Been Responsible for Kumbh-Like Gathering.' *Scroll.in*, 12 April. Available at https://scroll.in/article/992067/covid-19-imagine-the-headlines-if-any-other-religion-had-been-responsible-for-kumbh-like-gathering (accessed August 2022).

34. Singh, Namita. 2021. 'Calls for India to Release Kashmiri Political Prisoners During Devastating Second Covid Wave.' *Independent*, 30 May. Available at https://www.independent.co.uk/asia/india/kashmir-coronavirus-india-political-prisoners-b1856224.html (accessed August 2022).

35. Malik, Bismah. 2021. 'Concerned over Intimidation Tactics by Police, Potential Threat to Freedom of Expression: Twitter'. *The New Indian Express*, 27 May. Available at https://www.newindianexpress.com/business/2021/may/27/concerned-over-intimidation-tactics-by-police-potential-threat-to-freedom-of-expression-twitter-2308246.html (accessed August 2022).

36. *The Wire*. 2021. '"Time to Define Limits of Sedition", Particularly in Context of Media Freedom: SC', 31 May. Available at https://thewire.in/law/supreme-court-sedition-media-freedom-chandrachud-telugu-channel (accessed August 2022).

37. *Reuters*. 2021. 'Refugees in India, Elsewhere Hit Hard by COVID-19 Impact—Rights Report', 17 June. Available at https://www.reuters.com/world/india/refugees-india-elsewhere-hit-hard-by-covid-19-impact-rights-report-2021-06-16/ (accessed August 2022).

38. See the press briefing of the Office of the High Commissioner for Human Rights, dated 6 July 2021. Available at https://www.ohchr.org/en/2021/07/press-briefing-notes-india (accessed August 2022).

39. Iqbal, Naveed. 2021. '2,300 Booked Under UAPA in J&K since 2019, Nearly Half Still in Jail'. *The Indian Express*, 5 August. Available at https://indianexpress.com/article/india/2300-booked-under-uapa-in-jk-since-2019-nearly-half-still-in-jail-7438806/ (accessed August 2022).

40. See *The Indian Express*. 2021. 'Sedition Case against Bidar School: Police Questioning Kids Prima Facie Violated Rights, says Karnataka HC', 17 August. Available at https://indianexpress.com/article/india/sedition-case-against-bidar-school-police-questioning-kids-prima-facie-violated-rights-says-karnataka-hc-7457076/ (accessed August 2022).

41. See Agarwala, Tora. 2021. 'Two Dead as Assam Eviction Turns Violent; CM Orders Probe, Police Claims Self-Defence'. *The Indian Express*, 24 September. Available at https://indianexpress.com/article/north-east-india/assam/assam-eviction-drive-clashes-deaths-7530234/ (accessed December 2022). See also *The Hindu*. 2021. '2 Die in Assam Eviction Drive', 23 September. Available at https://www.thehindu.com/news/national/other-states/2-die-in-assam-eviction-drive/article36638255.ece (accessed December 2022).

42. See Bhalla, Gursharan. 2021. 'Mosques Vandalised, Shops Set On Fire, Houses Ransacked: Here's All That's Happening in Tripura'. *Indiatimes.com*, 27 October. Available at https://www.indiatimes.com/news/india/tripura-mosques-vandalised-bangladesh-552681.html (accessed December 2022).

43. See Sharma, Harikishan. 2021. 'PM Narendra Modi Says Sorry, Announces Repeal of Three Farm Laws'. *The Indian Express*, 20 November. Available at https://indianexpress.com/article/india/three-farm-laws-repealed-pm-modi-7630405/ (accessed December 2022).

44. See Siddique, Iram. 2021. 'Amidst BJP Tribal Push, Christian Schools, Churches, Feel the Heat in MP'. *The Indian Express*, 15 December. Available at https://indianexpress.com/article/political-pulse/christians-schools-churches-attack-mp-bjp-7674435/ (accessed December 2021).

45. See *The Wire*. 2021. 'Hindutva Leaders at Haridwar Event Call for Muslim Genocide', 22 December. Available at https://thewire.in/communalism/hindutva-leaders-dharma-sansad-muslim-genocide (accessed August 2022).

Annexure

Survey

Questionnaire on Identity, Citizenship and Nationality

Thou shalt not commit to social science nor submit to questionnaire.

When we examine the literature on identity, we find two relevant bodies of research: a larger, experimental school of literature on social identity theory and a smaller corpus on identity as understood through narrative. The narrative approach deals with the idea of identity as a process that is both shaped by and, in turn, shapes narrative discourse. These contexts of narrative draw on ideas from positioning theory, which postulates that individuals position themselves within a situation and that the narrative they then produce is based on that position. The narrative approach has helped develop an understanding of the ways in which identity is negotiated through narration and positioning. In this survey, the researchers used the same methodology across geographies so that a narrative could be developed on identity and citizenship.

Data has been collected through extensive interviews, conducted one-on-one with the researchers.

Ethnographers may spend months and years in the field and still not get 'truthful' answers. So depending on the situation, questions were phrased in a manner such that the participants did not feel vulnerable and could answer as authentically as possible.

Questionnaire

Level I

1. What is your name?
2. Gender

3. Address
4. Is there a 'permanent address'?
5. What is your profession/engagement?
6. How do you identify yourself? Through profession, community, caste, religion, gender, or all of them, or none of them.

Level II

1. What are the ways in which you express your Indianness?
2. What is patriotism according to you?
3. To what extent would you like your children to feel proud of their country?
4. What is Indianness for you? A piece of paper, or something else?
5. Have you ever felt like an outsider in your own country? How? When?

Level III

1. Is there a 'national identity'? If so, what is it?
2. What is a nation?
3. What is homeland?
4. Where is homeland for you?

TABLE A1: Survey Responses: Level I

Level I									
1. What is your name?	**Respondent 1**	**Respondent 2**	**Respondent 3**	**Respondent 4**	**Respondent 5**	**Respondent 6**	**Respondent 7**	**Respondent 8**	**Respondent 9**
2. Gender	Male	Male	Female	Female	Male	Female	Female	Male	Male
3. Is there a 'permanent address'?	Jammu District. Jammu and Kashmir	Salem, Tamil Nadu	Imphal, Manipur	Sunny Park, Calcutta	Chandigarh	Colva, Goa	I stay in Margao, I'm basically a Goan.	Dehradun, Uttarakhand	I have sold my house in Sangroor, now my permanent address is same as my current place of residence.
4. What is your profession/ engagement?	I am a student pursuing a B.A in International Relations.	Student. Former Law graduate.	I am a student.	Master's student.	Fighter Pilot in the Indian Air Force	Waiter	I am a pharmacist by profession. I have done my MPharm.	Technician at IBM.	I am a school bus driver. When I am free I teach driving. However, I want to become a stuntman and call myself that.

(Contd)

Table A1 (Contd)

Level I	Respondent 1	Respondent 2	Respondent 3	Respondent 4	Respondent 5	Respondent 6	Respondent 7	Respondent 8	Respondent 9
5. How do you identify yourself? Through profession/ community/ caste/ religion/ gender or all of them or none of them.	I am an individual associated with Jammu and Kashmir. Deeply attached to the state, I have spent early years in the state and believe that Jammu and Kashmir exists within me. I am fully immersed in the state and am concerned about the current conditions of lockdown in the state, and want to reach out to and help the people of Jammu and Kashmir. Currently, my identity is based on the fact that I want to help the people of Jammu and Kashmir. Caste and religion are not the dominant identities that I hold. I have cultivated good relations with people from different castes and religions, and now these friends are more like family.	My identity changes based on context, but mostly I identify myself as an Indian and then a Tamilian.	All of them.	A general identity would involve aspects of all of the above, but my definition would depend on what the situation calls for. I identify myself as an Indian, but with roots in Kashmir.	Through my profession.	First, I would give my name, then my father's name and my family background.	Actually, I identify myself as none of the above, you can say, because it depends on the place where I am, depends on the people. How they ask me about where I am from; it depends on that. So basically, on that basis I answer them.	Mostly through profession.	All of them, depending on the circumstance. If I have to sit in an interview, I will say I am a driver, but if asked in a sabha, I would say I am a Muslim.

TABLE A2: Survey Responses: Level II

Level II	Respondent 1	Respondent 2	Respondent 3	Respondent 4	Respondent 5	Respondent 6	Respondent 7	Respondent 8	Respondent 9
1. What are the ways in which you express your Indianness?	Every 15 August, I hang the national flag outside my house. That is my way of expressing my Indian values.	Unity and diversity, despite the fact that we are so diverse we are still together.	Through my knowledge of Hindi and also the familiarity we share with the music or the movie industries, languages and entertainment.	Rudimentary value systems, respect for cohabitation and a certain way of life represents my Indianness.	By being a good citizen of the country.	Just now I gave my vote.	I love my country. When the national anthem is going on, I always pay a tribute to it. I love cricket. I always support the Indian cricket team, and I usually don't go to work also when there's a match. And I love my country. There's a lot of diversity in it, and I respect each and every religion in it. I like to celebrate all the functions also. And I don't have limitations with my friends also. I have many friends who are Hindus, they're Muslims, they're Christians, and I attend their functions too.	By voting during the elections. Getting to decide who your representative will be is the first marker of expressing your Indianness.	What is there to express in it? You live like a law-abiding citizen. I don't think there are any signs to express whether you are an Indian or American. Speaking the language becomes an obvious sign, dressing in traditional dress may be another marker, but now all of us wear westerns. I don't believe in having overt signs of being Indian like painting a flag on my forehead.

(Contd)

Table A2 (Contd)

Level II	Respondent 1	Respondent 2	Respondent 3	Respondent 4	Respondent 5	Respondent 6	Respondent 7	Respondent 8	Respondent 9
2. What is patriotism according to you?	Not bringing shame to your country and improving the image of India. A true patriot will defend India's image from what foreigners perceive it to be. A true Indian will follow the Indian way of life, such as wearing Khadi clothing, which was popularised by Gandhiji. Having respect for the Indian Armed Forces who lay down their lives for the country. Although I feel that patriotism is a misconception. Today, being a patriot has become about speaking the government's language.	Patriotism for me is, anyone who understands national values and who makes all possible attempts to protect those values.	Patriotism, I think, is how you feel the need to change something for the better; you do not really have to support everything about your nation, but be concerned about your nation in a good way.	A sense of achievement and a willingness to sacrifice for it on an altruistic level.	Nation first, always and every time.	Patriotism is a feeling of love for your country.	Actually, patriotism is that you should love not only your religion, but you should also love—you should also respect—others' religions, I feel that. And you should equally participate in that and you should respect their feelings also.	Wanting good for my country and feeling proud about its decisions.	Not sure. Maybe it is the feeling the army-men have before they go in for a fight. It is like feeling that all wrongs have been done away with and all that is left to feel is pride.

(Contd)

Table A2 (Contd)

Level II	Respondent 1	Respondent 2	Respondent 3	Respondent 4	Respondent 5	Respondent 6	Respondent 7	Respondent 8	Respondent 9
3. To what extent would you like your children to feel proud of their country?	I would like my children to be proud of their great-grandparents and their grandparents who have lived through the freedom struggle against the British and have served in the Indian Armed Forces. I would like my children to respect the national flag and develop as truly secular and peace-loving individuals. I would say that I will become a successful father only if I have been able to instil the values of secularism in my children.	I want my children to feel proud, but at the same time, not to have any disparaging opinions about other countries.	I want my children to be proud when an achievement is made by the country collectively, rather than at small issues, how it is right now in India.	Their perception of patriotism and nationalism will come from their own derivations of how the country functions. They should be allowed the freedom to form their own opinions, be critical when necessary and pay attention to important details like national duties and paying taxes. But again, if there is something that they don't necessarily agree with, there should always be room for debate.	One should be proud of their country, their country, there is no extent required. India has been a role model for the rest of the world for centuries, the kind of unity and diversity we practice is not seen across the whole world. Europe is only 1/3rd our size and yet there is no European identity, whereas there is an identity of an Indian.	They should play for any club, for India or something. They should be proud of their country.	I have a son. In the future, if he travels to another country or is working abroad, he should always be supportive of his country's decisions. He should have equal love for it.	I want my children to have values, but I don't want them to get stuck in orthodoxy. I would rather have them settled abroad and live a healthy and easy life.	I would want my children to take pride in everything that the country does right. I don't want them to grow up thinking that killing other people, or harming animals, or abusing neighbours is a legitimate thing to do.

(Contd)

Table A2 (Contd)

Level II	Respondent 1	Respondent 2	Respondent 3	Respondent 4	Respondent 5	Respondent 6	Respondent 7	Respondent 8	Respondent 9
4. What is Indianness for you? A piece of paper or something else?	For me, holding an Indian passport or Aadhaar card doesn't define one as an Indian *per se.*	Indianness is an intangible thing. It is a sense of feeling. Even if you are a foreigner and you come to India and you adapt to the lifestyle in India, that makes you an Indian too. That is exactly how the Parsis came, adopted the culture and lived as Indians.	Right now, it is just my passport that makes me an Indian.	It is the smaller things and the tiny details, where we prefertea over coffee, and religiously watch cricket, and take immense pride in our national anthem, that defines our Indianness.	No, Indianness is the ability of everyone to stay within the rules of law and prosper and find happiness without trampling on anyone else's religion, custom, faith and practices. Irrespective of whether the person is rich or poor.	Not a piece of paper, but more like, I belong to this country and it's like, from Mahatma Gandhi they are all traditional and inde-pendence, its good. I love India.	More. It is something more. India is a country where you'll find a lot of diversity, and there is, like, you can see, in even a single state, you will find lots of diversity. Even in Goa, you will find different people speaking different languages and all. So, I feel, people should respect it.	No, Indianness for me is the variety of food. My father travelled a lot and one thing he complained about each time he went out was that no place has better varieties and taste of different food items than in India. What else do we live for? You go to any place, you cook for the person or you discuss how your cuisine is prepared that gives away how Indian you are.	Indianness is just an idea of being a part of the country. What else is it? Piece of paper, I am not sure. Papers can be taken away, they can get lost. Another way I can recall anything about Indianness is through Whatsapp jokes on how typical Indian men and women behave.

(Contd)

Table A2 (Contd)

Level II	Respondent 1	Respondent 2	Respondent 3	Respondent 4	Respondent 5	Respondent 6	Respondent 7	Respondent 8	Respondent 9
5. Have you ever felt like an outsider in your own country? How? When?	Recent events have made me feel like a foreigner in my own country, because of the recent abrogation of Article 370. I got a lot of snide remarks for being from Jammu and Kashmir. I got called a 'Pandit' and 'Having Separatist sentiments'. I did not appreciate the comments I was subjected to. This is the only time I felt this. Being in a fairly diverse college, I did not expect to hear such comments. Just because I do not speak the government's language, I have been made to feel like an outsider.	No, I have never felt like an outsider in my own country.	A lot of times. When you are with your own people and they deliberately make you feel alienated, in spite of you correcting them, they keep commenting that you are different. Also there is disparity in talk, for example when we have riots.	I have been perceived as an outsider, but when I began talking to them and I communicated with them, I was never made to feel like an outsider.	Never	No	No, I've never felt.	We are used to the *pahadi* language, which is spoken at my place. When I first came to Delhi, it was intimidating. I felt like I should run away and this is not my place. But now both of us have accepted each other.	We all feel like that when we move to another town or city. But during the Khalistani movement, I remember my dad came back home and shaved his beard. Someone in the neighbourhood had picked a fight with him and he was told, *tum log Pakistan ke liye bane ho humare desh ke liye nahi* ('you people have been made for Pakistan, not for our country'). That thought and fear stayed with me for very long. Our family had been living in Punjab for more than 200 years. During the Partition, many relatives moved to Pakistan, but it was a conscious decision of my family to be here. It was obviously because we respect the land. Our business and earnings were here.

TABLE A3: Survey Responses: Level III

Level III	Respondent 1	Respondent 2	Respondent 3	Respondent 4	Respondent 5	Respondent 6	Respondent 7	Respondent 8	Respondent 9
1. Is there a 'national identity'? If so, what is it?	For me, national identity is an individual who represents a secular identity and is a patriot.	Our national identity is a bit fluid in nature and it is more than a geographical construct.	Yes, there is a national identity, but for me it depends more than just on Indianness or a passport. For example, I am an Indian right now because I am a citizen of India, that's it.	Yes, I think there is a national identity, and it lies in the tiny details, from wearing handspun Khadi to every Indian's pride when it comes to our inclusivity and diversity.	National identity is the amalgamation of diverse cultures, languages, faiths, beliefs and the ability of every community to enjoy full freedom under the law and have full freedom to enjoy all festivities in any part of the land.	It is like each people has their own identity and nationality they belong to. And with that, we can make out the population of that country.	No, it is not like that.	Yes, everyone has one. Wherever you are born becomes your national identity. We don't have a say in it.	It is Indian. That's what the documents say.

(Contd)

Table A3 (Contd)

Level III	Respondent 1	Respondent 2	Respondent 3	Respondent 4	Respondent 5	Respondent 6	Respondent 7	Respondent 8	Respondent 9
2. What is a nation?	According to me, a nation is a country which is secular, tolerant and has freedom of speech.	Nation is a sense of Indianness.	A nation for me is where a group of people identify themselves with regards to a common ancestry.	A geographical area as governed by a central authority.	A nation is composed of people who have a cohesive and coherent viewpoint, irrespective of which part of the nation they come from.	It is made up of different religions, cultures.	As I have already said, a nation is not where there is only one religion, there is no one caste, there is no single state, there is a variety, you'll find different states in a nation and different varieties. So that is it. And one has to respect the other religion, their castes and other states also.	The larger place of which you are a part. Like if Dehradun is in India, then India is my nation.	Wherever you are born becomes your nation. It has a Constitution that is applicable to its people and not foreigners.

(Contd)

Table A3 (Contd)

Level III	Respondent 1	Respondent 2	Respondent 3	Respondent 4	Respondent 5	Respondent 6	Respondent 7	Respondent 8	Respondent 9
3. What is homeland?	Homeland, according to me, is Jammu and Kashmir because that's where I was born, and one thing I would like to say is that Jammu and Kashmir is a part of India and is very much a part of the motherland.	Indians should never subscribe to a homeland, it is a set of particular values that Indians must stick to.	Homeland is where you feel you belong.	Homeland would essentially be where you've been brought up or where you come from.	Homeland is strictly followed in the Western system, where they believe in Motherland and Fatherland and the rigidity of Borders. We don't have a concept of a Homeland like the Americans and the Russians.	Homeland is where you stay, like where you live.	Homeland is where you stay.	My village, where I grew up, is my homeland. Where I was born and raised.	Where one is born is homeland.

(Contd)

Table A3 (Contd)

Level III	Respondent 1	Respondent 2	Respondent 3	Respondent 4	Respondent 5	Respondent 6	Respondent 7	Respondent 8	Respondent 9
4. Where is homeland for you?	There is a popular quote that 'home is where the heart is' and my heart lies in Jammu and Kashmir, where I was born. That is for me my homeland, and my family and my friends have been longing to see peace in the Valley for a very long time now. I would be only able to call Jammu and Kashmir my homeland when peace has been restored, not just from one side, where the Muslims and the Pandits can livc together peacefully.	Anywhere in India.	Homeland for me is every region in Burma, India and Bangladesh, where my people have lived for centuries, those territories are my homeland.	In the hills, in Jammu.	Any part of my country is my home, which is given to us by the Constitution of India. And now after the abrogation of Article 370, even Jammu and Kashmir has been amalgamated into the rest of the country, like what was done by Sardar Patel immediately after Independence in August 1947. He merged 565 Princely states and formed the nation-state of India. A land of diverse topography, terrain and a land rich with natural resources—enough to sustain a population of 1.3 billion—and which has the capacity to sustain much more, provided we get our act together and ensure that all the landmass is gainfully utilised and resources not frittered away. It has been a land of plenty and opportunity since 2,000 BC and shall remain so for many years to come.	Goa.	Goa.	It's the same thing. Homeland is where you belong: for me, it is my village.	Punjab is my homeland. It is where I was born and now stay.

Report on the Survey

All interviewees gave their explicit consent to being interviewed and to being audio-recorded. They were informed of the context of the study and the use that would be made of their data. The respondents in the qualitative research analysis are geographically spread out, from the Indo-Bangladesh border to Goa, and from Kashmir to Tamil Nadu.

Level I—Identity

In the first level of the questionnaire, people were asked how they define themselves—through profession, community, caste, religion, gender, all of them, or none of these. Surprisingly, all the respondents said that their circumstances define their identity (suggesting that it is fluid)—for instance, when appearing for a job interview, they will associate themselves with a profession, whereas if they are a part of a religious gathering, religion may become their identifier. However, two respondents, both from Kashmir, added that they have a strong connection with the state and its people. For them, the dominant identity is that of being a Kashmiri.

Level II—The idea of 'Indianness'

In contrast to their responses on identity, when asked how people express their 'Indianness', or what makes them an Indian, their responses differed. These ranged from casting a vote to supporting the Indian cricket team. However, one person said that s/he does not believe in any overt signs of exhibiting Indianness. On the question of patriotism and how they experience it, all the respondents believe that patriotism is an act of feeling proud of one's country. Some of them go further to say that they need not take pride in all the decisions that the country takes, but only those steps that have been taken for the betterment of the people. The idea of patriotism, for them, does not go beyond its literal definition of achievements and pride in one's nation. Indianness is both tangible and intangible for the respondents. Some believe that documentary proof, such as a passport or an Aadhaar card, gives them a proof of their identity, while others think it is embedded in food, culture, language and their value systems. However, diversity of languages, physical features or clothing is not always welcomed, even within the same country. A majority of the respondents said that at some point in lives, they have felt like outsiders within their own country or even their state. They have been alienated and othered on the basis of their community, religion, looks or gender. They have also faced threats and intimidation, simply for being either different or a few in number. Despite this, they all want their children to feel proud of their country.

Level III—The idea of nation and homeland

In the third level of the questionnaire, respondents were asked about their idea of a nation and a homeland. Interestingly, the responses recorded on the idea of a nation are impersonal and detached. People view a nation as the larger space of which their homeland is a part. Their homeland is their place of birth or residence in most cases. Their associations with their homeland are more personal. This finding contradicts their responses to questions about nationality and patriotism, where they speak of taking pride in the entire country's diversity.

Citizens Speak

High-Caste Sylheti Muslim Man

H. Choudhury was initially apprehensive about sharing his thoughts, but gradually opened up, within his limits. There are off-record conversations with the interviewees that provide an insight into their problematic situations, while discussing the present crisis in terms of matters of citizenship and the idea of belongingness.

Address: Karimganj, 788781 (border area)
Interviewer: How do you identify yourself?
Interviewee: First and foremost, I am an Indian, and I want to identify myself as an Indian. In fact, I have got ample documents to prove my Indianness.
Interviewer: What are the ways in which you express your Indianness, do you hold any proof?
Interviewee: Of course, I do. (*Proudly shows his PAN card to the interviewer.*)

Interviewer: In an ideal world, to what extent would you feel like an Indian?
Interviewee: You see, I've got lots of documents—*dolil potro*—1951 NRC has the name of my *baap dada*; even the documents possessed [by us] are from the British era. If anything befalls us, we can confidently show it to them.
Interviewer: What are your expectations from India, being an Indian?
Interviewee: We want to remain Indian, but had to face a lot of instability, staying in a border area. It would have been good had there been no concept of a border. The idea of a free border, where Bangladesh, Pakistan and India encourage free international movement, without any constraints, would be an ideal one. [This is in conjunction with the earlier query of his view of an ideal world.]
Interviewer: Do you expect your children also to hold the same opinion as yours?
Interviewee: [My] children are mature enough. They'll have their own opinions to give.
Interviewer: How would you prove your Indianness?
Interviewer: Oh, I told you of these *dolil potro* I possess. However, I do also possess the LP school-leaving certificate of my mother, from 1937, back when Sylhet was a part of Assam.

The Sylheti community in Assam continues to bear an anxiety-ridden relationship with the state since 1947—they may not be under racist attack, but are predisposed to vulnerability as a linguistic group. The events of 19 May 1961 are a pioneering example of this, although the identity of the Sylheti community in Assam remains ambiguous, often conflated with either Bangladeshis, or with the Bengalis of West Bengal. The idea and identity of a 'Bengali', as understood by most people, is a Kolkata-centric identity. H. Choudhury clings to his account of proving his Indianness, laying emphasis on documents which highlight the Kafkaesque process wherein a piece of paper is made a marker of citizenship, propelled by the paranoia that always persists.

If we go back to 1961, when the 'Bhasha andolon' was at its peak, the Indian Sylhetis/Bengalis, particularly in the Barak Valley of Assam, asserted against the imposition of Assamese. While Bengali continued as a medium of education/instruction in this valley, the

Sylheti Bengalis became prone to Otherisation born out of '*Bongal kheda*' in the Brahmaputra Valley from the 1960s, culminating in the high-octane Assam Agitation of 1979. Although the mass movement was against illegal immigrants from Bangladesh, the targets were Bengalis in general. Coincidentally, the NRC is also the product of the Assam Accord, which appeared just before the Indian Sylheti/Bengali could gain momentum in asserting 'Sylheti' as a distinct identity.

In Conversation with a Sylheti Talukdar Man

Talukdars, in the Greater Bengal, term themselves as landowners and revenue collectors of the colonial era. However, while talking to a few Talukdar people, I realised that all of them consider themselves part of the peasant class in Barak Valley, and are disliked by others, like the Choudhuris.

Name: K. Talukdar
Gender: Male
Address: Karimganj (border area)

Interviewer: How would you like to identify yourself?
Interviewee: I'll identify myself as an Indian Muslim, given that I have so many documents, souvenirs, and antiques, which my forefathers left behind. I have preserved them in my house.
Interviewer: All right. Is it Indian Muslim or Indian Sylheti Muslim?
Interviewee: I am [an] Indian Sylheti Muslim.
Interviewer: What are the ways in which you express your Indianness?
Interviewee: Yes, of course, I have so many land property documents... that might surpass 100 years.
Interviewer: In an ideal world, to what extent do you feel that you are an Indian? Is it only confined to this region? Do you feel the same when you go to Guwahati, or beyond Assam?
Interviewee: When I am at home and in the surrounding areas of Karimganj, I feel Indian, but whenever I leave this place for Kolkata, Guwahati, I become doubtful about my citizenship. Other communities view me as an 'other', making me feel like a second-class citizen. I don't feel 100 per cent Indian there.
Interviewer: What expectations do you have from your children towards this country?

Interviewee: They are still in their childhood, but in due course of time—when they are mature enough—they'll understand and come across the same scene, which will make them realise that they aren't 'fully' Indian but second-class citizens.
Interviewer: Do you have any proof to prove your Indianness?
Interviewee: Well, I can show you my land properties' documents, which go back 100 years. My forefathers were sailors during the British era. I can even show you antiques bought by them.
Interviewer: During the Partition, did you want to migrate to the other side, and do you think that Sylhet should have been with India today?
Interviewee: Yes, during Partition, when India was divided into two, I was born at that time. We didn't go then, but after some years, say, before the liberation war of 1971, my father decided to leave Karimganj and go settle in [East] Pakistan. However, the war was unprecedented and Bangladesh attained liberation. The law and order situation of Bangladesh was not in our favour. So, eventually, we had to give up the idea of relocating.

In these short conversations with Choudhury and Talukdar, if scrutinised critically, we find that:

1. Both Choudhury and Talukdar were insistent on placing importance on their certificates and documents to prove their citizenship, albeit subconsciously, even though the questions sometimes asked were different, and were not related to documentary proof.
2. The above interview is with K. Talukdar, but the researcher also spoke to Choudhurys and other Talukdars in the region. It could be understood that the Talukdars of Barak Valley are also landowners, no matter what profession they embrace in post-colonial India. Talukdar's specific claim about 'land property documents that would surpass 100 years' is evidence to support the caste-profession. On the other hand, Hishab Talukdar, a government official, also possesses acres of ancestral land, where his two brothers grow crops to financially support themselves. So, are they socio-professionally the

peasant class, then, since most of them work on their ancestral lands? Does profession determine caste in Barak Valley? However, Talukdar mentions that his forefathers were sailors, from which it was somewhat clear that the Talukdars were in different professions, and that profession may not determine caste in Barak Valley directly, although this might have been the case in pre-colonial times.

3. Since both of them belong to the conceded part of Sylhet, they do relate to the Partition in 1947, as well as the issue of identity formed out of it, which further bifurcates into 'insider' and 'outsider' in the context of the past, emphasising it with the present.
4. The impulse to work hard to be recognised as an Indian citizen and the fear of being declared 'doubtful' is palpable. Given that Sylhet was with Assam (India) and not East Bengal (from 1874), and there was no similarity of language with West Bengal to enable any cultural or linguistic solidarity, it is not surprising that K. Talukdar feels like a second-class citizen even in West Bengal, or any other part of India where the global climate of Islamophobia is also a factor.

Sylheti Muslim Upper-Caste Woman

Interviewer: How do you identify yourself?
Interviewee: First of all, I'll identify myself as an Indian Sylheti woman. Second, I am a daughter of so-and-so. Third, as the wife of the man.
Interviewer: Okay. Would you define yourself as a Sylheti Muslim woman?
Interviewee: Yes, I meant that only.
Interviewer: First Indian and then Sylheti Muslim woman, right?
Interviewee: Ummm.... Yes.
Interviewer: What if I ask about your caste? Would you say whether you are Choudhury, Talukdar or Maimal?
Interviewee: I am a daughter of the Choudhury clan and married to a Talukdar man.
Interviewer: In between the two surnames, where do you stand?

Interviewee: As per the norm, women do not have a separate surname of their own. We ought to pick up the surname of our husbands.
Interviewer: What is a 'motherland' for you?
Interviewee: I believe it is the place where I was born; my land of birth. The place where [one] is born, is the birthplace of a child.
Interviewer: Where were you born?
Interviewee: At my father's place, Kamarkhai, Karimganj—border area.
Interviewer: What documents do you possess to prove your Indianness?
Interviewee: The first thing [is that] I was born in this land (in 1948), married an Indian man, parents are Indian, went for Haj in 2010, got a passport. And what was that? PRC? Bank account and all, whatever is needed, we have them all.
Interviewer: Do you ever feel that you are being mistreated by your country?
Interviewee: What feel about it? The entire world is witness to it. Extreme torment and mistreatment are the order of the day, to specifically mention about Muslims.
Interviewer: Do you think this applies to Sylhetiya Muslims, or Maimunsingha Muslims of Assam, or Muslims across the world?
Interviewee: Actually, all the Muslims. We ourselves are witness to it.
Interviewer: One thing is clear from our previous conversation, that you are a woman from the border area of Barak Valley. Have you ever felt any less Indian for this reason?
Interviewee: Yes, it is so. I have been away from that place for a long time [since her marital home is in Lakhimpur, but she visits her birthplace regularly]. [People in the] border areas suffer the brunt of marginalisation and the '*zulm*' meted out to Muslims is everywhere.
Interviewer: Do you feel the same for Sylheti Hindus, just like you feel for the Sylheti Muslims?
Interviewee: I haven't come across any such report yet, I am unaware. It is only when we speak of Sylheti-speaking Muslims, the government, as well as society, looks down upon us.
Interviewer: Did you ever feel that you are viewed as an immigrant from Bangladesh because of your linguistic identity?
Interviewee: What I feel is that when we shifted from Barak Valley to Assam Valley (Brahmaputra Valley), as per my experience, Sylheti Muslims were intimidated in Brahmaputra Valley. Which gives me

a clear indication that from the very beginning, Sylhetis have been suppressed. Sylheti language is not spoken in Brahmaputra Valley, [it is] the reason why Sylheti people are suppressed and being unheeded. They laugh at our language and culturally mock us, saying, '*Sylheti shidol khara*'. Their gestures, behaviour show it all.

Interviewer: During the time of the Assam agitation, you were in the Brahmaputra Valley. At that time, as a Sylheti, did you ever feel doubted or unwanted?

Interviewee: Every hour was spent with an irregular heartbeat. '*Sylheti bangali mane Bangladeshi*' ('Sylheti Bengali now means Bangladeshi'). Period.

Interviewer: People's perception, born out of the Assam agitation, right?

Interviewee: Umm… yes.

Interviewer: Neighbours made you feel that way?

Interviewee: (*Nodding her head in affirmation.*)

Interviewer: Were you suffering from any fear psychosis back then? Since it was the time of the anti-foreigner movement and 1983 Nellie genocide?

Interviewee: Yes, we were one family with four children, surrounded by non-Sylhetis. So, yes, fear was meandering around in the air. But even we were smart. We acquired all the techniques to live amidst them. They doubted us, neglected us, not just because we were Sylhetis, but also because they thought we were Bangladeshi.

Interviewer: Because you spoke in Bangla?

Interviewee: Everything boils down to that.

Interviewer: All right.

Interviewee: Although Calcutta's Bengalis were not looked down on, compared to the Sylhetis of Assam.

Interviewer: Do you think the reason is that once upon a time, Sylhet was surgically attached to Assam against the wishes of the Assamese, and that even after it was removed in 1947, the mentality of being the 'unwanted of Sylhet' prevailed?

Interviewee: Absolutely… [It] remained.

Interviewer: You said that you lived in a community where you felt unwanted; socio-economically, what sort of society was it?

Interviewee: It was the middle-class society.

Interviewer: Clerks, bosses, everyone lived [there]?

Interviewee: Yes… umm… semi-urban.
Interviewer: Was it in Guwahati?
Interviewee: Yes, Guwahati. Actually, we got to sense these things only after coming to Guwahati, not before that. After the Assam Andolon, matters became more sensitive. Earlier also it was there, but not as intense; it all began during the Assam agitation and perhaps will drag on until 'Qayamat' (the apocalypse).
Interviewer: The present time has brought about many policies and projects like the NRC. Does it take you back to the days of the Assam Andolon? Do you think these are exclusionary? You may not have been faced with a major problem [with the NRC], but looking at the arbitrary nature of harassment others face, do the days of Assam Andolon come back to your mind?
Interviewee: NRC itself is the product of Assam Accord (1985), which complicated the [communal] issue more. Politicians are happy as long as they enjoy power at the cost of dividing people.
Interviewer: Last question.
Interviewee: Ask more.
Interviewer: Give me one difference between NRC and Assam Andolon.
Interviewee: Post Andolon, the mind turned poisonous. [I am] speaking from my own perspective. And the Assam Accord is the root cause of all problems. Before the Agitation, we had a peaceful and pleasant atmosphere out here. I was married, and shifted to Lakhimpur (upper Assam), and we were happy there (in 1968). In fact, the Bangal khedao Andolon was not at its peak, but we got the feeling that something might befall us very shortly. No matter that they [referred to us with] the slur 'Bongal' at that time, but equally, they loved us. It was later, during the time of Andolon, that things were falling apart. Given the same context, whenever my children went to school, [I thought] '*Haay re amar jaaner khauf!*' Allah saved us, and our children.
Interviewer: You said that you were in decent society, living with your children and husband, who was a government employee. What do you think about those mothers who live in rural areas, with many kids, with the same religious linguistic identity of yours? Do you think that they should also have the right to feel secure?
Interviewee: Everyone is concerned about their children, be it Hindu or Muslim.

Interviewer: Do you hold the same for Hindus? Why Hindus? Are you talking about Sylheti Hindus or Muslims?
Interviewee: No, Assam Andolon was done by Assamese.
Interviewer: So you mean at that time, both Bengali Hindu and Bengali Muslims faced the same brunt?
Interviewee: Assamese Hindus were also in problem.
Interviewer: How so?
Interviewee: Trust issues between the two linguistic communities. Our kids went to the same school, you see.
Interviewer: But if we speak about Nellie or the Bodoland massacre, we have seen that Muslims of Bengali origin were worst hit by violence. Bengali Hindus suffered as well.
Interviewee: Actually, whatever happened in Nellie, we were not there on the ground. We were in Kahilipara, Guwahati. We got to learn about it from *India Today* (confirms with her relative sitting next to her). It happened in a remote area, and personally nobody harassed us like that (physically). We dealt with them (neighbours) very tactfully… we lived in government quarters. We weren't direct, but indirect victims.
Interviewer: Psychologically scared?
Interviewee: Fear loomed over us. We lived with it. My husband attended to his duty during the high time of Assam agitation. It was tortuous for him as well as for us. If he skipped work, the government enforced a pay-cut, and on the other hand, if he went to office, 'Chhatra Sanshtha' [the All Assam Students' Union (AASU)] would beat him up in the middle of the streets, pull him off the rickshaw, undress him, slap him, take off his watch, and do other such demeaning acts…. '*Government duty korle, public e marto, aar duty na korle, government pay-cut korto*' (If you went for your government duty, the public would beat you, and if you did not go for your duty, the government would cut your pay). Well, in this entire process, women and children were the worst sufferers. If there's no food at home, what would we eat?
Interviewer: Do you think the same for Assamese mothers as well?
Interviewee: No, not at all. Probably, they may also have thought that we would also inflict pain on their children as they do to us. Well, that's my perception…. There's a rule in Assam. The moment one movement dies, another takes birth. That is how the Assam agitation inserted the issue of language within communal complexities.

Interviewer: So, you mean that by the time the language movement died, religious communalism was on the rise, and now there is this issue of NRC?
Interviewee: Assam Andolon itself started with '*Aa hoi aah! Ulaai aah! Khed! Khed! Bidehik khed!*' After all, what did it boil down to? Nothing. As a matter of fact, it turned our souls poisonous towards each other. Nobody is considerate towards each other. Nowadays, if there's a party in a Hindu household, we don't go. We are apprehensive that they will look at us [with suspicion]. It is a dilemma. Hence, we don't go!

Interview with Sylheti Muslim Lower-Caste Woman

Name: I. Begum
Caste: Born Maimal (fisherman caste), married a Talukdar
Gender: Female
Address: Latu (Karimganj, Barak Valley)

Interviewer: How would you identify yourself?
Interviewee: Wholeheartedly an Indian. Born, brought up and married on Indian soil. Natively, from Assam.
Interviewer: Would you like to introduce yourself, region-wise?
Interviewee: I am an Assamese. (*Thinks for a while.*) I am a Muslim. My state is Assam.
Interviewer: Which place in Assam?
Interviewee: My homeland is in Latu (border area in Barak Valley). I was brought up in Guwahati. Whenever I am at my place, I feel at peace. The feeling can't be quantified with my stay at Brahmaputra Valley.
Interviewer: May I know your caste?
Interviewee: We are no Choudhuris. We are peasant-class people. We do not link ourselves with Choudhuris, nor do we want to. We are a labouring people. Our work defines us, not caste. Islam taught us to pay heed to work. Islam taught us to perform one's duties well, to love one's motherland.
Interviewer: So, you are all against caste discrimination as well?
Interviewee: Undoubtedly. When our men go to the Masjid, everyone stands equal, shoulder to shoulder, to prostrate before Allah.
Interviewer: You have put emphasis on your Indianess. How would you prove that?

Interviewee: I was born in India. My father was a government employee. He pursued education in school. We went to government schools and colleges (she was hinting at certificates).
Interviewer: When were you born?
Interviewee: 1969, May.
Interviewer: Where were you born?
Interviewee: Latu. We shifted from place to place [since the father's job was transferable].
Interviewer: What is patriotism for you?
Interviewee: Patriotism means to love the place where one stays. I stay in Assam, India. I have been breathing its air. Living on its soil. So, I ought to love this land. Although things aren't as steady these days, with political parties spreading bile to pollute the environment. Consequently, there emerges fear at the face of communal onslaught.
Interviewer: When you were in Guwahati, did you experience the Assam Andolon days?
Interviewee: I was in Class 8. Every other day, there either used to be *bandh*, hunger strike or black day. I hardly remember if I properly attended even fifteen days of my school amidst the political tension. We were scared that if AASU people saw us on the streets, they may admonish us or may even go to the extent of physically harming us. We were not so young [that we could not] rationally fathom what might follow. Maa-Baba were concerned, so were we.
Interviewer: How did you know that people would find out about your linguistic identity?
Interviewee: Why wouldn't they? We went to a Bangla-medium school. The uniforms signified [our identity]. At that time, we had only 2–3 Bangla-medium schools in the whole of Guwahati.
Interviewer: What expectations do you have from your children towards the nation?
Interviewee: My children ought to love their country, considering they breathe its air. I always ask them to do their duties effectively, no matter how justice is served.
Interviewer: Are your children of college-going age?
Interviewee: Yes, they are in universities now.
Interviewee: Do your children tell you about the ongoing political crisis?
Interviewee: Yes, they do. Let me tell you. In 2008, when the insurgent group under Ranjan Daimary, NDFB, was held responsible in the

serial Guwahati bomb blasts, it was initially believed to be the work of 'jihadis' or the Indian Mujahideen and Muslims were targeted. But it turned out that one of the worst cases of violence was perpetrated by indigenous people of Assam against themselves.

Interviewer: You mean to say all the kids of this specific religious identity faced the spectre of doubt? Bengali Muslims, Assamese Muslims?

Interviewee: Bengali Muslims are the worst-hit, to measure the degree of psychological violence inflicted upon them.

Interviewer: All right. You said you are an Indian first. What specific documents can immediately prove your nationality?

Interviewee: Matric certificate (in lieu of birth certificate), degree certificate with my Baba's name on it. Baba was in a good post at his office and knew how to take care of those certificates.

Interviewee: The present topic of NRC, do you think the less privileged have been suffering more than others?

Interviewee: Without any doubt. The economically backward section is the worst hit in this project. We must understand how material conditions work here and how limited accessibility has landed them in wretchedness.

Interviewer: Now we are seeing flooding around the area, with many videos popping up about affected people in this phase where documents are everything. What do you think about this?

Interviewee: Yes, people are more worried about their papers than life. The other day, I saw on a news channel how a poor man, who stood still on the water, was holding his documents. The situation is such: '*Jaan jaye, jauk. Maan potro thik rakte lagbo*' ('If we lose our lives, so be it. But our documents have to be kept safe').This sort of ruthlessness prevails in this land! I'm appalled!

Interviewer: Did you ever feel like an outsider in your country?

Interviewee: I feel like an outsider when these political parties exercise despotism under the façade of community-division. I suffer from fear psychosis, thinking that if the other Muslims may face it, then I am no exception to be lynched some other day. Else, I always carry an identity card along with me. Because my Baba had a stable job, we lived a life of security and didn't have to die of hunger. My heart goes out to those who couldn't afford the same.

Interviewer: Did you ever feel like an outsider in Assam?

Interviewee: Yes, during my college days. The majority of the students were Assamese, and they didn't like the Bengalis. Step-motherly treatment, we received.

Interviewer: You said that you visited and stayed in many places—Calcutta, Delhi, Chennai—did you ever feel like an outsider in those places?

Interviewee: No, I didn't feel much of anything, since I hardly interacted with people around there. I was occupied with running my own errands.

Interviewer: What is national identity for you?

Interviewee: In my opinion, identity is formed out of one's education. Based on the contemporary crisis, when certificates are the markers of 'nationality', education is a must for self-preservation. Education, then, will drive nation building, by helping people to assert an identity for themselves that will be recognised by the nation. [She was particularly gesturing at the miserable socio-economic conditions of the minorities, and how she wants them to methodically lift themselves up the ladder in order to be nationally recognised as a legitimate identity.]

Interviewer: What is homeland for you?

Interviewee: Homeland is my birth place. Where I have my relatives.... It's in Latu.

Interviewer: You even stayed in Guwahati for years. Did you ever feel at home there?

Interviewee: No. Home is Latu.

Interviewer: What is the difference between Barak Valley and Brahmaputra Valley?

Interviewee: I grew up in Brahmaputra Valley, but at the back of my mind, Latu (Barak Valley) was my home. I have my own people in Latu, it is homely and not just home. I was in Guwahati for some years, but my heart was in Latu.

Interviewer: Did you face problems with language in Brahmaputra Valley?

Interviewee: Initially, yes. It was difficult to assimilate in a host culture, but we did it. So, the taunts like '*Bongal kheda*' and '*Bongal Oxomiya hikibo ahise*' eventually stopped. We were kids back then, and whenever we went out to play with them in the evening, we were asked why we had celebrated Eid, or why we were jubilant when hosting guests, even after being forbidden by AASU from celebrating Bihu or any festivals.

Interviewer: Did you face the same situation ever in Barak Valley?

Interviewee: Of course not.

From these two interactions, what we can understand is:

1. They are subaltern voices who possess a notion of community, with a different experience of living, dissimilar to the mainstream projection of the majority.
2. There is a pinch of caste flexibility in terms of their marriages with men from other castes.
3. Among the women I interacted with in Barak Valley, almost no one described their identity as a Sylheti or Bengali, but Indian, keeping the religious identity as a secondary marker. For example, the statement: '*Shorbo prothom, ami ekjon Indian Muslim mohila*' ('First and foremost, I am an Indian Muslim woman'). This is contrary to what we saw in the 1920s, when they wanted their identity to be articulated as Sylheti/Bengali of Assam. Here, history is in complete denial of the stringent agendas of contemporary issues. The same can be observed in Brahmaputra Valley with the Miyas. The term 'Miya' is being used with pride now, and they refer to themselves as a distinctly non-Bengali identity in Assam, while another section of Bengali Muslims has merged or assimilated with the larger Assamese community for recognition.
4. It has been found, not only from the subaltern voices of women but also from academics, that non-Assamese Muslims of both valleys have been 'Othered' after 1947. This is validated by the insufficient representation of Muslim voices in literature. For instance, the memories of Partition (in the Barak Valley), passed down to the youth, are finding means of articulation through the translation of literary pieces, if not through nuanced research. However, if we closely observe these Partition-memoirs, we find an overrepresentation of Hindu voices from Sylhet, while there is hardly any literary representation of Muslims to enunciate the disrupted social

ties (caused by geographical demarcation), nor is there any caste or gendered dimension in terms of women's voices and their experiences vis-à-vis the partition of Sylhet.

5. Can we say that the Indian Sylheti identity is compromised forever, with the NRC silencing such identity assertions and the Citizenship Amendment Act making the communal situation more complex? At that crucial time, when the Barak Valley was resentful towards both Bengal and Assam for geocultural reasons, would the new political dilemmas—brought about by sub-nationalist movements and projects—give birth to another meta-narrative of Otherisation?
6. These women and men see themselves as second-class citizens in the Brahmaputra Valley, which is perhaps because of a sustained subnational assertion by various groups, who come together in Othering them and denying them their legitimate space and identity.

Index